EDUCATION

Assessment, Evaluation and Remedial

EDUCATION

Assessment, Evaluation and Remedial

Editors
Sarita Kumari
D.S. Srivastava

ISHA BOOKS
DELHI-110 033

ISBN : 978-81-8205-170-6

Published, 2018
Published by

Isha Books
D-69, New Gupta Colony,
Near DDA Market
Delhi – 110009
Ph.: +91-9212142040.

PREFACE

Student evaluation and assessment are central to every school and classroom. It is how teachers find out what students are learning, how they are progressing, and how teachers can make improvements for their future development. With requirements for testing and standards-based instruction at an all-time high, effective student evaluation is more essential today than ever. Both research and current practices support the use of structured assessment and placement of students in remedial courses.

Assessment and evaluation serve to enhance student education and to improve teacher instruction. Often, teachers, students, parents and guardians differentiate between assessment and evaluation. It may be appropriate to see assessment as the preliminary phase in the evaluation process. It is the gathering of information on student progress. Various techniques are employed to collect the information. Evaluation, on the other hand, is the weighing of assessment information against a standard in order to make a judgement or evaluation.

Keeping accurate, up-to-date records of student achievement is crucial to meeting the principles of evaluation. Teachers are encouraged to use a wide range of assessment techniques to track student progress and facilitate future learning. The teacher determines the instructional strategy and method that will be used to achieve the education objectives and correlates them to the appropriate type of assessment strategy.

Teachers use their professional judgement to decide which

strategies will best suit the specific purposes of the evaluation. Just as no one teaching strategy will apply, nor will one evaluation formula. This exercise also gives students, parents and guardians the language they need to discuss learning progress. When parents understand educational jargon, they feel more comfortable asking questions before, during and after summative evaluation. Clear communication of expectations and evaluation can help parents and guardians support student achievement.

The book examines the essential concepts of assessment and evaluation, and how they can enhance student learning and motivation. It provides a detailed account of various types of tests and gives guidance to teachers about the essential factors taken into consideration while constructing them. The methods of grading, reporting student achievement and importance remediation and reinforcement mechanism are also discussed. This work is destined to become an essential reference tool for practising teachers, student-teachers, school administrators and parents.

Editor

CONTENTS

1

ASSESSMENT AND EVALUATION

Evaluation process is not necessarily sequential, it can by seen as a cyclical process including four phases: preparation, assessment, evaluation and reflection. The evaluation process involves the teacher as a decision maker throughout the process. Development assessments can improve cognitive ability and enhance self-esteem. Assessment and evaluation are key components of teaching and Education. Assessment and evaluation serve to enhance student Education and to improve teacher instruction. It is important; however, that teachers, students, parents and guardians differentiate between assessment and evaluation.

It may be appropriate to see assessment as the preliminary phase in the evaluation process. It is the gathering of information on student progress. Various techniques are employed to collect the information. Evaluation, on the other hand, is the weighing of assessment information against a standard (such as a curriculum learning objective) in order to make a judgement or evaluation.

TYPES OF EVALUATION

There are three main types of student evaluation:

Diagnostic evaluation

Diagnostic evaluation is used when the teacher decides that information is needed about student knowledge or skills prior to deciding on the most effective instruction. Diagnostic evaluation then, informs instruction.

Formative evaluation

Formative evaluation provides information for both teacher and student about the progress of that student so that corrective action may be taken to help achieve the desired learning outcome.

Summative evaluation

Summative evaluation provides information to be used in making judgements about a student's achievement. Summative evaluation occurs primarily at the end of a unit of study. Its purpose is to inform students, teachers and parents of progress made over a period of time. Involving students in the selection of more specific or more precise words will help to make the criteria more meaningful and clearer to them.

GUIDING PRINCIPLES OF STUDENT EVALUATION

Recognizing the value of evaluation in the process of teaching and learning, Saskatchewan Learning has developed five general guiding principles, which are linked closely to the *Evaluation in Education*, 1990, report and provide a framework to assist teachers in planning for student evaluation.

— Evaluation is an integral part of the teaching- learning process, and is a planned, continuous activity, that reflects the outcomes of the curriculum.

— A variety of assessment strategies should be used to accommodate the individual needs of the students and to provide ongoing, relevant programming.

— Evaluation plans should be fair and equitable, taking into account students' socio-demographic differences such as culture, gender and geographic location; it should be free of bias.

— Evaluation plans should be communicated in advance. Students should have opportunities for input into the evaluation process opportunities to demonstrate the extent of their knowledge, understandings, skills and attitudes.

— Evaluation should help students by providing positive feedback and encouraging them to actively participate in their own learning.

Gathering Information and Keeping Records

Keeping accurate, up-to-date records of student achievement is crucial to meeting the principles of evaluation. Easy access to accurate data facilitates student confidence and teacher decision making. Teachers are encouraged to use a wide range of assessment techniques to track student progress and facilitate future learning. The teacher determines the instructional strategy and method that will be used to achieve the Education objectives and correlates them to the appropriate type of assessment strategy.

Teachers use their professional judgement to decide which strategies will best suit the specific purposes of the evaluation. Just as no one teaching strategy will apply, nor will one evaluation formula. This exercise also gives students, parents and guardians the language they need to discuss learning progress. When parents understand educational jargon, they feel more comfortable asking questions before, during and after summative evaluation. Clear communication of expectations and evaluation can help parents and guardians support student achievement.

Student Self-Assessment

Self-assessment is a basic metacognitive function. It is a form of appraisal that fosters life long-learning. In students establish personal learning goals, aside from those the curriculum sets for them. Hence, it is important that students have opportunities to develop the skills necessary for self-assessment. The teacher can assist in this process by modelling goal setting and helping students to articulate their own objectives. While some students are unrealistic about the quality of their work, Dynesson and Gross 1995, agree that the value of self-assessment out weighs the difficulty. They concur that, "... studies of self-evaluation indicate that correlations between students' and teachers' marks are.60 to.80, certainly high enough to justify self-grading, especially since students learn from such opportunities." Even so, students need clear guidelines and structure to experience success in self-assessment. Developing the evaluation should be part of the exercise. Students, working alone or in groups, make the initial suggestions and these are modified in consultation with the teacher.

Peer Assessment

Like self-assessment, peer assessment is used with an emphasis on student growth and self-understanding, rather than on arriving at a final grade. Having students involved in developing criteria also serves to deepen their knowledge of the expectations concerning their work. Engaging students in consultation about each other's performance and making suggestions for improvement requires them to think analytically. In turn, their analytical skills may extend their thinking to their own work. Peer evaluation should be structured to ensure that students are descriptive rather than judgmental. Students are encouraged to be consistent, realistic, positive and reflective when providing feedback to one another.

Teachers can assist peer evaluators by modeling the behaviour and the language used in their own assessments. Self and peer evaluation should be reserved for those situations where student self-knowledge about the Education process is important. Major projects involving a mix of Education skills such as researching, planning, drafting and bringing to completion are good examples.

Communicating Evaluation to Students, and Parents or Guardians

In order to achieve the principles of evaluation it is important that students, parents and guardians are well informed about the evaluation process. The teacher can facilitate this process by establishing expectations from the start.

Assessment of problem solving/decision-making

It is difficult, if not impossible, to evaluate students' solutions to a problem or a decision. There are; however, particular skills students develop in the process. Teachers may consider the following when assessing problem solving and decision making.

- Consider the quality and quantity of ideas generated when students identify possible solutions. Flexibility and originality should be given more weight than quantity.
- Consider students' ability to identify and rank criteria upon which solutions are based.
- Consider students' ability to explain their reasons for choosing a particular solution. Thinking about the basis for choice allows students to develop understanding of the subtle forces that lead them to make one choice over another.
- Consider students' ability to articulate or write down the process that they used to solve the problem.
- Consider the extent to which students can apply the problem-solving process to another situation. Hypothetical problems lend themselves to this process.

Assessment of values and attitude objectives

Values objectives in the curriculum guide call for students to respect, appreciate, understand or empathize with aspects of Aboriginal life. While the curriculum does not expect students to adopt Aboriginal values, it does expect students to respect those values. Historically, Aboriginal values were misrepresented, or not represented at all, in curricula and Education materials. The use of almost exclusively Aboriginal content fills a need that has been missing from curricula. Assessing students' values poses the same conundrum as assessing problem solving and decision making; however, it also offers a similar solution. Rating scales used periodically over the duration of the Native Studies course can give students and teachers a picture of growth and development. Teachers may ask students to self-assess and peer-assess on occasion. Or, teachers my use an observation check list to assess growth and development during selected activities.

Story completion and role plays

Having students complete or add an ending to a story (or picture interpretation) may assess attitudes. Typically, story completion rests on a criterion related to the students' ability to comprehend the nature of the social issue or conflict and to deal with it reasonably and effectively. Prior to the story completion exercises, the student would receive instruction regarding the use of democratic processes, or some form of moral reasoning, that could be generally applied to almost any situation involving controversy or conflict. This instruction can be completed individually or in a group through class discussions, in committees or in paired exercises between two students. A valuable modification here is to have students role play the possible conclusion(s) to the story, event or problem being studied. Precise evaluation is difficult, but teachers can gain valuable insights into student beliefs and attitudes by observation and from subsequent class discussion of the action. When such skits or role plays are employed, they can be especially helpful in formative evaluations, indicating emphases and options that may be in order for an entire class or the needs of certain students.

Portfolios

Porfolios are collections of relevant work that reflect students' individual efforts, development and progress over a designated period of time. Portfolios provide students, teachers, parents and administrators with a broad picture of each student's growth over time, including abilities, knowledge, skills, processes and attitudes. Students should be involved in selecting the items to be included, setting goals for further personal learning, and self-assessment and reflection. Teachers can encourage critical and reflective thinking by having students decide which of their works to include in their portfolios and explain why they have chosen those particular items.

Instruction and assessment are integrated as students and teachers collaborate to compile relevant and individual portfolios representing each student's progress. Some guidelines for developing and using portfolio assessment include:

— Brainstorm with students to discover what they already know about portfolios (e.g., designers and architects use them to collect samples of their best work to show prospective employers).

— Explain the purposes of portfolio assessment, and share samples of portfolios with students. Teachers may need to create examples if student samples are not available; however, samples should be as authentic as possible.

— Collaborate with students to develop guidelines for the contents of their portfolios, and to establish evaluation criteria for their portfolio collections.

Consider the following for discussion with students:

— What is the purpose of the portfolio? (Is it the primary focus of their assessment or is it supplemental?)

— Will it be used to determine a mark for the unit, or will it simply be used to inform students, teachers and parents about student progress?

— Who will be the audience(s) for the portfolio?

— What will be included in the portfolio (e.g., projects, checklists, research assignments)?

— What are the criteria for selecting items for inclusion?

— When, or at what intervals in the unit, should those selections be made?

— Who will determine what items are included in the portfolio (e.g., the student, the teacher, student and teacher in collaboration)?

— When should items be added or removed?

— How should the contents be organized and documented in the portfolio (e.g., similar assignments grouped, chronologically by date, representative range of work)?

— Where will the portfolios be stored? Will students be allowed to take their portfolios home to share with their parents, or to do further work on them?

— What will be the criteria for evaluating each portfolio collection? Are students aware of these criteria prior to beginning to collect their portfolio items?

— What form will feedback to the students take (e.g., written summaries, oral interviews or conferences)? Will the portfolios be assigned a number value?

— Assemble examples of work that represent a wide range of students' developing abilities, skills, knowledge, thinking and research processes, and attitudes. Select items that demonstrate their oral and written abilities.

— Date all items for effective organization and easy access.

— Inform parents/guardians about the use and purposes of portfolios (e.g., send home letters describing portfolio assessment, display samples on meet-the-teacher nights).

Consider the following for organization and inclusion:

— criteria for content selection

— table of contents or captioned labels that briefly outline the contents

— samples of a variety of student work (e.g., both oral and written products, evidence of effort and/or achievement of a process or skill, self-assessment checklists)

— evidence of student self-assessment

— audio and video tapes of student

— performances and presentations

— photographs

— computer disks

— collaborative projects.

Formats for portfolio assembly should provide for easy organization, storage and accessibility. Some possibilities include:

— Keep file folders or accordion folders in a classroom filing cabinet or cupboard, or in boxes.

— Use three-ring binders for ease of adding and removing items as students' progress.

— Store scrapbooks in boxes or crates.

Evaluating Student Portfolios

At the end of the unit, term, semester or year, when portfolios are submitted for summative evaluation, it is useful to review the contents as a whole. Data can be recorded using previously established criteria outlined on a rating scale or rubric. Modelling the presentation procedure will give students a good idea about how to conduct a portfolio presentation. Giving students the opportunity to rehearse the portfolio presentation with their classmates prior to presenting to parents and teachers may alleviate anxiety some students might feel.

Methods of Data Recording

Anecdotal records

Anecdotal records are written descriptions of daily student progress. The teacher may decide to keep anecdotal records of students' ability to work in groups, conduct themselves appropriately for an invited speaker or complete a research project.

Observation checklists

Observation checklists, once developed, are a quick way of assessing knowledge, specific skills, learning processes or attitudes. A list of criteria gives the teacher the opportunity to assess several students over a short time. Students should be aware of the criteria before observation assessment takes place.

Rating scales

Rating scales have the same use as observation checklists with one essential difference. While checklists record the presence or absence of a particular knowledge item, skill or process, rating scales record the degree to which they are found or the quality of the performance. A rating scale can easily be adapted into a rubric.

Ongoing student activities

Ongoing student activities include learning activities that students are engaged in on a daily basis.

Written Assignments

Teachers may collect student progress information by having students plan, organize, and produce a written product.

Presentations

The educational curriculum covers a vast amount of content so students are often asked to present their findings to their classmates. Hence, while teachers may use checklists, rating scales and anecdotal records to assess presentation, they may also enlist the help of those students acting as audience.

Performance assessment

Teachers may collect assessment data on various types of performances. The students may be asked to role play a discriminatory incident, or create a graphic organizer that displays their understanding of the concept of identity, for example.

Homework

Homework may be assigned as an instructional strategy or an assessment technique. The teacher may ask students to watch the news for a week and analyze the Aboriginal content. Assigning homework is most effective when students are interested in the project and when the teacher requires specific assessment information.

Quizzes and tests

Quizzes and tests should allow students to demonstrate their knowledge of the subject matter, and, depending on the quality of the test items, they may be used to assess processes, skills and attitudes.

ASSESSMENT OF STUDENT LEARNING

Assessment of student learning can be conducted using a variety of available instruments and methods. Many experts believe that a combination of assessment approaches can be the most effective way to measure student learning. Fortunately for assessment planners, many departments on campus and at other institutions have acquired some experience with many of the more commonly used instruments. Faculty in a variety of academic programs at large and small research universities have tested and used a wide range of assessment methods to determine whether students were attaining prescribed educational goals.

Direct Indicators of Learning

Capstone Course Evaluation

Capstone courses integrate knowledge, concepts, and skills associated with an entire sequence of study in a program. This method of assessment is unique because the courses themselves become the instruments for assessing student teaching and learning. Evaluation of students' work in these courses is used as a means of assessing student outcomes. For academic units where a single capstone course is not feasible or desirable, a department may designate a small group of courses where competencies of completing majors will be measured.

Capstone courses provide students with a forum to combine various aspects of their programmatic experiences. For departments and faculty, the courses provide a forum to assess student achievement in a variety of knowledge and skills-based areas by integrating their educational experiences. Also, these courses can provide a final common experience for student in the discipline. Many research universities are currently using capstone courses in a variety of academic disciplines including general education programs and other academic units in the

Arts and Sciences. Departments at other research institutions using this instrument to gather information about student learning in the major include many general education programs, chemistry, political science, physics, music, religious studies, theatre, history, and foreign languages.

Course-Embedded Assessment

Assessment practices embedded in academic courses generate information about what and how students are learning within the program and classroom environment. Course-embedded assessment takes advantage of already existing curricular offerings by using standardized data instructors already collect or by introducing new assessment measures into courses. The embedded methods most commonly used involve the development and gathering of student data based on questions placed in course assignments. These questions, intended to assess student outcomes, are incorporated or embedded into final exams, research reports, and term papers in senior-level courses. The student responses are then evaluated by two or more faculty to determine whether or not the students are achieving the prescribed educational goals and objectives of the department.

This assessment is a separate process from that used by the course instructor to grade the exam, report, or term paper. There are a number of advantages to using course-embedded assessment. First, student information gathered from embedded assessment draw on accumulated educational experiences and familiarity with specific areas or disciplines. Second, embedded assessment often does not require additional time for data collection, since instruments used to produce student learning information can be derived from course assignments already planned as part of the requirements. Third, the presentation of feedback to faculty and students can occur very quickly creating a conducive environment for ongoing programmatic improvement. Finally, course-embedded assessment is part of the curricular structure and students have a tendency to respond seriously to this method. Departments at other research institutions using embedded assessment include general education programs, classics, economics, English, film studies, geography, fine arts, history, kinesiology, philosophy, political science, physics, and religious studies.

Tests and Examinations

In most cases, a test will be one part of a fully developed assessment plan. Tests are commonly used in association with cognitive goals in order to review student achievement with respect to a common body of knowledge associated with a discipline or program. Departments have traditionally used tests in assessment programming to measure whether students have acquired a certain process- and content-related knowledge. Using this approach, there are two primary testing alternatives; first, locally developed/ faculty generated tests and examinations, and commercially produced standardized tests and examinations. Locally developed testing and examinations are probably the most widely used method for evaluating student progress. For assessing the validity of an academic program, examinations designed by the instructors who set the educational goals and teach the courses is often the best approach. Cost benefits, interpretation advantages, and quick turnaround time all make using locally designed tests an attractive method for assessing student learning.

Tests designed for a specific curriculum can often prove more valuable when assessing student achievement than commercial instruments. These tests focus on the missions, goals, and objectives of the departments and permit useful projections of student behavior and learning. A well-constructed and carefully administered test that is graded by two or more judges for the specific purpose of determining program strengths and weaknesses remains one of the most popular instruments for assessing most majors.

Departments at other research institutions using locally designed tests and examinations include mathematics, physical education, psychology, and English. Commercially generated tests and examinations are used to measure student competencies under controlled conditions. Tests are developed and measured nationally to determine the level of learning that students have acquired in specific fields of study. For example, nationally standardized multiple-choice tests are widely used and assist departments in determining programmatic strengths and weaknesses when compared to other programs and national data. Compilations of data on the performance of students who voluntarily take national examinations such as GRE and MCAT enable faculty to discover useful data that often leads to programmatic improvements.

When using commercially generated tests, national standards are used as comparative tools in areas such as rates of acceptance into graduate or professional school, rates of job placement, and overall achievement of students when compared to other institutions. In most cases, standardized testing is useful in demonstrating external validity. There are a number of advantages for using commercial/standardized tests and examinations to measure student achievement;

— first, institutional comparisons of student learning are possible.

— second, very little professional time is needed beyond faculty efforts to analyze examinations results and develop appropriate curricular changes that address the findings.

— third, in most cases, nationally developed tests are devised by experts in the discipline.

— fourth, tests are traditionally given to students in large numbers and do not require faculty involvement when exams are taken by students.

As part of their assessment efforts, many institutions and programs already use a multitude of commercially generated examination and tests. Some of the more commonly used national tests include:

— *ACT - COMP (College Outcome Measures Program)*: This is an assessment instrument that measures knowledge and skills acquired by students in general education courses. Administered by ACT, Iowa City, IA.

— *GRE (Graduate Record Examinations)*: The GRE is widely used by colleges, universities, departments, and graduate schools to assess verbal and quantitative student achievement. Also, many discipline-specific examinations are offered to undergraduate students in areas such as Biology, Chemistry, Education, Geology, History, Literature, Political Science, Psychology, and Sociology. The GRE is published and administered by Educational Testing Services, Princeton, New Jersey.

— *Major Field Achievements Tests*: Major field examinations are administered in a variety of disciplines. They often are given to student upon or near completion of their major field of study. These tests assess the ability of students to analyze and solve problems, understand relationships, and interpret material. Major field exams are published by Educational Testing Services, Princeton, New Jersey.

Departments with a successful history in using commercial tests and examinations include many general education programs, mathematics, chemistry, biology, computer science, geology, physics, psychology, sociology, education, engineering, foreign languages, music, exercise science, and literature.

Portfolio Evaluation

Portfolios used for assessment purposes are most commonly characterized by collections of student work that exhibit to the faculty and the student the student's progress and achievement in given areas. Included in the portfolio may be research papers and other process reports, multiple choice or essay examinations, self-evaluations, personal essays, journals, computational exercises and problems, case studies, audiotapes, videotapes, and short-answer quizzes. This information may be gathered from in-class or as out-of-class assignments.

Information about the students' skills, knowledge, development, quality of writing, and critical thinking can be acquired through a comprehensive collection of work samples. A student portfolio can be assembled within a course or in a sequence of courses in the major. The faculty determine what information or students' products should be collected and how these products will be used to evaluate or assess student learning. These decisions are based on the academic unit's educational goals and objectives. Portfolio evaluation is a useful assessment tool because it allows faculty to analyze an entire scope of student work in a timely fashion.

Collecting student work over time gives departments a unique opportunity to assess a students' progression in acquiring a variety of learning objectives. Using student portfolios also gives faculty the ability to determine the content and control the quality of the assessed materials. Portfolios at other research institutions are widely used and have been a part of student outcomes assessment for a long time. Departments using portfolio evaluations include English, history, foreign languages, fine arts, theatre, dance, chemistry, communications, music, and general education programs.

Pre-test/Post-test Evaluation

Pre-test/post test assessment is a method used by academic units where locally developed tests and examinations are administered at the beginning and at the end of courses or academic programs. These test results enable faculty to monitor student progression and learning throughout prescribed periods of time. The results are often useful for determining where skills and knowledge deficiencies exist and most frequently develop. Academic departments at other research institutions currently using this form of assessment to measure student learning include communications, economics, geography, linguistics, theatre, and dance.

Thesis Evaluation

A senior or graduate student thesis, research project, or performance paper that is structured by the department to give students an opportunity to demonstrate a mastery of an array of skills and knowledge appropriate to the major can be a useful assessment instrument. Thesis evaluation has been used effectively for program improvement in such disciplines as foreign languages, literature, and the sciences.

Videotape and Audiotape Evaluation

Videotapes and audiotapes have been used by faculty as a kind of pre-test/post-test assessment of student skills and knowledge. Disciplines, such as theatre, music, art, communication, and student teaching, that have experienced difficulty in using some of the other assessment methods have had significant success in utilizing videotapes and audiotapes as assessment tools.

INDIRECT INDICATORS OF LEARNING

External Reviewers

Peer review of academic programs is a widely accepted method for assessing curricular sequences, course development and delivery, and the effectiveness of faculty. Using external reviewers is a useful way of analyzing whether student achievement correlates appropriately with departmental goals and objectives. In numerous instances, recommendations initiated by skilled external reviewers have been instrumental in identifying program strengths and weaknesses leading tc substantial curricular and structural changes and improvements

Student Surveying and Exit Interviewing

Student surveying and exit interviews have become increasingly important tools for understanding the educational needs of students. When combined with other assessment instruments, many departments have successfully used surveys to produce important curricular and co-curricular information about student learning and educational experiences. During this process, students are asked to reflect on what they have learned as majors in order to generate information for program improvement. Through using this method, universities have reported gaining insight into how students experience courses, what they like and do not like about various instructional approaches, what is important about the classroom environment that facilitates or hinders learning, and the nature of assignments that foster student learning.

In most cases, student surveys and exit interviews are conducted in tandem with a number of other assessment tools. In many universities where surveys have been adopted as a method of program assessment, findings have results in academic and service program énhancement throughout campus. Among the departments currently using these methods are general education programs, mathematics, philosophy, social work, speech and hearing science, chemistry, biology, fine arts, geology, kinesiology, and engineering.

Alumni Surveying

Surveying of alumni is a useful assessment tool for generating data about student preparation for professional work, program satisfaction, and curriculum relevancy. As an assessment supplement, alumni surveying provides departments with a variety of information that can highlight program areas that need to be expanded or enhanced. In most cases, alumni surveying is an inexpensive way to gather data and for reestablishing relationships with individuals that want to help the program continually improve.

Employer Surveying

Employer surveys can provide information about the curriculum, programs, and students that other forms of assessment cannot produce. Through surveys, departments traditionally seek employer satisfaction levels with the abilities and skills of recent graduates. Employers also assess programmatic characteristics by addressing the success of students in a continuously evolving job market. The advantages in using employer surveys include the ability to obtain external data that cannot be produced on campus, and the responses are often useful to help students discern the relevance of educational experiences and programs.

CLASSROOM ASSESSMENT TECHNIQUES

In the 1990's, educational reformers are seeking answers to two fundamental questions: (1) How well are students learning? and (2) How effectively are teachers teaching? Classroom Research and Classroom Assessment respond directly to concerns about better learning and more effective teaching. Classroom Research was developed to encourage college teachers to become more systematic and sensitive observers of learning as it takes place every day in their classrooms. Faculty have an exceptional opportunity to use their classrooms as laboratories for the study of learning and through such study to develop a better understanding of the learning process and the impact of their teaching upon it.

Classroom Assessment, a major component of Classroom Research, involves student and teachers in the continuous monitoring of students' learning. It provides faculty with feedback about their effectiveness as teachers, and it gives students a measure of their progress as learners. Most important, because Classroom Assessments are created, administered, and analyzed by teachers themselves on questions of teaching and learning that are important to them, the likelihood that instructors will apply the results of the assessment to their own teaching is greatly enhances. Through close observation of students in the process of learning, the collection of frequent feedback on students' learning, and the design of modest classroom experiments, teachers can learn much about how students learn and, more specifically, how students respond to particular teaching approaches.

Classroom Assessment helps individual college teachers obtain useful feedback on what, how much, and how well their students are learning. Faculty can then use this information to refocus their teaching to help students make their learning more efficient and more effective. College instructors who have assumed that their students were learning what they were trying to teach them are regularly faced with disappointing evidence to the contrary when they grade tests and term papers. Too often, students have not learned as much or as well as was expected. There are gaps, sometimes considerable ones, between what was taught and what has been learned. By the time faculty notice these gaps in knowledge or understanding, it is frequently too late to remedy the problems.

To avoid such unhappy surprises, faculty and students need better ways to monitor learning throughout the semester. Specifically, teachers need a continuous flow of accurate information on student learning. For example, if a teacher's goal is to help students learn points "A" through "Z" during the course, then that teacher needs first to know whether all students are really starting at point "A" and, as the course proceeds, whether they have reached intermediate points "B," "G," "L," "R," "W," and so on. To ensure high-quality learning, it is not enough to test students when the syllabus has arrived at points "M" and "Z." Classroom Assessment is particularly useful for checking how well students are learning at those initial and intermediate points, and for providing information for improvement when learning is less than satisfactory.

Through practice in Classroom Assessment, faculty become better able to understand and promote learning, and increase their ability to help the students themselves become more effective, self-assessing, self-directed learners. Simply put, the central purpose of Classroom Assessment is to empower both teachers and their students to improve the quality of learning in the classroom. Classroom Assessment is an approach designed to help teachers find out what students are learning in the classroom and how well they are learning it. This approach has the following characteristics:

— *Learner-Centered*: Classroom Assessment focuses the primary attention of teachers and students on observing and improving learning, rather than on observing and improving teaching. Classroom Assessment can provide information to guide teachers and students in making adjustments to improve learning.

— *Teacher-Directed*: Classroom Assessment respects the autonomy, academic freedom, and professional judgement of college faculty. The individual teacher decides what to assess, how to assess, and how to respond to the information gained through the assessment. Also, the teacher is not obliged to share the result of Classroom Assessment with anyone outside the classroom.

— *Mutually Beneficial*: Because it is focused on learning, Classroom Assessment requires the active participation of students. By cooperating in assessment, students reinforce their grasp of the course content and strengthen their own skills at self-assessment. Their motivation is increased when they realize that faculty are interested and invested in their success as learners. Faculty also sharpen their teaching focus by continually asking themselves three questions: "What are the essential skills and knowledge I am trying to Teach?" "How can I find out whether students are learning them?" "How can I help students learn better?" As teachers work closely with students to answer these questions, they improve their teaching skills and gain new insights.

— *Formative*: Classroom Assessment's purpose is to improve the quality of student learning, not to provide evidence for evaluating or grading students. The assessment is almost never graded and are almost always anonymous.

— *Context-Specific*: Classroom Assessments have to respond to the particular needs and characteristics of the teachers, students, and disciplines to which they are applied. What works well in one class will not necessary work in another.

— *Ongoing*: Classroom Assessment is an ongoing process, best thought of as the creating and maintenance of a classroom "feedback loop." By using a number of simple Classroom Assessment Techniques that are quick and easy to use, teachers get feedback from students on their learning. Faculty then complete the loop by providing students with feedback on the results of the assessment and suggestions for improving learning. To check on the usefulness of their suggestions, faculty use Classroom Assessment again, continuing the "feedback loop." As the approach becomes integrated into everyday classroom activities, the communications loop connecting faculty and students — and teaching and learning — becomes more efficient and more effective.

— *Rooted in Good Teaching Practice*: Classroom Assessment is an attempt to build on existing good practice by making feedback on students' learning more systematic, more flexible, and more effective. Teachers already ask questions, react to students' questions, monitor body language and facial expressions, read homework and tests, and so on. Classroom Assessment provides a way to integrate assessment systematically and seamlessly into the traditional classroom teaching and learning process

As they are teaching, faculty monitor and react to student questions, comments, body language, and facial expressions in an almost automatic fashion. This "automatic" information gathering and impression formation is a subconscious and implicit process. Teachers depend heavily on their impressions of student learning and make important judgments based on them, but they rarely make those informal assessments explicit or check them against the students' own impressions or ability to perform. In the course of teaching, college faculty assume a great deal about their students' learning, but most of their assumptions remain untested.

Even when college teachers routinely gather potentially useful information on student learning through questions, quizzes, homework, and exams, it is often collected too late — at least from the students' perspective - to affect their learning. In practice, it is very difficult to "de-program" students who are used to thinking of anything they have been tested and graded on as being "over and done with." Consequently, the most effective times to assess and provide feedback are before the chapter tests or the midterm an final examinations. Classroom Assessment aims at providing that early feedback.

Classroom Assessment is based on seven assumptions:

— The quality of student learning is directly, although not exclusively, related to the quality of teaching. Therefore, one of the most promising ways to improve learning is to improve teaching.

— To improve their effectiveness, teachers need first to make their goals and objectives explicit and then to get specific, comprehensible feedback on the extent to which they are achieving those goals and objectives.

— To improve their learning, students need to receive appropriate and focused feedback early and often; they also need to learn how to assess their own learning.

— The type of assessment most likely to improve teaching and learning is that conducted by faculty to answer questions they themselves have formulated in response to issues or problems in their own teaching.

— Systematic inquiry and intellectual challenge are powerful sources of motivation, growth, and renewal for college teachers, and Classroom Assessment can provide such challenge.

— Classroom Assessment does not require specialized training; it can be carried out by dedicated teachers from all disciplines.

— By collaborating with colleagues and actively involving students in Classroom Assessment efforts, faculty (and students) enhance learning and personal satisfaction.

To begin Classroom Assessment it is recommended that only one or two of the simplest Classroom Assessment Techniques are tried in only one class. In this way very little planning or preparation time and energy of the teacher and students is risked. In most cases, trying out a simple Classroom Assessment Technique will require only five to ten minutes of class time and less than an hour of time out of class. After trying one or two quick assessments, the decision as to whether this approach is worth further investments of time and energy can be made. This process of starting small involves three steps:

Step 1: Planning - Select one, and only one, of your classes in which to try out the Classroom Assessment. Decide on the class meeting and select a Classroom Assessment Technique. Choose a simple and quick one.

Step 2: Implementing - Make sure the students know what you are doing and that they clearly understand the procedure. Collect the responses and analyze them as soon as possible.

Step 3: Responding - To capitalize on time spent assessing, and to motivate students to become actively involved, "close the feedback loop" by letting them know what you learned from the assessments and what difference that information will make.

Five suggestions for a successful start:

1. If a Classroom Assessment Techniques does not appeal to your intuition and professional judgement as a teacher, don't use it.

2. Don't make Classroom Assessment into a self-inflicted chore or burden.

3. Don't ask your students to use any Classroom Assessment Technique you haven't previously tried on yourself.

4. Allow for more time than you think you will need to carry out and respond to the assessment.
5. Make sure to "close the loop." Let students know what you learn from their feedback and how you and they can use that information to improve learning.

EXAMPLES OF ASSESSMENT TECHNIQUE

Background Knowledge Probe

Description

At the first class meeting, many college teachers ask students for general information on their level of preparation, often requesting that students list courses they have already taken in the relevant field. This technique is designed to collect much more specific, and more useful, feedback on students' prior learning. *Background Knowledge Probes* are short, simple questionnaires prepared by instructors for use at the beginning of a course, at the start of a new unit or lesson, or prior to introducing an important new topic. A given *Background Knowledge Probe* may require students to write short answers, to circle the correct response to multiple-choice questions, or both.

Step-by-step procedure

— Before introducing an important new concept, subject, or topic in the course syllabus, consider what the students may already know about it. Recognizing that their knowledge may be partial, fragmentary, simplistic, or even incorrect, try to find at lease one point that most students are likely to know, and use that point to lead into others, less familiar points.

— Prepare two or three open-ended questions, a handful of short-answer questions, or ten to twenty multiple-choice questions that will probe the students' existing knowledge of that concept, subject, or topic. These questions need to be carefully phrased, since a vocabulary that may not be familiar to the students can obscure your assessment of how well they know the facts or concepts.

— Write your open-ended questions on the chalkboard, or hand out short questionnaires. Direct student to answer open-ended questions succinctly, in two or three sentences if possible. Make a point of announcing that these *Background Knowledge Probes* are not tests or quizzes and will not be graded. Encourage students to give thoughtful answers that will help you make effective instructional decisions.

— At the next class meeting, or as soon as possible, let students know the results, and tell them how that information will affect what you do as the teacher and how it should affect what they do as learners.

Minute Paper

Description

No other technique has been used more often or by more college teachers than the *Minute Paper*. This technique — also known as the *One-Minute Paper* and the *Half-Sheet Response* — provides a quick and extremely simple way to collect written feedback on student learning. To use the *Minute Paper*, an instructor stops class two or three minutes early and asks students to respond briefly to some variation on the following two questions: "What was the most important thing you learned during this class?" and "What important question remains unanswered?" Students they write their responses on index cards or half-sheets of scrap paper and hand them in.

Step-by-step procedure

— Decide first what you want to focus on and, as a

consequence, when to administer the *Minute Paper*. If you want to focus on students' understanding of a lecture, the last few minutes of class may be the best time. If your focus is on a prior homework assignment, however, the first few minutes may be more appropriate.

— Using the two basic questions from the "Description" above as starting points, write *Minute Paper* prompts that fit your course and students. Try out your *Minute Paper* on a colleague or teaching assistant before using it in class.

— Plan to set aside five to ten minutes of your next class to use the technique, as well as time later to discuss the results.

— Before class, write one or, at the most, two *Minute Paper* questions on the chalkboard or prepare an overhead transparency.

— At a convenient time, hand out index cards or half-sheets of scrap paper.

— Unless there is a very good reason to know who wrote what, direct students to leave their names off the papers or cards.

— Let the students know how much time they will have (two to five minutes per question is usually enough), what kinds of answers you want (words, phrases, or short sentences), and when they can expect your feedback.

Muddiest Point

Description

The *Muddiest Point* is just about the simplest technique one can use. It is also remarkable efficient, since it provides a high information return for a very low investment of time and energy. The technique consists of asking students to jot down a quick response to one question: "What was the muddiest point in........?" The focus of the *Muddiest Point* assessment might be a lecture, a discussion, a homework assignment, a play, or a film.

Step-by-step procedure

— Determine what you want feedback on: the entire class session or one self-contained segment? A lecture, a discussion, a presentation?

— If you are using the technique in class, reserve a few minutes at the end of the class session. Leave enough time to ask the question, to allow students to respond, and to collect their responses by the usual ending time.

— Let students know beforehand how much time they will have to respond and what use you will make of their responses.

— Pass out slips of paper or index cards for students to write on.

— Collect the responses as or before students leave. Stationing yourself at the door and collecting "muddy points" as students file out is one way; leaving a "muddy point" collection box by the exit is another.

— Respond to the students' feedback during the next class meeting or as soon as possible afterward.

One-Sentence Summary

Description

This simple technique challenges students to answer the questions "Who does what to whom, when, where, how, and why?" (represented by the letters WDWWWWHW) about a given topic, and then to synthesize those answers into a simple informative, grammatical, and long summary sentence.

Step-by-step procedure

— Select an important topic or work that your students have recently studied in your course and that you expect them to learn to summarize.

— Working as quickly as you can, answer the questions "Who Did/Does What to Whom, When, Where, How and Why?" in relation to that topic. Note how long this first step takes you.

— Next, turn your answers into a grammatical sentence that follows WDWWWWHS pattern. Not how long this second step takes.

— Allow your students up to twice as much time as it took you to carry out the task and give them clear direction on the One-Sentence Summary technique before you announce the topic to be summarized.

What's the Principle?

Description

After students figure out what type of problem they are dealing with, they often must then decide what principle or principles to apply in order to solve the problem. This technique focuses on this step in problem solving. It provides students with a few problems and asks them to state the principle that best applies to each problem.

Step-by-step procedure

— Identify the basic principles that you expect students to learn in your course. Make sure focus only on those that students have been taught.

— Find or create sample problems or short examples that illustrate each of these principles. Each example should illustrate only one principle.

— Create a *What's the Principle?* form that includes a listing of the relevant principles and specific examples or problems for students to match to those principles.

— Try out your assessment on a graduate student or colleague to make certain it is not too difficult or too time-consuming to use in class.

— After you have make any necessary revisions to the form, apply the assessment.

BASIC ASSESMENT CONCEPTS FOR TEACHERS AND SCHOOL ADMINISTRATORS

Several authors have argued that there are a number of essential assessment concepts, principles, techniques, and procedures that teachers and administrators need to know, there continues to be relatively little emphasis on assessment in the preparation or professional development of teachers and administrators. Nevertheless, guidance is provided through established professional standards for assessment skills of teachers (Standards for Teacher Competence in Educational Assessment of Students, a framework of assessment tasks for administrators, the Code of Professional Responsibilities in Educational Measurement, the Code of Fair Testing Practices in Education, and the new edition of Standards for Educational and Psychological Testing.

Assessment is inherently a process of professional judgement: Professional judgment is the foundation for all assessment. The measurement of student performance may seem "objective," given such practices as machine scoring and multiple—choice test items, but even these approaches are based on professional assumptions and values. Whether that judgment occurs in constructing test questions, scoring essays, creating rubrics, grading participation, combining scores, or interpreting standardized test scores, the essence of the process is making professional interpretations and decisions.

Assessment is based on separate but related principles of measurement evidence and evaluation: It is important to understand the difference between measurement evidence (differentiating degrees of a trait by description or by assigning scores) and evaluation (interpreting the description or scores). Essential measurement evidence skills include the ability to understand and interpret the meaning of descriptive statistical procedures, including variability, correlation, percentiles, standard scores, growth—scale scores, norming, and principles of combining scores for grading. A conceptual understanding of these techniques is needed (not necessarily knowing how to compute statistics) for such tasks as interpreting student strengths and weaknesses, examining reliability and validity evidence, determining grades, and making admissions decisions.

Schafer has indicated that these concepts and techniques comprise part of an essential language for educators. They also provide a common basis for communication about results, interpretation of evidence, and appropriate use of data. This is increasingly important given the pervasiveness of standards—based, high—stakes, large-scale assessments. Evaluation concerns merit and worth of the data as applied to a specific use or context. It involves what Shepard has described as the systematic analysis of evidence to interpret evidence effectively and make value judgments about the meaning of the results.

Assessment dicission making is influenced by a series of tensions: Competing purposes, uses, and pressures result in tensions for teachers and administrators as they make assessment—related decisions. For example, good teaching incorporates assessments that motivate and engage students in ways that are consistent with teachers' philosophies of teaching and learning and with theories of development, learning and motivation. Most teachers want to use constructed-response assessments because they believe this kind of testing is best to ascertain student understanding.

On the other hand, factors external to the classroom, such as mandated large—scale testing, promote different assessment strategies, such as using selected—response tests and providing practice in objective test—taking. Further examples of tensions include formative (informal and ongoing) vs. summative (formal and at the end), criterion—referenced vs. norm-referenced, traditional vs. alternative, authentic vs. contrived, and standardized tests vs. classroom tests. Decisions about assessment are best made with a full understanding of how different factors influence the nature of the assessment.

Assessment influences Student motivation and learning: The nature of assessment influences what is learned and the degree of meaningful engagement by students in the learning process. While Wiggins contends that assessments should be authentic, with feedback and opportunities for revision to improve, rather than simply audit learning, the more general principle is understanding how different assessments affect students. Will students be more engaged if assessment tasks are problem-based? How do students study when they know the test consists of multiple—choice items? What is the nature of feedback, and when is it given to students? How does assessment affect student effort? Recent research summarized by Black & Wiliam, for example, shows that student self-assessment skills, learned and applied as part of formative assessment, enhance student achievement.

Assessment contains error: Teachers and administrators need to know not only that there is error in all classroom and standardized assessments, but also, more specifically, how reliability is determined and how much error is likely. With so much emphasis today on high-stakes testing for promotion, graduation, teacher and administrator accountability, and school accreditation, it is critical that all educators understand such concepts as standard error of measurement, reliability coefficients, confidence intervals, and standard setting. Two reliability principles deserve special attention:

1. Reliability refers to scores, not instruments;
2. Typically, error is underestimated.

Good assessment enhances instruction: Just as assessment affects student learning and motivation, it also influences the nature of instruction in the classroom. When assessment is integrated with instruction, it informs teachers about what activities and assignments will be most useful, what level of teaching is most appropriate, and how summative assessments provide diagnostic information. During instructional activities, informal, formative assessment helps teachers know when to move on, when to ask more questions, when to give more examples, and how to respond to student questions. Standardized test scores, when used appropriately, help teachers understand student strengths and weaknesses in order to target further instruction.

Good assessment is valid: As with reliability, validity has certain technical terms and issues associated with it that are essential in helping teachers and administrators make reasonable and appropriate inferences from assessment results (e.g., types of validity evidence, validity generalization, construct underrepresentation, construct—irrelevant variance, and discriminate and convergent evidence). Of critical importance is the concept of evidence based on consequences, a new major validity category in the recently revised Standards. Both intended and unintended consequences of assessment need to be examined with appropriate evidence that supports particular arguments or points of view. Of equal importance is getting teachers and administrators to understand their role in gathering and interpreting validity evidence.

Good assessment is fair and ethical: Arguably, the most important change in the recently published Standards is an entire new major section entitled "Fairness in Testing." The Standards presents four views of fairness: as absence of bias (e.g., offensiveness and unfair penalization), as equitable treatment, as equality in outcomes, and as opportunity to learn. It includes entire chapters on the rights and responsibilities of test takers, testing individuals of diverse linguistic backgrounds, and testing individuals with disabilities or special needs. Three additional areas are also important:

1. Student knowledge of learning targets and the nature of assessments prior to instruction (e.g., what will be tested, how it will be graded, scoring criteria, anchors, exemplars);
2. Student prerequisite knowledge and skills, including test-taking skills; and
3. Avoidance of stereotypes.

Good assessments use multiple methods: Assessment that is fair, leading to valid inferences with a minimum of error, is a series of measures that show student understanding through multiple methods. A complete picture of what students understand and can do is put together in pieces comprised by different approaches to assessment. While testing experts and testing companies stress that important decisions should not be made on the basis of a single test score, some educators at the local level, and some politicians at the state and national levels, seem determined to violate this principle. There is a need to understand the entire range of assessment techniques and methods and their limitations.

Good assessment is efficient and feasible: Teachers and school administrators have limited time and resources. Consideration must be given to the efficiency of different approaches to assessment, balancing needs to implement methods required to provide a full understanding with the time needed to develop and implement the methods and score results. Teacher skills and knowledge are important to consider, as are the levels of support and resources.

Good assessment appropriately incorporates technology: As technology advances and teachers become more proficient in the use of technology, there will be increased opportunities for teachers and administrators to use computer—based techniques (e.g., item banks, electronic grading, computer—adapted testing, computer—based simulations),Internet resources, and more complex, detailed ways of reporting results. There is, however, a danger that technology will contribute to the mindless use of new resources, such as using items online developed by some companies without adequate evidence of reliability, validity, and fairness, and crunching numbers with software programs without sufficient thought about weighting, error, and averaging.

To summarize, what is most essential about assessment is understanding how general, fundamental assessment principles and ideas can be used to enhance student learning and teacher effectiveness. This will be achieved as teachers and administrators learn about conceptual and technical assessment concepts, methods, and procedures, for both large-scale and classroom assessments, and apply these fundamentals to instruction.

IMPROVING TEACHER EVALUATIONS

Teacher evaluations are often designed to serve two purposes: to measure teacher competence and to foster professional development and growth. A teacher evaluation system should give teachers useful feedback on classroom needs, the opportunity to learn new teaching techniques, and counsel from principals and other teachers on how to make changes in their classrooms. To achieve these goals, evaluators must first set specific procedures and standards. The standards should

- relate to important teaching skills,
- be as objective as possible,
- be clearly communicated to the teacher before the evaluation begins and be reviewed after the evaluation is over, and
- be linked to the teacher's professional development.

Evaluators should consider a variety of teaching skills. If the evaluators use several sources of information about a teacher's performance, they can make a more accurate evaluation. Some procedures evaluators can use are to:

- *Observe classroom activities*: This is by far the most common form of data collection for evaluation. The goal of class observations is to obtain a representative sample of a teacher's performance in the classroom. Evaluators cannot accomplish this goal with a sample of only a few hours of observation or with an observation of only one class. Observations can be formal and planned or informal and unannounced. Both forms of evaluation can provide valuable information.

— *Review lesson plans and classroom records*: Lesson plans can reflect how well a teacher has thought through instructional goals. Looking at classroom records, such as tests and assignments, can indicate how well a teacher has linked lesson plans, instruction, and testing.

— *Expand the number of people involved in the evaluations*: Most often principals or department supervisors conduct evaluations. Again, many state laws and collective bargaining agreements specify that teacher's supervisors evaluate their performance. This system works well if the only goal of evaluation is to determine competence. If the goal of the evaluation is to promote growth, however, other evaluators should participate. Self-evaluations give teachers' perspective on their work. Surprisingly, few school systems require self-evaluations. Peer and student evaluations, if schools administer them properly, can also benefit teachers.

Teachers who want to improve their teaching are eager to know how other teachers and their students view them. These are the people who interact with the teacher everyday; their perspective should not be ignored during the evaluation process.

A post-observation conference can give teachers feedback on their strengths and weaknesses. Evaluators must remember to:

— deliver the feedback in a positive and considerate way;

— offer ideas and suggest changes that make sense to the teacher;

— maintain a level of formality necessary to achieve the goals of the evaluation;

— maintain a balance between praise and criticism; and

— give enough feedback to be useful but not so much that the teacher is overwhelmed.

Linking evaluation and development is a difficult task for teachers, evaluators, and principals. Although there are few easy answers, evaluation can be used to

— work with teachers to set specific, achievable goals;

— provide constructive criticism and suggestions to improve weak areas and amplify strengths; and

— enlist experienced teachers to help improve the performance of less experienced teachers.

Experienced teachers often state that evaluations are not productive. Some of this dissatisfaction is based on experiences which can be avoided:

— Teachers not having any input into the evaluation criteria. Other professionals (doctors, lawyers, engineers) control the criteria for entering and maintaining membership in their profession. Teachers, on the other hand, often do not have that privilege. State laws or school boards decide the focus of the evaluation. This leads teachers to distrust the evaluation process and to question the validity of the results it produces.

— Evaluators not spending enough time on the evaluation. Teachers complain that the principal, or whoever is conducting the evaluation, does not have the time to gather quality information and provide useful feedback. After a teacher's first year evaluation, he or she may not have another evaluation for two or three years, sometimes longer.

— Evaluators not being well trained. Teachers complain that few evaluators have any special training to help them plan and carry out a successful evaluation. Even worse, many have had little or no recent experience in the classroom. The criteria for evaluations are often vague, subjective, and inconsistent. This robs the evaluator of the credibility needed to carry out an effective evaluation.

— Results of evaluations not being used to further teacher development. For many teachers, the evaluation process can be a dead end. The results do not figure into salary increases, promotions, or any meaningful program for professional development. Few districts have established a clear link between teacher evaluation and teacher development.

TEACHER MENTORING

Mentoring is the establishment of a personal relationship for the purpose of professional instruction and guidance. In education, the value of mentoring has been recognized in the use of teachers and other professionals in one-on-one instruction of students for vocational education, science, and reading. Mentoring programs have been implemented recently for beginning teacher induction and continuing staff development.

Characteristcs and activities of mentoring

From the literature on mentoring in professions, Bova and Phillips compiled a list of ten characteristics inherent in any mentor-protege relationship.

1. Mentor-protege relationships grow out of voluntary interaction.
2. The mentor-protege relationship has a life cycle: introduction; mutual trust-building; teaching of risk-taking, communication, and professional skills; transfer of professional standards; and dissolution.
3. People become mentors to pass down information to the next generation.
4. Mentors encourage proteges in setting and attaining short- and long-term goals.
5. Mentors guide technically and professionally. Mentors teach proteges skills necessary to survive daily experiences and promote career-scope professional development.
6. Mentors protect proteges from major mistakes by limiting their exposure to responsibility.
7. Mentors provide opportunities for proteges to observe and participate in their work.

8. Mentors are role models.
9. Mentors sponsor proteges organizationally and professionally.
10. Mentor-protege relationships end, amiably or bitterly.

Some school systems have formalized mentoring processes as part of newly developed induction programs, thus compromising some of the mentor-protege relationship characteristics. Voluntary participation becomes mandatory for the protege. At the same time the sphere of influences in which the mentor would ordinarily affect the protege is decreased by time and authority restrictions. The mentor cannot regulate the beginning teacher's levels of responsibility. The mentor does not have the freedom to direct the protege's activities nor the time to adequately oversee developing classroom performance. The mentoring relationship can be supported by creating a school environment which openly offers assistance and provides the means to expand the initiate's repertoire of teaching techniques and classroom management skills.

Benefits of mentoring

As an interactive system, mentoring benefits all participants: the mentor, the protege, and the school system. Mentors gain the satisfaction of being able to transfer skills and knowledge accumulated through extensive professional practice. Much of this knowledge is intangible and is not contained in teacher preparation programs. It might be lost entirely if it were not rediscovered by each beginner. The questions from beginning teachers provide opportunities for mentor teachers to reexamine their own classroom practices and the effects of accepted instructional techniques on the teaching/learning process. The protege benefits in three major ways: fast assimilation into the school environment, establishment of professional competence, and introduction to teaching as a continually developing, lifelong career. One of the most recognized uses of mentoring is the conveyance of operating procedures to the beginner.

The school administration provides an introduction to the rules but the mentor teaches the skills necessary to comply and cope with them. The mentor provides the protege with opportunities to develop professional competence through a cycle of observation/assessment/practice/assessment. This permits continuous communication and constant feedback to the protege. Classroom skills develop under the mentor's constant and consistent assistance. The mentor also guides the protege though the maze of local and state administration systems which potentially influence the practices of the classroom teacher. Finally, the mentor directs the protege to professional organizations for academic and professional development.

The school district benefits both directly and indirectly from mentoring programs. A school which enthusiastically welcomes beginning teachers and initiates them to active participation in the educational processes potentially reduces its teacher attrition rate. Furthermore, close supervision of the beginning teacher catches problems which may affect the instructional process or discourage the teacher. Involving experienced teachers in the program and providing them the opportunity to pass on their expertise further demonstrates long-term professional interest in the faculty and provides an environment conducive to lifelong professional careers.

Confusing "assessment" with "evaluation" provides a common cause of mentor program failure. An effective mentoring process is built on a foundation of mutual trust. The objective of the process is assistance. Both trust and assistance are placed in serious jeopardy if the mentor is saddled with evaluation responsibilities. Assessment, however, is an important part of the mentoring process which allows the protege self-criticism and direction for improvement. Programs can resolve this conflict by appointing separate evaluators who meet with the protege and mentor to discuss performance evaluations.

Mandatory program participation could cause problems in the mentoring process, but surveys of post-program proteges and mentors repeatedly report enthusiastic support of organized mentoring programs. This seems to indicate that schools can establish an environment for effective mentoring in mandatory programs. Finding criteria and methods for choosing mentors is a problem common to all programs. Some criteria and methods for mentor selection are suggested by Driscoll in her description of the Utah Teacher Evaluation Program. The California Teacher Mentor Program and the Model School Project of Louisville offer additional mentor characteristics. Proteges become good teachers by assimilating the desirable skills, attitudes, and professional outlook of their mentors.

The latter is unlikely unless the beginning teachers are matched judiciously with prequalified senior teachers who share professional interests, expressed educational philosophies, and compatible personalities. Using a mentoring program to fulfill state-mandated and district-required certification, induction, and staff development programs loads mentoring with obligations that the technique is not designed to handle. The mentor is a guide to the profession, not a stand-in for administration. Krupp describes one of few wholly mentoring programs. This experimental program conducted in Connecticut elementary and secondary schools cultivated the spontaneous formation of mentoring relationships among teachers. An introductory seminar for all school staff motivated an interest in the mentoring process.

Successive workshops for volunteer program participants provided information and guidance to mentor teachers and their proteges. In most teacher mentoring programs, mentoring forms a basic component of a multipurpose teacher induction program. Many induction programs seek to qualify a new teacher for certification and permanent employment, necessitating evaluation of teaching skills and providing programs to improve those skills to preset standards. The literature provides many examples of these mentoring-evaluation program hybrids. Another purpose for supporting the teacher mentor/protege relationship with additional induction activities is to restore some of the benefits of professional mentoring which are necessarily curtailed by the teaching environment: time constraints and limitations of personnel interaction.

Driscoll et al. discuss the problems common to the adaptation of the traditionally idealistic relationship of mentor and protege to the teacher's real world of limited time and structured activities. The multipurpose programs come in two varieties: those using mentoring as a part of an induction process and those using mentoring as a tool for general staff development. The Charlotte-Mecklenburg Schools Career Development Program is representative of teacher induction programs which assign each new teacher to an induction committee. This "Advisory/Assessment Team" consists of a school administrator, an instructional consultant (often from a teacher preparation program of a nearby college), and a peer teacher who acts as a mentor to the beginner. These programs back up both the mentor and the protege with separate supporting activities. The system has received favorable reviews, despite the misleading use of the term "assessment": the final team "assessment" determines the employment status for the protege.

Examples of programs which use mentoring as a general approach to staff development are the California Mentor Teacher Program and the proposed Model School System of Louisville, Kentucky. In these specific programs, the use of "mentor" is a misnomer. Both programs professionalize the mentoring process by training senior teachers as master teachers to instruct beginning and experienced teachers in advanced instructional techniques and classroom skills. Each trained "mentor" is assigned a group of "proteges." The mentor also is responsible for curriculum development and the exploration of new instructional techniques.

The concept of training experienced teachers to advise and monitor a group of other teachers does not evolve from developments in the use of mentoring as much as it is derived from twenty years of induction program development. The

California and Louisville programs borrow the best of master teacher programs and combine it with the less personal aspects of mentoring. The success of mentoring programs has been documented largely by opinion survey. Most of the programs using teacher mentoring are less than four years old.

Long-term objectives, including the retention of new teachers and development of experienced ones, have had insufficient time to be realized. However, surveys of perceptions of program success overwhelmingly conclude that beginning teachers expand their techniques, improve teaching skills, and learn classroom management. Furthermore, mentors do appreciate the opportunity to and do pass their expertise on to new teachers. The varieties of mentoring programs described in the literature should allow any school district to find a model which fits its budget, time, and spatial constraints.

TOWARDS GOOD EVALUATION

Doing good evaluation is like doing good research. In both cases, you are trying to answer some important questions about an important topic. The key to doing both activities well is (a) identifying the right questions to ask and (b) figuring out how to answer them.

What are the key questions in the evaluation of teaching? Basically they are: "How well am I teaching? Which aspects of my teaching are good and which need to be improved?" The first question attempts to provide a global assessment, while the second is analytical and diagnostic in character. Before moving to the task of figuring out how to answer these questions, we should look at the reasons for taking time to evaluate. There are five basic sources of information that teachers can use to evaluate their teaching. All evaluation efforts use one or more of these basic sources. Each of these five sources has a unique value as well as an inherent limitation.

Techniques for Good Evaluation

Self-monitoring

Self-monitoring is what people do semi-automatically and semi-consciously whenever they teach. Most of their mental activity is concerned with making the presentation or leading the discussion. But one portion of their mental attention is concerned with "How is it going?" "Are they with me?" "Am I losing them?" "Are they interested or bored?"

Unique Value: The first value of this is that it is immediate and constant. You do not have to wait a week or a day or even an hour to get the results. It happens right away. Hence adjustments are possible right away. The second value is that this information is automatically created in terms that are meaningful to the teacher because it is the teacher who creates the information. It is the teacher, not someone else, who looks at the situation and says "This is what is happening." This does not mean that we always know why it is happening, or what to do about it if it is something we do not like. But we do have our own sense of what is happening.

Frequency: This does and should happen all the time. We may only take a mental pause every few minutes to size up the situation. But by comparison with the other sources of information discussed below, this takes place continuously.

Appropriate Response: What can be done about the subjectivity of self-monitoring? Turn to an objective source of information, one without subjective bias.

Audiotape and Videotape Recordings

Modern technology has given us relatively inexpensive and easy access to audio and video recordings of what we do as teachers. We can put a small audio recorder on the teachers desk or put a video recorder on the side of the classroom and let it run during a class session. Then later we can listen to or view it.

Information from Students

As the intended beneficiaries of all teaching, students are in a unique position to help their teachers in the evaluation process.

Special value: If we want to know whether students find our explanations of a topic clear, or whether students find our teaching exciting or dull, who else could possibly answer these kinds of questions better than the students themselves? Of the five sources of information described here, students are the best source for understanding the immediate effects of our teaching, i.e., the process of teaching and learning. This information can be obtained in two distinct ways: questionnaires and interviews, each with its own relative values.

Questionnaires. The most common method of obtaining student reactions to our teaching is to use a questionnaire. Lots of different questionnaires exist but most in fact ask similar kinds of questions: student characteristics (e.g., major, GPA, reasons for taking the course), the students characterization of the teaching (e.g., clear, organized, interesting), amount learned, overall assessment of the course and/or the teacher (e.g., compared to other courses or other teachers, this one is ...), and sometimes, anticipated grade. The special value of questionnaires, compared to interviews, is that they obtain responses from the whole class and they allow for an anonymous (and therefore probably more candid) response. The limitation of questionnaires is that they can only ask a question once, i.e., that cannot probe for further clarification, and they can only ask questions that the writer anticipates as possibly important.

Questionnaires can be given at three different times: the beginning, middle and end of a course. Some teachers use questionnaires at the beginning of a course to get information about the students, e.g., prior course work or experience with the subject, preferred modes of teaching and learning, and special problems a student might have (e.g., dyslexia). Many use mid-term questionnaires to get an early warning of any existing problems so that changes can be made in time to benefit this set of students. The advantage of end-of-term questionnaires is that all the learning activities have been completed. Consequently, students can respond meaningfully to questions about the overall effectiveness of the course.

Interviews. The other well-established way of finding out about student reactions is to talk to them. Either the teacher(if sufficient trust and rapport exist) or an outside person (if more anonymity and objectivity are desired) can talk with students for 15-30 minutes about the course and the teacher. The special value of interviews is that students often identify unanticipated strengths and weaknesses, and the interviewer can probe and follow-up on topics that need clarification. The limitation of course is that a professor can usually only interview a sub-set of the class, not the whole class. This leaves some uncertainty as to whether their reactions represent the whole class or not.

General limitation: Returning to the general issue of information from students, regardless of how such information is collected, one needs to remember that this is information from students. Although they know better than anyone what their own reactions are, they can also be biased and limited in their own perspectives. They occasionally have negative feelings, often unconsciously, about women, people who are ethnically different from themselves, and international teachers. Perhaps more significantly, students usually do not have a full understanding of how a course might be taught, either in terms of pedagogy or content. Hence they can effectively address what is, but not what might be.

Appropriate response: As with the other limitations, the appropriate response here is to seek another kind of information. In this case, we need information from someone with a professional understanding of the possibilities of good teaching.

Students' Test Results

Teachers almost always give students some form of graded

exercise, whether it is an in-class test or an out-of-class project. Usually, though, the intent of the test is to assess the quality of student learning. We can also use this same information to assess the quality of our teaching.

Special value: The whole reason for teaching is to help someone else learn. Assuming we can devise a test or graded exercise that effectively measures whether or not students are learning what we want them to learn, the test results basically tell us whether or not we are succeeding in our whole teaching effort. This is critical information for all teachers.

Frequency: How often should we give tests? Many teachers follow the tradition of two mid-terms and a final. In my view this is inadequate feedback, both for the students and for the teacher. Weekly or even daily feedback is much more effective in letting students and the teacher know whether they are learning what they need to learn as the course goes along. If the teacher's goal is to help the students learn, this is important information for both parties. And remember, not all tests need to be graded and recorded!

Limitation: It might be hard to imagine that this information has a limitation. After all, this is what it's all about, right? Did they learn it or not? The problem with this information is its lack of a causal connection: we don't know why they did or did not learn. Did they learn because of, or in spite of, our teaching? Some students work very hard in a course, not because the teacher inspires or motivates them but because their major requires a good grade in the course and the teacher is NOT effective. Therefore they work hard to learn it on their own.

Appropriate response: If we need to know whether one's actions as a teacher are helpful or useless in promoting student learning, we need a different source of information, such as the students themselves.

Outside Observer

In addition to the two parties directly involved in a course, the teacher and the students, valuable information can be obtained from the observations of a third party, someone who brings both an outsider's perspective and professional expertise to the task.

Special value: Part of the value of an outside observer is that they do not have a personal stake in the particular course, hence they are free to reach positive and negative conclusions without any cost to themselves. Also, as a professional, they can bring an expertise either in content and/or in pedagogy that is likely to supplement that of both the teacher and the students. A variety of kinds of observers exist: a peer colleague, a senior colleague, or an instructional specialist. Peer colleagues, e.g., two TA's or two junior professors, can visit each others classes and share observations. Here the political risk is low and each one can empathize with the situation and challenges facing the other. Interestingly, the person doing the observing in these exchanges often finds that they learn as much as the person who gets the feedback.

Senior colleagues can be of value because of their accumulated experience. Although one has to be selective and choose someone who is respected and with whom the political risk is low, experienced colleagues can offer ideas on alternative ways of dealing with particular topics, additional examples to illustrate the material, etc. A third kind of outside observer, an instructional consultant, is available on many campuses. They may or may not be able to give feedback on the clarity and significance of the content material, but their expertise in teaching allows them to comment on presentation techniques, discussion procedures, and ideas for more active learning.

Frequency: Beginning TA's and beginning faculty members should consider inviting one or more outside observers to their classes at least once a semester for two or three years. They need to get as many new perspectives on teaching as soon as possible. After that, more experienced teachers would probably benefit from such feedback at least once every year or two. We change as teachers; as we do, we need all the feedback and fresh ideas we can find.

Limitations: Again, the strength of being an outsider is also its weakness. Outside observers can usually only visit one or two class sessions and therefore do not know what happens in the rest of the course. Apart from this general problem, each kind of observer has its own limitation. The peer colleague may also have limited experience and perspectives; the senior colleague may be someone who makes departmental decisions about annual evaluations and tenure; and the instructional consultant may have limited knowledge of the subject matter.

Appropriate response: As with the other sources, the response to these limitations is to use a different source, either a different kind of outside observer or one of the other sources described above.

A COMPREHENSIVE EVALUATION SCENARIO

For exampler in the case of Professor X, he is a relatively young person, only two years into his tenure track position at University Would Be Good. This fall he will be teaching a junior level course on International Trade. He once attended a workshop on Evaluating Your Own Teaching, so he knows what he should do. On the first day of class, he keeps his eyes and ears open (self-monitoring) to see what sort of personality this year's class has. In addition, he asks students to fill out a short questionnaire about business or international experience they have had, prior course work in related areas, and what they hope to get out of the course. From this he discovers a wide range of backgrounds.

Some students have extensive international experience and others have none at all. Perhaps he can use the former as a resource for the latter. A few weeks into the course, he brings a small cassette recorder into class and makes an audio recording. After listening to it, he feels reasonably good about his presentation but notes there is little student participation. Class time consists mainly of "teacher-talk." The weekly quizzes are turning out okay, but he had hoped that, since they were upper division students, the class would be getting into it a bit more. After thinking about this awhile and talking to one of his departmental colleagues, he decides to call the university instructional development program and request a class review. His colleague said these people actually make some good suggestions once in awhile.

The consultant, who was recently hired into the program because of her doctorate in instructional communication, meets with the professor, visits his class twice, and then shares her observations with him. Her reaction is that the lectures seem good enough, but there is just too much of the same thing day after day: lecture, lecture, lecture. She suggests using some active learning strategies. After hearing the reaction of the consultant, Professor X decides to use a mid-term questionnaire available from the instructional development program to see if the students feel the same way. The consultant helps him interpret the results, which indicate a degree of boredom with the steady diet of lectures.

The consultant gives him a handout on "enhanced lectures" that shows how to intersperse some active learning activities in between shorter lecture segments. They also discuss some possible larger modifications for next semester. On the end-of-semester course evaluation, Professor X adds some special questions about the changes he has made. The responses indicate that students like the changes, and the overall results, while not yet outstanding, are appreciably higher than in previous terms. The point of this scenario is to illustrate that a thorough evaluation of teaching can be effective in identifying important changes that can be made, and that such evaluation is much more extensive than simply looking at one comparative statistic on an end-of-semester questionnaire.

But how costly is a comprehensive evaluation plan in terms of the time required? Based on the above example following estimate of the time required beyond what happens anyway in normal teaching:

Task	Additional Time (hrs)
Self-monitoring	0 (did automatically anyway)
Initial questionnaire	1 (writing, interpreting)
Audio-recording	1 (reviewing afterwards)
Weekly quizzes	0 (did this anyway)
Visit with consultant	3 (three times)
Mid-term questionnaire	1 (constructing, interpreting)
End-of-term questionnaire	1(for added questions)
Total	7 hours

The seven hours required for a comprehensive evaluation is an addition of about 5% to the total time required for teaching one three-credit hour course in one semester. This amounts to less than 1/2 hour per week for the whole term. This is a small but wise investment that informed Professor X of an important area of his teaching that needed improving. This investment will pay big dividends in effectiveness and satisfaction in a major area of his professional life for many years.

Sources of Assistance

Professors should not think that they have to do it alone when it comes to evaluating their teaching. Following are some sources of assistance that are available for two important activities: constructing or selecting a questionnaire and figuring out how to make needed improvements.

Student questionnaires

The first option for getting a questionnaire to use in class is to write it yourself. At institutions with instructional development programs, consultants can help in this process. Custom-made questionnaires can focus on specific questions the professor has about his or her teaching. Or they can be open-ended, asking questions like: How satisfied are you with what you are learning?

What do you like most about the course? If you could change one thing about the course, what would it be?

A second source is often the institution itself. Many institutions have questionnaires that are available, or required, for end-of-term use. These have the advantage of being ready-made, but they also frequently allow the professor to add his own questions. The third option is to use a nationally available questionnaire.

Ideas for improving

How to find out what one's strengths and weaknesses are as a teacher? But having identified them, a professor still needs ideas and assistance on how to make needed improvements. Four resources can be helpful with this: selected colleagues, books and journals, institutionally-based instructional development programs, and off-campus workshops. The handiest resource is undoubtedly colleagues who are creative and effective in their own teaching. They are usually flattered by requests to visit their classes, review their course materials, and discuss their teaching strategies and philosophy.

A wide variety of reading material is available on teaching and ways to improve it. Several disciplines have journals with articles on teaching a specific subject matter. Some are focused specifically on college-level teaching. A third resource, which is available on many campuses, is an instructional development program. During the last two decades more and more institutions have seen fit to sponsor such a program as an appropriate investment in the single most costly and important factor in a university's quality: the faculty. The professional staff in these programs can offer selected reading material, share their own ideas, and provide classroom observations and feedback to faculty members.

Finally, a number of disciplinary associations, regional consortia, and entrepreneurial persons at various universities now offer workshops, often in the summer, for regional and national audiences of faculty members wanting to learn how to become better teachers. These range from a few days to a few weeks in length. They give participants a chance to hear new ideas, systematically study a wide range of issues and topics, and practice new possibilities in a low-risk setting with feedback from understanding and sympathetic peers.

2

ROLE OF EVALUATION IN TEACHING-LEARNING PROCESS

Evaluation is a core part of the educational delivery process. Many practitioners in the higher education system are reasonably skilled in the art (and science) of evaluating teaching and learning. Yet, many lack essential skills of evaluation. This module is to provide learning experiences for the "experts" and "novices" alike. Dison and De Groot have stressed the need for compatibility between content, teaching methods and assessment procedures. It is only when these are in tandem that learning can be appropriately assessed. The outcome-based evaluation (OBE) model of student assessment in higher education is now gaining wide acceptance. After completing the module, you should be able to :

— explain concepts used in evaluation

— develop techniques for evaluating the performance of your student;

— analyse and interpret learner's assessment results ; and

— conduct self evaluation of your teaching.

NATURE OF EVALUATION

Evaluation varies based on its nature, which may be quantitative or qualitative . In the field of education, evaluation is usually of a quantitative nature. Grades and ordered categories (A,B,C,D) used to measure the scope of results scored by learners relate to a quantitative type of evaluation. For example, the quantitative evaluation of the internal efficiency of an academic year may be quantitatively evaluated based on :

— the ratio between the number of degree holders and the number of registered learners

— the ratio between the number of repeaters and the total enrollment figure.

Evaluation may also be qualitative. For instance, the internal efficiency of an academic year may be qualitatively evaluated by :

— comparing skills acquired by the end of the school year with learners' skills in the beginning of the year,

— comparing targeted skills with acquired skills.

A teacher has arranged the content of his annual courses in modules. He gives tests at the end of each module. The teacher has in mind a double objective: 1°. To compare all learners' performance levels and to classify them based on their achievements with each test ; 2°. To provide each learner with adequate information to help him improve his performances. What is the type of tests organised by the teacher at the conclusion of each module?

EVALUATION TOOLS IN HIGHER EDUCATION

The major tools used to evaluate learning are :

— Tests

— Questionnaires

— Observation Schedules

— Interview Guides

The major tool of evaluation in higher institutions are tests. Tests can be of various types. They can be classified on the following basis :

By Kind of item

— Choice items (true-false, multiple choice, matching)

— Completion items

— Short answer items

— Essay items

By how observations are scored

— Objectives tests

— Subjective tests

By degree of standardization

— Standardised tests

— Non standardised tests

By administrative conditions

— Individual tests

— Group tests

By language emphasis of response

— Verbal tests

— Performance tests

By emphasis on time

— Power tests

— Speed tests

By score-referencing scheme

— Norm-referencing

— Criterion-referencing

By what attribute is measured

— *Achievement tests*

— Survey batteries

— Specific subject tests

— *Aptitude tests*

— General scholastic aptitude tests

— Readiness tests

— Tests of specific aptitudes

— *Personality and adjustment measures*

— Projective techniques

— Structured tests

— Self-report questionnaires

— *Interest inventories*

— Vocational or career interests

— Other interest inventories

— *Attitude and values questionnaires*

Description of Tests

Tests can be described in a variety of ways:

— Group and individual tests differ in the number of persons to whom they are simultaneously administered as well as in the manner of their administration. Group tests sacrifice maximum examinee-examiner interaction, personalised testing conditions, and clinical observations for cost and efficiency.

— Tests differ in their objectivity – the extent to which every observer of the examinee's performance on the test will give exactly the same report of what was observed. The scoring of a test is subjective if the report of the observed performance varies a great deal from one observer to the next.

— Standardisation is the extent to which a test's observational procedures, equipment and materials, and scoring rules are pre-established so that exactly the same testing procedure can be followed at different times and in different places. This view of standardisation has nothing to do with whether norm-referenced data are provided. It provides a way to improve a test's objectivity and the interpretation of the examinee's performance on the test.

— Verbal tests focus on the verbal responses of examinees, while performance tests focus on non-verbal responses. Verbal ability may be necessary to understand the directions on performance tests and to mediate the non-verbal responses.

— If a test is designed to measure speed of responding, then the items are generally not difficult under unspeeded conditions. Many tests are concerned with assessing the amount of knowledge or understanding an individual possesses, independent of speed, and testing conditions are essentially untimed. Such tests are called power tests. Many tests in education are partially speeded; often this is unknown to both the examinee and examiner.

— Norm-referenced tests describe the examinee by stating where an examinee is located in a specified group of persons. Criterion-referenced tests describe the performance repertoire of an examinee, independent of group membership.

— The questions on a test are called items, and a test can be described in terms of the types of items it contains. There are choice items: true-false, multiple-choice, and matching exercises. There are also supply items: completion, short answer, and essay. No item type has a uniformly distinct advantage under all circumstances.

— Tests are described also in terms of the attributes they are designed to observe. Among these attributes are academic achievements; scholastic – and other – aptitudes; personality traits; and interests, attitudes, and values.

EVALUATION OF TEACHING AND LEARNING IN HIGHER EDUCATION

A decision-making definition of evaluation is very appropriate for higher education. Whatever definition of evaluation one uses however, the following three components of the evaluation process remain valid:

— The entity to be evaluated which could be a product, a process or a performance.

— Measurement of the entity to arrive at a score, grade or other quantitative representation.

— Evaluating the quantitative measure by putting a value on it. The value could take various forms such as pass/fail, first class/second class/third class/pass/fail.

Evaluation of Teaching

Evaluation of teaching of individual teachers may be based on:

— The extent to which he or she displays expected teacher behaviour

— The extent to which achievement of his or her pupils attain expected levels.

— Expected teacher behaviour includes such things as punctuality to class, regularity of attendance to give lectures, adequacy of preparation of lectures given, appropriateness of classroom interaction with students, efficiency; promptness and reliability in grading students' tests and examinations.

— Student achievement may be measured by the various tools listed in section 5.0.

— If we regard the raw scores as being criterion-referenced and plot the frequency curves for each course taken, three basic curves may be obtained.

  i. Positively skewed

  ii. Normal

  iii. Negatively skewed

The most commonly obtained curve with traditional teaching especially with large classes is the normal curve. Bloom in his exposition of Mastery learning says:

"There is nothing sacred about the normal curve. It is the distribution most appropriate to chance and random activity. Education is a purposeful activity, and we seek to have the students learn what we have to teach. If we are effective in our instruction, the distribution of achievement should be very different from the normal curve. In fact, we may even insist that our educational efforts have been unsuccessful to the extent that the distribution of achievement approximates the normal distribution."

In the area of teaching and learning, the UNESCO regional workshop held in Dakar, Senegal, in March 1999 provided useful basic evaluation concepts, the various forms of evaluation and the qualities of good evaluation tools. The forms of evaluation identified by the Dakar workshop included: coursework, written examinations (essays, multiple choice, etc) oral and aural examinations, project work, laboratory reports, class tests, direct observations (clinical education, teaching practice, practicum), term papers and theses. The features and the qualities of a good evaluation tool are as follows: validity, reliability, fairness, practicability, relevance and economical.

In a teaching and learning situation, evaluation has accrued benefits to both the teacher and the learner in that it enables:

— the teacher to identify what the learners know or do not know in order to facilitate him/her to teach more effectively, and

— the learner to learn more effectively.

In addition to the above benefits, evaluation enables the institutions to make summative judgement about the adequacy of the learner's performance in the form of:

— grading

— classification

— certification

A major problem for approximately 95% of the Kenya universities and middle level college staff, other than those in the faculties of education, is that they have no pedagogical training and therefore lack skills in the development of evaluation items. These deficiencies lead to the following negative effects:

— teachers' misconception of both the purpose of evaluation and the various forms of evaluation;

— teachers' setting of cognitively less demanding tasks that encourage students to reproduce subject matter;

— teachers' misuse of examinations to instil fear among students.

In addition, given the current large class sizes, lecturers have not been effective in:

— giving students feedback on their performance

— indicating to students what they could have done to improve their performance,

— providing adequate face -to-face interaction

Some possible solutions to these deficiencies could be found for example through:

— provision of in -service training on theories and practices in education;

— In-building quality in evaluation the provision of in-service training on item writing·, moderation and marking system;

— Utilizing group evaluation facilitates acquisition on interpersonal skills, teamwork skills;

— Using a mix of different tasks would give students the best opportunity to demonstrate the quality of their learning, and

— Making students know what is expected of them.

Assessing Academic Staff

The problem connected with evaluating teaching methods is less attributed to the lack or inadequacy of appropriate pedagogic techniques than to the negative attitudes of certain teachers in this respect. Such evaluation can inevitably be done by observing the performance of teachers because an objective assessment can be made only on the basis of their conduct. With regard to the objectives of training, qualification and assessment of lessons taught and their feed-back, the evaluation can induce the academic staff to improve their performance and thus enhance the quality of teaching; it also helps to ascertain whether the objectives of a coure or a study programme have been attained or to discover the discrepancies between the students' expectations, the teacher's intentions and the demands of the discipline.

All the same, with what tools can one make an objective assessment of a teacher's performance? There is in the first place the video technique which not only allows for the observation of the teacher's performance by a third person, but also encourages self-observation. There is also the practice of course inspection by a high-ranking professor or expert, analysis of syllabi by an administrative body and course evaluation by students.

The assessment of teachers' performance has often been resisted by some teachers and this deserves attention. The refusal can be explained as a resistance to pedagogic innovation, a mean of averting the risks of upsetting the "master" image which the teacher enjoys and the established monopoly of learning power which the master arrogates to himself in the classroom. However, this lack of conformity to the pedagogic practice of evaluation seems to be linked to the cultural context, educational system, the manner in which institutions and their teachers have been made to consider the notions of learning, knowledge and teaching in terms of aptitude, competence and training, the last element being a measurable product of planning. It is also linked to the level of students' participation in managing their studies and in running their school, the quality of instructional information given to teachers which underscores the significance of evaluating their services and skills.

The inherited educational system actually allows for the assessment of teachers in tertiary institutions only on the basis of their research works. Such evaluation has the merit of trying to define certain objective criteria for assessment such as publications and theses, and forcing young graduate assistants or assistant lecturers to distinguish themselves in a discipline before occupying positions of responsibility. On the other hand, it accounts for the preference given to scientific research to the detriment of teaching. Most of the teacher who took part in the debate on scientific research and teaching reached a consensus on the need for training through and for research even though some of them wondered about the place of educational research in the training institutions.

This explains the fact that, in the countries where teachers' performance is assessed, the practice is attributed to the search for the institutions' internal efficiency on account of the economic crisis and/or the phenomenon of student unrest. The revival of educational practices as well as the evaluation of teachers and teaching derives from this situation. That is why students now indulge in making a quasi-systematic evaluation of their teachers. If it more or less provides information on the quality of the pedagogic relationship (criteria for teaching and research: characteristics of a course), it scarcely helps to evaluate the contents and their level of assimilation – at least because the assessments are based on human relations, the sole guarantee, in the eyes of the learners, for efficient teaching. This experience now reveals that students' assessments can measure the level of conviviality and human warmth!

However, the assessment that students make of the instruction received is a source of vital information for every lecturer who cares about improving his course. This practice is fruitful because it is rare to find instances where no deductions are made from the remarks given or from the analysis of their comments for improvement. A policy on this type of evaluation can only be incorporated into a comprehensive effort by an institution determined to provide quality education. This practice indeed goes beyond the questionnaires filled by students to take into account all the other pedagogic parameters. With all precautions taken (agreement on the validity of questionnaires, objectiveness in data gathering), it is possible to ask the teachers deserving promotion to submit an evaluation report on their performance in order to reinforce the pedagogic judgement or opinion of his peers, which cannot be ignored.

3

EDUCATIONAL OBJECTIVES

BLOOM'S TAXONOMY OF EDUCATIONAL OBJECTIVES

One of the most widely used ways of organizing levels of expertise is according to Bloom's Taxonomy of Educational Objectives. Bloom's Taxonomy uses a multi-tiered scale to express the level of expertise required to achieve each measurable student outcome. Organizing measurable student outcomes in this way will allow us to select appropriate classroom assessment techniques for the course. There are three taxonomies. Which of the three to use for a given measurable student outcome depends upon the original goal to which the measurable student outcome is connected. There are *knowledge-based* goals, *skills-based* goals, and *affective* goals (affective: values, attitudes, and interests); accordingly, there is a taxonomy for each. Within each taxonomy, levels of expertise are listed in order of increasing complexity. Measurable student outcomes that require the higher levels of expertise will require more sophisticated classroom assessment techniques.

To determine the level of expertise required for each measurable student outcome, first decide which of these three broad categories (knowledge-based, skills-based, and affective) the corresponding course goal belongs to. Then, using the appropriate Bloom's Taxonomy, look over the descriptions of the various levels of expertise. Determine which description most closely matches that measurable student outcome. Bloom's

Table 1: Bloom's Taxonomy of Educational Objectives for Knowledge-Based Goals

Level of Expertise Outcome	Description of Level	Example of Measurable Student
1. Knowledge	Recall, or recognition of terms, ideas, procedure, theories, etc.	When is the first day of Spring?
2. Comprehension	Translate, interpret, extrapolate, but not see full implications or transfer to other situations, closer to literal translation.	What does the summer solstice represent?
3. Application	Apply abstractions, general principles, or methods to specific concrete situations.	What would Earth's seasons be like if its orbit was perfectly circular?
4. Analysis	Separation of a complex idea into its constituent parts and an understanding of organization and relationship between the parts. Includes realizing the distinction between hypothesis and fact as well as between relevant and extraneous variables.	Why are seasons reversed in the southern hemisphere?
5. Synthesis	Creative, mental construction of ideas and concepts from multiple sources to form complex ideas into a new, integrated, and meaningful pattern subject to given constraints.	If the longest day of the year is in June, why is the northern hemisphere hottest in August?
6. Evaluation	To make a judgment of ideas or methods using external evidence or self-selected criteria substantiated by observations or informed rationalizations.	What would be the important variables for predicting seasons on a newly discovered planet?

Table 2: Bloom's Taxonomy of Educational Objectives for Skills-Based Goals

Level of Expertise	Description of Level	Example of Measurable Student Outcome
Perception	Uses sensory cues to guide actions	Some of the colored samples you see will need dilution before you take their spectra. Using only observation, how will you decide which solutions might need to be diluted?
Set	Demonstrates a readiness to take action to perform the task or objective	Describe how you would go about taking the absorbance spectra of a sample of pigments?
Guided Response	Knows steps required to complete the task or objective	Determine the density of a group of sample metals with regular and irregular shapes.
Mechanism	Performs task or objective in a somewhat confident, proficient, and habitual manner	Using the procedure described below, determine the quantity of copper in your unknown ore. Report its mean value and standard deviation.
Complex Overt Response	Performs task or objective in a confident, proficient, and habitual manner	Use titration to determine the Ka for an unknown weak acid.
Adaptation	Performs task or objective as above, but can also modify actions to account for new or problematic situations	You are performing titrations on a series of unknown acids and find a variety of problems with the resulting

		curves, e.g., only 3.0 ml of base is required for one acid while 75.0 ml is required in another. What can you do to get valid data for all the unknown acids?
Organization	Creates new tasks or objectives incorporating learned ones	Recall your plating and etching experiences with an aluminum substrate. Choose a different metal substrate and design a process to plate, mask, and etch so that a pattern of 4 different metals is created.

Table 3: Bloom's Taxonomy of Educational Objectives for Affective Goals

Level of Expertise	Description of Level	Example of Measurable Student Outcome
Receiving	Demonstrates a willingness to participate in the activity	When I'm in class I am attentive to the instructor, take notes, etc. I do not read the newspaper instead.
Responding	Shows interest in the objects, phenomena, or activity by seeking it out or pursuing it for pleasure	I complete my homework and participate in class discussions.
Valuing	Internalizes an appreciation for (values) the objectives, phenomena, or activity	I seek out information in popular media related to my class.
Organization	Begins to compare different values, and resolves conflicts between them to form an internally consistent system of values	Some of the ideas I've learned in my class differ from my previous beliefs. How do I resolve this?
Characterization by a Value or Value Complex	Adopts a long-term value system that is "pervasive, consistent, and predictable"	I've decided to take my family on a vacation to visit some of the places I learned about in my class.

Taxonomy is a convenient way to describe the degree to which we want our students to understand and use concepts, to demonstrate particular skills, and to have their values, attitudes, and interests affected.

Though the most common form of classroom assessment used in introductory college courses—multiple choice tests—might be quite adequate for assessing knowledge and comprehension, this type of assessment often falls short when we want to assess our students knowledge at the higher levels of synthesis and evaluation. Multiple-choice tests also rarely provide information about achievement of skills-based goals. Similarly, traditional course evaluations, a technique commonly used for affective assessment, do not generally provide useful information about changes in student values, attitudes, and interests.

Thus, commonly used assessment techniques, while perhaps providing a means for assigning grades, often do not provide us (or our students) with useful feedback for determining whether students are attaining our course goals. Usually, this is due to a combination of not having formalized goals to begin with, not having translated those goals into outcomes that are measurable, and not using assessment techniques capable of measuring expected student outcomes given the levels of expertise required to achieve them. Using the CIA model of course development, we can ensure that our curriculum, instructional methods, *and* classroom assessment techniques are properly aligned with course goals.

Note that Bloom's Taxonomy need not be applied exclusively after course goals have been defined. Indeed, Bloom's Taxonomy and the words associated with its different categories can help in the goals-defining process itself. Thus, Bloom's Taxonomy can be used in an iterative fashion to first state and then refine course goals. Bloom's Taxonomy can finally be used to identify which classroom assessment techniques are most appropriate for measuring these goals.

Learning Domains or Bloom's Taxonomy

There is more than one type of learning. A committee of colleges, led by Benjamin Bloom, identified three domains of educational activities. The three domains are cognitive, affective, and psychomotor. Since the work was produced by higher education, the words tend to be a little bigger than we are normally used to. Domains can be thought of as categories. Cognitive is for mental skills (Knowledge), affective is for growth in feelings or emotional areas (Attitude), while psychomotor is for manual or physical skills (Skills). Trainers often refer to these as KAS, SKA, or KSA (Knowledge, Attitude, and Skills). This taxonomy of learning behaviors can be thought of as "the goals of the training process." That is, after the training session, the learner should have acquires these new skills, knowledge, or attitudes.

The committee then produced an elaborate compilation for the cognitive and affective domains, but none for the psychomotor domain. Their explanation for this oversight was that they have little experience in teaching manual skills within the college level. This compilation divides the three domains into subdivisions, starting from the simplest behavior to the most complex. The divisions outlined are not absolutes and there are other systems or hierarchies that have been devised in the educational and training world. However, Bloom's taxonomy is easily understood and is probably the most widely applied one in use today.

Cognitive

The cognitive domain involves knowledge and the development of intellectual skills. This includes the recall or recognition of specific facts, procedural patterns, and concepts that serve in the development of intellectual abilities and skills. There are six major categories, which are listed in order below, starting from the simplest behavior to the most complex. The categories can be thought of as degrees of difficulties. That is, the first one must be mastered before the next one can take place.

Knowledge: Recall of data.	Examples: Recite a policy. Quote prices from memory to a customer. Knows the safety rules. Key Words: defines, describes, identifies, knows, labels, lists, matches, names, outlines, recalls, recognizes, reproduces, selects, states.
Comprehension: Understand the meaning, translation, interpolation, and interpretation of instructions and problems. State a problem in one's own words.	Examples: Rewrites the principles of test writing. Explain in one's own words the steps for performing a complex task. Translates an equation into a computer spreadsheet. Key words: comprehends, converts, defends, distinguishes, estimates, explains, extends, generalizes, gives examples, infers, interprets, paraphrases, predicts, rewrites, summarizes, translates.
Application: Use a concept in a new situation or unprompted use of an abstraction. Applies what was learned in the classroom into novel situationsin the workplace.	Examples: Use a manual to calculate an employee's vacation time. Apply laws of statistics to evaluate the reliability of a written test. Key Words: applies, changes, computes, constructs, demonstrates, discovers, manipulates, modifies, operates, predicts, prepares, produces, relates, shows, solves, uses.
Analysis: Separates material or concepts into component parts	Examples: Troubleshoot a piece of equipment by using logical

so that its organizational structure may be understood. Distinguishes between facts and inferences.	deduction: Recognize logical fallacies in reasoning. Gathers information from a department and selects the required tasks for training. Keywords: analyzes, breaks down, compares, contrasts, diagrams, deconstructs, differentiates, discriminates, distinguishes, identifies, illustrates, infers, outlines, relates, selects, separates.
Synthesis: Builds a structure or pattern from diverse elements. Put parts together to form a whole, with emphasis on creating a new meaning or structure.	Examples: Write a company operations or process manual. Design a machine to perform a specific task. Integrates training from several sources to solve a problem. Revises and process to improve the outcome. Keywords: categorizes, combines, compiles, composes, creates, devises, designs, explains, generates. modifies, organizes. plans, rearranges, reconstructs, relates, reorganizes, revises, rewrites, summarizes, tells, writes.
Evaluation: Make judgments about the value of ideas or materials.	Examples: Select the most effective solution. Hire the most qualified candidate. Explain and justify a new budget. Keywords: appraises, compares, concludes, contrasts, criticizes, critiques, defends, describes, discriminates, evaluates, explains, interprets, justifies, relates, summarizes, supports.

Affective

This domain includes the manner in which we deal with things emotionally, such as feelings, values, appreciation, enthusiasms, motivations, and attitudes. The five major categories listed in order are:

Receiving phenomena: Awareness, willingness to hear, selected attention.	Examples: Listen to others with respect. Listen for and remember the name of newly introduced people. Keywords: asks, chooses, describes, follows, gives, holds, identifies, locates, names, points to, selects, sits, erects, replies, uses.
Responding to phenomena: Active participation on the part of the learners. Attends and reacts to a particular phenomenon. Learning outcomes may emphasize compliance in responding, willingness to respond, or satisfaction in responding (motivation).	Examples: Participates in class discussions. Gives a presentation. Questions new ideals, concepts, models, etc. in order to fully understand them. Know the safety rules and practices them. Keywords: answers, assists, aids, complies, conforms, discusses, greets, helps, labels, performs, practices, presents, reads, recites, reports, selects, tells, writes.
Valuing: The worth or value a person attaches to a particular object, phenomenon, or behaviour. This ranges from simple acceptance to the more complex state of commitment. Valuing is based on the internalization of a set of specified values, while clues to these values are expressed in the learner's	Examples: Demonstrates belief in the democratic process. Is sensitive towards individual and cultural differences (value diversity). Shows the ability to solve problems. Proposes a plan to social improvement and follows through with commitment. Informs management on matters that one feels strongly about.

overt behaviour and are often identifiable.	Keywords: completes, demonstrates, differentiates, explains, follows, forms, initiates, invites, joins, justifies, proposes, reads, reports, selects, shares, studies, works.
Organization: Organizes values into priorities by contrasting different values, resolving conflicts between them, and creating an unique value system. The emphasis is on comparing, relating, and synthesizing values.	Examples: Recognizes the need for balance between freedom and responsible behaviour. Accepts responsibility for one's behaviour. Explains the role of systematic planning in solving problems. Accepts professional ethical standards. Creates a life plan in harmony with abilities, interests, and beliefs. Prioritizes time effectively to meet the needs of the organization, family, and self. Keywords: adheres, alters, arranges, combines, compares, completes, defends, explains, formulates, generalizes, identifies, integrates, modifies, orders, organizes, prepares, relates, synthesizes.
Internalizing values (characterization): Has a value system that controls their behaviour. The behaviour is pervasive, consistent, predictable and most importantly, characteristic of the learner. Instructional objectives are concerned with the student's general patterns of adjustment (personal, social, emotional).	Examples: Shows self-reliance when working independently. Cooperates in group activities (displays teamwork). Uses an objective approach in problem solving. Displays a professional commitment to ethical practice on a daily basis. Revises judgments and changes behaviour in light of new evidence. Values people for what they are, not how they look.

	Keywords: acts, discriminates, displays, influences, listens, modifies, performs, practices, proposes, qualifies, questions, revises, serves, solves, verifies.

Psychomotor

The psychomotor domain includes physical movement, coordination, and use of the motor-skill areas. Development of these skills requires practice and is measured in terms of speed, precision, distance, procedures, or techniques in execution. The seven major categories listed in order are:

Perception: The ability to use sensory cues to guide motor activity. This ranges from sensory stimulation, through cue selection, to translation.	Examples: Detects non-verbal communication cues. Estimate where a ball will land after it is thrown and then moving to the correct location to catch the ball. Adjusts heat of stove to correct temperature by smell and taste of food. Adjusts the height of the forks on a forklift by comparing where the forks are in relation to the pallet. Keywords: chooses, describes, detects, differentiates, distinguishes, identifies, isolates, relates, selects.
Set: Readiness to act. It includes mental, physical, and emotional sets. These three sets are dispositions that predetermine a person's response to different situations (sometimes called mindsets).	Examples: Knows and acts upon a sequence of steps in a manufacturing process. Recognize one's abilities and limitations. Shows desire to learn a new process (motivation). NOTE: This subdivision of Psychomotor is closely related with the "Responding to phenomena" subdivision of the Affective domain.

	Keywords: begins, displays, explains, moves, proceeds, reacts, shows, states, volunteers.
Guided response: The early stages in learning a complex skill that includes imitation and trial and error. Adequacy of performance is achieved by practicing.	Examples: Performs a mathematical equation as demonstrated. Follows instructions to build a model. Responds hand-signals of instructor while learning to operate a forklift. Keywords: copies, traces, follows, react, reproduce, responds
Mechanism: This is the intermediate stage in learning a complex skill. Learned responses have become habitual and the movements can be performed with some confidence and proficiency.	Examples: Use a personal computer. Repair a leaking faucet. Drive a car. Keywords: assembles, calibrates, constructs, dismantles, displays, fastens, fixes, grinds, heats, manipulates, measures, mends, mixes, organizes, sketches.
Complex Overt Response: The skillful performance of motor acts that involve complex movement patterns. Proficiency is indicated by a quick, accurate, and highly coordinated performance, requiring a minimum of energy. This category includes performing without hesitation, and automatic performance. For example, players are often utter sounds of satisfaction or expletives as soon as they hit a tennis ball or throw a football, because they can tell by the feel of the act what the result will produce.	Examples: Maneuvers a car into a tight parallel parking spot. Operates a computer quickly and accurately. Displays competence while playing the piano. Keywords: assembles, builds, calibrates, constructs, dismantles, displays, fastens, fixes, grinds, heats, manipulates, measures, mends, mixes, organizes, sketches. NOTE: The key words are the same as Mechanism, but will have adverbs or adjectives that indicate that the performance is quicker, better, more accurate, etc.
Adaptation: Skills are well developed and the individual can modify movement patterns to fit special requirements.	Examples: Responds effectively to unexpected experiences. Modifies instruction to meet the needs of the learners. Perform a task with a

	machine that it was not originally intended to do (machine is not damaged and there is no danger in performing the new task). Keywords: adapts, alters, changes, rearranges, reorganizes, revises, varies.
Origination: Creating new movement patterns to fit a particular situation or specific problem. Learning outcomes emphasize creativity based upon highly developed skills.	Examples: Constructs a new theory. Develops a new and comprehensive training programming. Creates a new gymnastic routine. Keywords: arranges, builds, combines, composes, constructs, creates, designs, initiate, makes, originates.

As mentioned earlier, the committee did not produce a compilation for the psychomotor domain model, but others have. The one discussed above is by Simpson (1972). There are two other popular versions:

R.H. Dave's (1970):

Imitation: Observing and patterning behavior after someone else. Performance may be of low quality. Example: Copying a work of art.

Manipulation: Being able to perform certain actions by following instructions and practicing. Example: Creating work on one's own, after taking lessons, or reading about it.

Precision: Refining, becoming more exact. Few errors are apparent. Example: Working and reworking something, so it will be "just right."

Articulation: Coordinating a series of actions, achieving harmony and internal consistency. Example: Producing a video that involves music, drama, color, sound, etc.

Naturalization: Having high level performance become natural, without needing to think much about it. Examples: Michael

Jordan playing basketball, Nancy Lopez hitting a golf ball, etc.

Harrow's:

— *Involuntary movement* - reaction

— *Fundamental movements* - basic movements

— *Perception* - response to stimuli

— *Physical abilities* - stamina that must be developed for further development

— *Skilled movements* - advanced learned movements

— *No discursive communication* - effective body language

Knowing the three types of learning and what they represent will aid you when selecting learning strategies.

Mastery Learning

John B Carroll inaugurated a fundamental change in thinking about the characteristics of instruction in 1963 when he argued for the idea that student aptitudes are reflective of an individuals' learning rate. In this new paradigm, Carroll suggested that instruction should focus more on the time required for different students to learn the same material. This was in contrast with the classic model in which all students are given the same amount of time to learn and the focus is on differences in ability. He called this learning rate, LR, the degree of learning, which is demonstrated in the formula:

LR = f (time spent learning / time needed to learn)

This describes that the learning rate is a function of the time a learner has to learn to the time he actually needs to learn a given situation of instruction. Carroll's new theory was based on the idea that all learners can have the potential to learn any instruction given, but take different amounts of time to do so. So when a learner's aptitude is seem the context as an index or the learning rate then students are not seen a good or bad learners, but as fast or slow learners.

Carroll identified two factors that affected the learning rate of a student, perseverance of the student, and the opportunity to learn. The first is controlled by the student, that is, how much time they spend on learning, the former is the time allotted to learn by the classroom, or access to materials, etc. However, it was Bloom in 1968 who fully developed the concepts now known as Mastery Learning. In the 1960s, Benjamin Bloom was involved in research on individual differences as applied to learning. Impressed with Carrolls ideas, he took them further by concluding that if,

(1) aptitude could predict a learner's learning rate, then he believed that it should be able to set the degree of learning expected of a student to some level of mastery performance. Then,

(2) see to the instructional variables under an instructors control, such as the opportunity to learn and the quality of the instruction. Thus,

(3) the instructor should be able to ensure that each learner can attain the specified objective. Bloom concluded that given sufficient time and quality instruction, nearly all students could learn.

The theories of Mastery Learning resulted in a radical shift in responsibility for teachers; the blame for a student's failure rests with the instruction not a lack of ability on the part of the student. In this type of learning environment, the challenge becomes providing enough time and employing instructional strategies so that all students can achieve the same level of learning.

How to instruct for mastery:

1. Clearly state the objectives representing the purposes of the course.

2. The curriculum is divided into relatively small learning units, each with their own objectives and assessment.

3. Learning materials and instructional strategies are identified; teaching, modeling, practice, formative evaluation, reteaching, reinforcement, and summative evaluation are included.

4. Each unit is preceded by brief diagnostic tests, or formative assessments.

5. The results of formative tests are used to provide supplementary instruction, or corrective activities to help the learner overcome problems.

As a matter of curriculum development, mastery learning does not focus on content, but on the process of mastering it. Curriculum materials can be designed by inhouse Instructional designers, or via a team approach various professionals in a given setting either in a school, industry, or military. Or instructional materials can be obtained via prepared materials from an outside commercial source. A combination of this is also apparent. However, the instructional materials are developed or obtained, the teachers must evaluate the materials they plan to use to ensure that they match the instructional objectives set up for a given course of instruction.

The mastery learning model is closely aligned with the use of instructional objectives and the systematic design of instructional (ISD) programs. The Criterion Referenced Instruction (CRI) model of Mager of evaluating terminal behaviors is an attempt to implement the mastery learning model. Here the instructor can assess students progress based on the objectives of the instruction rather the traditional norm-referenced test. In addition, the theoretical framework of Skinner with its emphasis on individualized learning and the importance of feedback (reinforcement) is also relevant to mastery learning. Mastery learning ensures numerous feedback loops, based on small units of well-defined, appropriately sequenced outcomes.

Mastery Learning, ML, is an instructional strategy based on the principle that all students can learn a set of reasonable objectives with appropriate instruction and sufficient time to learn. ML puts the techniques of tutoring and individualized instruction into a group learning situation and brings the learning strategies of successful students to nearly all the students of a given group. In its full form it includes a philosophy, curriculum structure, instructional model, the alignment of student assessment, and a teaching approach.

Advantages:

1. Students have prerequisite skills to move to next unit
2. Requires teachers to do task analysis, thereby becoming better prepared to teach the unit
3. Requires teachers to state objectives before designating activities
4. Can break cycle of failure (especially important for minority and disadvantaged students)

Disadvantages (easily dealt with in most cases):

1. Not all students will progress at same pace; this requires students who have demonstrated mastery to wait for those who have not or to individualize instruction
2. Must have a variety of materials for remediation:
3. Must have several tests for each unit
4. If only objective tests are used, can lead to memorizing and learning specifics rather than higher levels of learning

METHODS OF STATING OBJECTIVES

— An objective is a description of a performance you want learners to be able to exhibit before you consider them competent.

— An objective describes an intended result of instruction, rather than the *process* of instruction itself.

When clearly defined objectives are lacking, there is no sound basis for the selection or designing of instructional materials, content, or methods. If you don't know where you are going, it is difficult to select a suitable means for getting there. A second important reason for stating objectives sharply has to do with finding out whether the objective has, in fact, been accomplished. Test or examination s are the mileposts along the road of learning and are supposed to tell instructors and students whether they have been successful in achieving the course objectives. But unless objectives are stated clearly and are fixed in the minds of both parties, tests are at best misleading; at worst, they are irrelevant, unfair, or uninformative.

Test items designed to measure whether important instructional outcomes have been accomplished can be selected or created intelligently only when those instructional outcomes have been made explicit. A third advantage of clearly defined objectives is that they provide students with a means to organize their own efforts toward accomplishment of those objectives. Experience has shown that with clear objectives in view, students at all levels are better able to decide what activities on their part will help them get to where it is important for them to go.

Qualities of Useful Objectives

Useful objectives contain and Audience, Behavior (performance), a Condition, and a Degree (criterion).

— *Audience* : The who. Your objectives had better say, "The student will be able to..."

— *Behavior*: An objective always says what a learner is expected to be able to do. The objective sometimes describes the product or result of the doing. Ask yourself, what is the learner doing when demonstrating achievement of the objective?

— *Condition*: An objective always describes the important conditions (if any) under which the performance is to occur.

— *Degree*: Wherever possible, an objective describes the criterion of acceptable performance by describing how well the learner must perform in order to be considered acceptable.

Behavior

The verb used to describe a desirable behaviour in an instructional objective must be observable.

Overt versus Covert Behaviors

But wait a minute. Something may be a little fishy here. Can you tell whether people are adding? Suppose they were standing perfectly still and claimed to be adding in their heads. Would adding still qualify as a performance?

Overt refers to any kind of performance that can be observed directly, whether that performance be visible or audible. Covert refers to performance that cannot be observed directly, performance that is mental, invisible, cognitive, or internal. Overt performance can be observed by the eye or ear. Covert performance can be detected only when asking someone to say something or to do something.

A performance can be *covert* (mental, internal, invisible, cognitive) as long as there is a direct way determining whether it satisfies the objective. *"A direct way"* means a single behavior that will indicate the covert skill. There is an easy way to handle the matter in stating an objective, a way that helps to avoid arguments about just what ought or ought not to be called a covert performance. Simply follow this rule:

Whenever the performance stated in a n objective is covert, add and indicator behavior to the objective. What that means is this: You want student to be able to add? And adding seems like a covert performance? Then just add an indicator behavior to show the *one single visible thing* students could dont demonstrate mastery of the objective. For example:

— Be able to add numbers (write the solutions) written in binary notation.

— Be able to identify (underline or circle) misspelled words on a page of news copy.

Identifying is a covert skill. You can't see anyone doing it. But you could see a person doing activities that were either associated with the identifying or that were the result of the identifying. So, all you do is add a word or two to your objective to let everyone know what directly visible behavior you would accept as an indicator or the existence of the performance.

Overt/Covert Practices

Below are a few expressions; some describe covert performance, and some describe overt performance.

Here is what to do: On a piece of paper, number five lines 1 through 5 (one line for each expression below). Place check marks (oa O.K.) beside the expressions that describe performances that you can see or hear.

Beside those that describe covert performances, write the simplest indicator behaviors that you can think of that would let you know the covert performances existed. (In other words, what visible thing could you ask someone too that would tell you whether he or she were performing as you desired?)

Behaviour Summary

— An instructional objective describes an intended outcome of instruction rather than an instructional procedure.

— An objective always states a performance, describing what the learner will be DOING when demonstrating mastery of the objective.

— To prepare and objective describing an instructional intent:

a) Write a statement that describes the main intent or performance you expect of the student.

b) If the performance happens to be covert, add an indicator behavior to the objective by which the main performance can be known. Make the indicator the simplest and most direct one possible.

Condition

To state an objective clearly, you will sometimes have to state the conditions you will impose when students are demonstrating their mastery of the objective. Here are some examples:

— Given a problem of the following type...

— Given a list of...

— Given any reference of the learner's choice...

— Given a matrix of intercorrelations...

— When provided with a standard set of tools...

— Given a properly functioning...

— Without the aid of references...

— With the aid of references...

— Without the aid of a calculator...

— Without the aid of tools...

How detailed should you be in your description? Detailed enough to be sure the desired performance would be recognized by another competent person, and detailed enough so that others understand your intent as YOU understand it. Here are some questions you can ask yourself about your objectives as a guide to your identifying important aspects o f the target, or terminal performances you wish to develop:

— What will the learner be allowed to use?

— What will the learner be denied?

— Under what conditions will you expect the desired performance to occur?

— Are there any skills that you are specifically NOT trying to develop? Does the objective exclude such skills?

Degree

If you can specify the acceptable level of performance for each objective, you will have a standard against which to test your instruction. Therefore, you will have the means for determining whether your instruction is successful in achieving your instructional intent. You would know, and the student would know, the quality of performance necessary to work for or exceed. What you must try to do, then, is indicate in your objectives what the acceptable performance level will be by adding word s that describe the criterion of success.

If the thought that now pops into your mind is something like, "*Many of the things I teach are intangible and cannot be evaluated,*" consider this. Maybe so. But if you are teaching things that cannot be evaluated, you are in the awkward position of being unable to demonstrate that you are teaching anything at all. The issue here is not whether all important things can be measured or evaluated. The issue is simply whether you can improve the usefulness of an objective by making clear how well the student must be able to perform to be considered acceptable. Sometimes such a criterion is critical. Sometimes it is of little or no importance at all. But adding a degree to an objective is a way of communicating an important aspect of what it is you want your students to be able to do.

Examples of degrees: time limits, accuracy, quality.

Condtion and degree summary

— A successful objective will specify the important conditions or constraints under which you want the student to perform.

— A successful objective will include a statement that indicates how well that student must perform to satisfy the instructor.

Common pitfalls of Objective writing

1. False performance

— Have a thorough understanding of particle physics.

— Demonstrate a comprehension of the short-story form.

— Be able to relate to others in a demonstration of empathy.

— Be able to understand individual differences in patients.

The above statements have the appearance of objectives, but contain no performances. They are not objectives.

2. Fase givens

— Given three days of instruction...

— Given that the student has completed six laboratory experiments on...

— Given that the student is in the category of gifted...

— Given adequate practice in...

These are words or phrases that follow the word given in an objective but that describe something other than specific conditions the learner must have or be denied when demonstrating achievement of the objective. Most typically, the words describe something about the instruction itself. don't describe the instructional procedure in your objective. You'll have the chance to do that in your mini-lesson.

3. Teaching point

Be able to choose an art print or photo that illustrates a theme of your choice and explain how it illustrates that theme. Similar to a false given, this statement describes a teaching point, a practice exercise, or some other aspect of classroom activity. Don't describe a classroom activity and call it an objective. The main function of an objective is to help course planners decide on instructional content and procedure. If the objective describes a teaching procedure, it will fail to perform its primary purpose because it will be describing instructional practice rather than important instructional outcomes.

Other examples: Be able to discuss in class the case histories handed out by the instructor.

4. Gibberish

— Manifest an increasing comprehensive understanding...

— Demonstrate a thorough comprehension...

— Relate and foster with multiple approaches...

— Have a deep awareness and thorough humanizing grasp...

— The student must be able to demonstrate an ability to develop self- confidence and self-respect...

Leave out the "Ed-speak." It gets in the way of communication. It is noise.

5. Instroctor Performance

— The teacher will provide an atmosphere that will promote the development of self-esteem, confidence, and security in students.

— Demonstrate to students the proper procedures for completing FORM 321.

An instructional objective describes student performance. It avoids saying anything about instructor performance.

6. False criteria

— To the satisfaction of the instructor.

— Must be able to make 80% on a multiple choice exam.

— Must pass a final exam.

Students know who they have to perform for. With the second, you are only giving half of the picture. Eighty percent has no substance. It doesn't tell the student anything. Eighty percent of how many questions? What's in the questions? What exactly is it that they are performing here? The ability to get 80%?

4

Tests and Their Construction

To test or not to test? That is the question evoking substantial debate, as well as various responses within the home schooling community. While there are different ways to teach children and very many different curricula to use in that process, there really are only two positions to take in answering the question of testing. First, consider the position of non-testing. Parents who do not wish to formally test their students usually hold that testing is not needed for three main reasons. First, they feel they can know their children's academic accomplishments through repeated involvement and observation. Secondly, they prefer the lack of pressure that their untested students experience.

Finally, the position is held that the standardized process of evaluation is not something that independent home educators desire for their particular situations. All these views are understood. However, when you look at testing differently, you can see its great benefit. Simply put, testing provides the litmus of discovery - objectively boiling down the process of determining whether your student has actually achieved in certain academic areas. Testing provides the tools needed to verify the student's accomplishments in his or her educational experience. Good tests, including The Diagnostic Prescriptive Assessment, avoid all undue pressure, while recognizing that it is unrealistic to expect the avoidance of any pressure when the determination of accomplishment is the objective. (In fact, most folks will attest that, all of life is composed of a series of choices involving some element of "pressure", whether great or little.)

In fact, The Diagnostic Prescriptive Assessment imposes no time limits on many of its test items and those that do have time limits have been devised in such a way as not be be unduly restrictive. Furthermore, students with attention disorders or learning disabilities are instructed to disregard the time limits. Testing also consolidates subjects, promotes self-confidence and thinking skills and therefore, stimulates academic progression. Outside testing relieves the teaching parent of undue and unrealistic pressure by not requiring the parent to wear the hat of "expert" in the field of evaluation. So, the answer here at DPS to the question is, "Do test, but use the correct measure".

Once you have decided that testing really is a good choice, the question immediately arises, "What test do I have my child take?" It is here that the view can become blurred and confused because of the different kinds of testing available to the homeschooler today. That calls for a consideration of the different kinds of...

GENERAL PRINCIPLES OF TEST CONSTRUCTION

Planning the test

To plan a test, you prepare a two-way table, called a *test blueprint*. The names of the major categories of a taxonomy head the table columns while the row heading indicates the major topics of the subject matter to be tested. In the body of the table, the "cells", formed by a combination of a particular taxonomy category and a particular subject-matter topic, contain specific instructional objectives. Thus, the blueprint serves as a double-entry classifying scheme for specific objectives. After objectives are classified, the number of test items that will be used to test each objective is recorded in the table. Thus, the test blueprint serves as a plan which assures that all important objectives are included and that they receive the proper emphasis on the test.

Hints for Constructing Essay-type Tests

— Define the behaviour the examinee is expected to exhibit or describe the process to be exhibited before beginning to write the essay question.

— Ask questions that require the examinee to demonstrate the ability to use essential knowledge and to do so in situations that are new or novel for the examinee, rather than simply recalling information from a textbook or a classroom.

— Ask questions that are relatively specific or focused, and which require relatively brief responses.

— If a test includes several essay questions, be sure that they cover the appropriate range of topics and complexity of behavior called for in the test blueprint, but be sure that the complexity of the questions are within the educational maturity level of the examinees.

— Require all examinees to answer the same questions; don't give optional questions.

— Word questions so that all examinees will interpret the task the way you intend.

— Word questions so that all examinees know the limits of the tasks, their purposes, and can answer them in the time allotted.

— Word questions so that experts can agree on the correctness of an examinee's response.

— Word questions calling for examinee opinion on controversial matters so that they ask the examinee to give evidence to support the opinion and evaluate the examinee's response in terms of the evidence presented rather than the opinion or position taken.

— Word questions so the examinee can judge the approximate length of the answer desired and knows the point-value of weight each will be given.

Phrasing Essay-type Questions

The following are some hints in phrasing essay-type questions

Comparing:

Describe the similarities and differences between.......

Compare the following two methods for........

Relating Cause and Effect:

What are major causes of ....?

What would be the most likely effects of ...?

Justifying:

Which of the following alternative would you favour and why?

Explain why you agree or disagree with the following statement:

Summarising:

State the main points included in ....

Briefly summarise the contents of ....

Generalising:

Formulate several valid generalisations from the following data.

State a set of principles that can explain the following events.

Inferring:

In light of the facts presented, what is most likely to happen, when...?

What deductions can you make from the statement of....?

Classfying:

Group the following items according to....

What do the following items have in common?

Creating:

List as many ways as you can think of for....

Write a list of questions that should be answered before....

Applying:

Using the principle of.... As a guide, describe how you would solve the following problem situation.

Describe a situation that illustrates the principle of...

Analysing:

Describe the reasoning errors in the following paragraph.

List and describe the main characteristics of...

Describe the relationship between the following parts of...

Synthesising:

Describe a plan for proving that...

Write a well-organised report that shows...

Write a set of specifications for building a...

Evaluating:

Criticise or defend each of the following statements.

Describe the strengths and weaknesses of the following...

Using the criteria developed in class, write a critical evaluation of...

Hints for Scoring Essay-type Answers

Prepare some type of scoring guide (e.g., an outline, an "ideal" answer, or "specimen" responses)

Grade all responses to one question before moving on to the next question.

Periodically re-score previously scored papers.

Score papers without reference to the identity (e.g. registration or matriculation number or name) of the student.

Provide students with feedback on the strengths and weaknesses of their responses.

When the grading decision is crucial, have two or more readers score the essays independently.

Hints for writing short-answer (completion) items

Use the question form of the short-answer variety if possible.

Word each item in specific terms with clear meanings so that the intended answer is the only one possible, and so that the answer is a single word, brief phrase, or number.

Word each item so that the blank or answer space is toward the end of the sentence.

Avoid copying statements verbatim from texts or classroom materials.

Omit important rather than trivial words.

Avoid "butchered" or "mutilated" sentences; use only one or two blanks in a completion sentence.

Keep the blanks of equal length and arrange the items so the answers are placed in a column at the right or left of the sentences.

State the precision, numerical units, or degree of specificity expected of the answer.

Word the items to avoid irrelevant clues or specific determiners.

Hints for writing true-false items

Make sure the item is either definitely true or definitely false.

Avoid verbal clues (specific determiners) that give away the answer.

Test important ideas, knowledge, or understanding (rather than trivia, general knowledge, or common sense).

Keep the word-length of true statements about the same as that of false statements.

Avoid copying sentences directly from textbook and other written materials.

Avoid presenting items in a repetitive or easily learned pattern.

Hints for constructing matching exercising

Within a single matching exercise, make the premises and responses homogeneous.

Write directions that explain completely the intended basis for matching.

Check to see that all the responses function as plausible options to each premise.

Keep the list of premises and responses within a single matching exercise relatively short.

Avoid creating "perfect matching" in which each response matches only one premise.

Place the longer phrases (sentences) in the premise list and the shorter phrases, words, or symbols in the response list.

If at all possible, arrange the responses in a logical, meaningful order.

Use numbers to identify the premises and letters to identify the responses.

Avoid using incomplete sentences for premises.

Keep all the premises and responses belonging to a single matching exercise on the same page.

Hints for constructing multiple-choice items (with emphasis on how to formulate the stem of the item)

To Do	***To Avoid***
If possible, write as a direction question. If an incomplete sentence is used, be sure it implies a direct question.	Avoid extraneous, superfluous, and non-functioning words and phrases that are mere "window dressing."
The alternatives come at the end (rather than in the middle) of the sentence.	Avoid (or use sparingly) negatively worded items.
Control the wording so that vocabulary and sentence structure are at a relatively low and of an option.	Avoid phrasing the item so that the personal opinion of the examinee is non-technical level.
In items testing definitions, place the word or item in the stem and use definitions or descriptions as alternatives	Avoid textbook wording and "textbookish" or stereotyped phraseology.
	Avoid "clueing" and "linking" items (i.e., having the correct answer to one item be clued or

	linked to the correctness of the answer to a previous item

Hints for improving the quality of the alternatives in multiple-choice items

To Do	*To Avoid*
1. In general strive to create three to five functional Alternatives.	1. Avoid overlapping alternatives.
2. All alternatives should be homogeneous and appro-	2. Avoid making the alternatives a priate to the stem collection of true-false items.
3. Put repeated words and phrases the stem.	3. Avoid using "not given", "none of the above", etc, as an alternative in best-answer type of items (use only with correct-answer variety).
4. Use consistent and correct punctuation in relation	4. Avoid using "all of the above"; limit to the stem. Its use to the correct-answer variety.
5. Arrange alternatives in a list format rather than in Alternatives.	5. Avoid using verbal clues in the tandem.
6. Arrange alternatives in a logical or meaningful order.	6. Avoid using technical terms, unknown words or names, and "silly" terms or names as distractors.
7. All distractors should be grammatically correct with	7. Avoid making it harder to eliminate a respect to the stem. Distractor than to choose the keyed alternative.

The requirements or criteria of evaluating tests

The ultimate goal of any evaluation should be to collect relevant valid, reliable and economical information for decisions to be appropriately made. Relevance, validity, reliability and the economical aspect are currently the most expected requirements or criteria for any evaluation test.

The relevance of data collected implies that the subject under evaluation precisely and specially corresponds to the objectives targeted by the evaluation. For example, the relevance of examination tests at the end of a given curriculum makes it necessary to differentiate between examinations meant to evaluate learners' qualification for promotion to an upper class or to move into the job market and active life.

The validity of data collected implies that the evaluation has actually been focused on the subject initially targeted for evaluation. For instance, for the sake of validity, learners' written and oral skills cannot be evaluated with the same tests.

The reliability of data collected implies that they are not determined by the free will and choice of the individual who collected them. For example, the double grading of examination papers is meant to consolidate and further ascertain reliability.

Data analysis and interpretation

Data analysis follows the administration or taking of tests. Data collected at the end of a quantitative evaluation or a qualitative evaluation may nearly always be amenable to statistical processing.

Distribution of scores: Scores of groups can be summarised and interpreted by tabulating a frequency distribution and/or plotting a histogram or polygon. Special terms describe the shapes of distributions including their symmetry, modality, peakedness, and skewness. These graphs can also be used to compare two or more distributions of scores.

Measures of central tendency: Among the summary numbers or statistics used with test scores are those that reflect the average or typical score of the group. Among these are the mode, median, and mean. These indices may be used jointly as well as singly to describe a distribution of scores.

Score variability: Statistics describing the variability or spread of scores are important in understanding a group's score distribution. Of these, the standard deviation has been the most frequently used with educational and psychological tests. This index, a type of average of the deviations from the mean, measures the extent to which persons' scores differ from each other.

Relative location in a distribution of scores: Individuals' scores can be interpreted in terms of their relative location in a distribution. Scores which express this relative standing directly are called norm-referenced scores. Among those described are simple rank in the group; percentile rank, or percent of the group that person's score exceeded; and a linear standard score called the z-score.

The correlation coefficient: The degree of relationship between two sets of scores is quantitatively described by the correlation coefficient. The correlation quantifies the relationship between the z-score on two test. This relationship can be displayed in a scatter diagram, also.

A group of 19 students scored the following grades :

15 ; 13 ;7 ;8 ;9 ;12 ;11 ;10 ;8 ;17 ;18 ;19 ;10 ;12 ;13 ;16 ;5 ;12 ;13

1. Give the frequency table of the 19 grades
2. What is or what are the modes of the 19 grades
3. What is the median of the 19 grades
4. What is the mean or average of the 19 grades
5. Calculate the typical gap of the 19 grades
6. Calculate the standardised grade of each of the 19 grades.

TYPES OF TESTS

In the area of test types, there are generally three kinds that homeschoolers give to their students. They are:

(1) Informal - often, parentally devised daily, weekly, and monthly

(2) Standardized - Norm referenced

(3) Diagnostic - criterion referenced.

*Informal Test:*The Informal testing has the advantages of being tailored both to the certain curriculum and parental evaluation of the student.. Also, it may be designed to be more or less rigorous in its items and requirements. Its disadvantages are in the facts that its designers usually do not possess the expertise found among the devisers and administrators of formal standardized and diagnostic tests. Such a lack of expertise can cause substantial oversight regarding test items, procedures, and goals, with the result that the student is not properly tested according to all grade level requirements.

Standardized Tests: Examples of this kind of test include, The Iowa Test of Basic Skills and the Stanford Achievement Test. Certain states' laws require that homeschoolers take a standardized test with a designated frequency. Home schooled students usually do well on these kinds of tests. Homeschoolers do well on these kinds of tests because of their basic content in math and reading. Homeschoolers do well because they, as a group, are in the top bracket of quality education, all myths aside. Be that as it may, the questions arise, "What is a standardized test and what does it tell me about my student"?

A standardized test is an assessment that has been devised *from* a sample of primarily public school students of a certain grade and age in a particular area. After the test has been duly administered to this group, an average of the group's score is determined as the "standard" for that grade and age. Each student of the same grade and age who thereafter takes the test is assessed according to the average of the sample peer group - hence "norm-referenced" or simply "normed" testing. The foregoing is easy enough to understand. When it comes to understanding the way that a student's answers are *scored* on standardized tests, other confusing rules apply. The scoring system used by these tests is a three-tiered one, called "percentile rank", "stanine", and "grade equivalent".

The "percentile rank" is the most accurate of the three. However, it does not reveal the percent that your child got correct but rather ranks him to the sample peer group of children his age who took the same test. For example, if your child scores in the 75th percentile in Reading Comprehension, this means that he scored as well as or better than 75 percent of the sample peer group of students who took the same test. "Stanine" scores range in numbers from 1-9. Numbers 4-6 are average. These scores place your child within a range of the percentile ranks. The "grade equivalent" scores cause the most excitement among homeschoolers. They are also the most misleading. These scores measure development from year to year.

More importantly though, they do not indicate the grade level that your child is in or should be in. Rather, their scores are relational. For example, if your child who is in 5th grade scored on a 7.6 grade level in math, this does not mean that your child knows all 7th grade math skills or should be placed in 7th grade math. It only means that the score your child received would be the same score that a 7th grader in the sixth month of 7th grade would make when he took the same 5th grade math test.

A big difference - indeed! *Added to all of this* is the fact that standardized tests are devised to include extra-year test items on their grade level tests. In other words, if your student is in 3rd grade, standardized tests are devised in such a way to include some 2nd grade items and some 4th grade items in his 3rd grade test. Okay, so you understand that standardized tests may place your 5th grade student in the 75th percentile with a high stanine score and that he did as well as a 7th grader who took the 5th grade test. What exactly does that tell you? What precisely have you discovered? Not very much. To make matters worse, parents are rarely allowed to view the tests themselves to see what exactly their child did poorly on in order to remediate the weaknesses. It was because of all of the issues addressed above that Mrs. Dixon devised The Diagnostic Prescriptive Assessment, which is a diagnostic test. Next, then, consider diagnostic testing.

Diagnostic Tests: Unlike standardized tests, diagnostic tests are criterion referenced. This means that the test items and goals are determined according to a fixed set of requirements. They are scored using true test score criteria. This means that they are not averaged or normed. Each test is scored based only on the student's own performance regarding his or her grade level requirements. Because of this feature, diagnostic tests have the added advantage of being able to pinpoint specific grade level strengths and weaknesses. Beyond this, revealed weaknesses can be properly targeted for remediation. This feature is lacking regarding standardized tests because of their broadness and vagueness regarding specific grade level test item criteria.

The Diagnostic Prescriptive Assessment is designed to be parentally administered any time of the year; that is, the need for professional or paraprofessional administration is excluded and the tests can be purchased at any time of the year and not just during certain times. Also, there is no need for outside help at all because each test comes complete with lucid instructions for administration and contains a grade-key. So, there are no lengthy periods of waiting for professionals to score and interpret the tests and return them to you.

An invaluable feature of the tests is that each one contains a remedial strategies section for the remediation of specific weaknesses discovered through the test. This feature is unknown in standardized tests, not only because of their aforementioned vagueness, but also because those tests, unlike ours, are not parentally administered. Parental administration also has the added advantage of parents gaining first hand knowledge of their student's methods, procedures, and accomplishments during test taking. Most diagnostic tests are produced by publishers and sometimes are tied to their specific curriculum. This is a definite disadvantage to most test-takers. The tests do not suffer from this limitation because they are not tied to any specific curriculum or set of curricula and are universal in scope. Mrs. Dixon devised each test with both a high criteria of mastery and superior educational qualifications. They possess no "normed" standards but only reveal true test scores.

The result is that when each student successfully completes his or her specific test, they will have, indeed, mastered the grade level requirements for that particular grade. Tests can also be used for record keeping as they fulfill the need for IEPs and portfolios that are required by some states. They can also be used as a pre-assessment for grade placement and are used by some parents for this purpose. By giving the test before the year begins, parents can discover direction for subject/grade placement, as well as target weaknesses for correction.

Human beings make tests. They decide what topics to include on the test, what kinds of questions to ask, and what the correct answers are, as well as how to use test scores. Tests can be made to compare students to each other (norm-referenced tests) or to see whether students have mastered a body of knowledge (criterion or standards-referenced tests). This fact sheet explains what NRTs are, their limitations and flaws, and how they affect schools. Norm-referenced tests (NRTs) compare a person's score against the scores of a group of people who have already taken the same exam, called the "norming group." When you see scores in the paper which report a school's scores as a percentage — "the Lincoln school ranked at the 49th percentile" — or when you see your child's score reported that way — "Jamal scored at the 63rd percentile" — the test is usually an NRT.

Most achievement NRTs are multiple-choice tests. Some also include open-ended, short-answer questions. The questions on these tests mainly reflect the content of nationally-used textbooks, not the local curriculum. This means that students may be tested on things your local schools or state education department decided were not so important and therefore were not taught. Commercial, national, norm-referenced "achievement" tests include the California Achievement Test (CAT); Comprehensive Test of Basic Skills (CTBS), which includes the "Terra Nova"; Iowa Test of Basic Skills (ITBS) and Tests of Academic Proficiency (TAP); Metropolitan Achievement Test (MAT); and Stanford Achievement Test (SAT, not to be confused with the college admissions SAT). "IQ," "cognitive ability," "school readiness," and developmental screening tests are also NRTs.

Creating the bell curve

NRTs are designed to "rank-order" test takers — that is, to compare students' scores. A commercial norm-referenced test does not compare all the students who take the test in a given year. Instead, test-makers select a sample from the target student population (say, ninth graders). The test is "normed" on this sample, which is supposed to fairly represent the entire target population (all ninth graders in the nation). Students' scores are then reported in relation to the scores of this "norming" group. To make comparing easier, testmakers create exams in which the results end up looking at least somewhat like a bell-shaped curve (the "normal" curve, shown in the diagram). Testmakers make the test so that most students will score near the middle, and only a few will score low (the left side of the curve) or high (the right side of the curve).

Scores are usually reported as percentile ranks. The scores range from 1st percentile to 99th percentile, with the average student score set at the 50th percentile. If Jamal scored at the 63rd percentile, it means he scored higher than 63% of the test takers in the norming group. Scores also can be reported as "grade equivalents," "stanines," and "normal curve equivalents." One more question right or wrong can cause a big change in the student's score. In some cases, having one more correct answer can cause a student's reported percentile score to jump more than ten points. It is very important to know how much difference in the percentile rank would be caused by getting one or two more questions right.

In making an NRT, it is often more important to choose questions that sort people along the curve than it is to make sure that the content covered by the test is adequate. The tests sometimes emphasize small and meaningless differences among testtakers. Since the tests are made to sort students, most of the things everyone knows are not tested. Questions may be obscure or tricky, in order to help rank order the testtakers. Tests can be biased. Some questions may favor one kind of student or another for reasons that have nothing to do with the subject area being tested.

Non-school knowledge that is more commonly learned by middle or upper class children is often included in tests. To help make the bell curve, testmakers usually eliminate questions that students with low overall scores might get right but those with high overall scores get wrong. Thus, most questions which favor minority groups are eliminated. NRTs usually have to be completed in a time limit. Some students do not finish, even if they know the material. This can be particularly unfair to students whose first language is not English or who have learning disabilities. This "speededness" is one way testmakers sort people out.

How accurate is that test score?

The items on the test are only a sample of the whole subject area. There are often thousands of questions that could be asked, but tests may have just a few dozen questions. A test score is therefore an estimate of how well the student would do if she could be asked all the possible questions. All tests have "measurement error." No test is perfectly reliable. A score that appears as an absolute number — say, Jamal's 63 — really is an estimate. For example, Jamal's "true score" is probably between 56 and 70, but it could be even further off. Sometimes results are reported in "score bands," which show the range within which a test-takers' "true score" probably lies.

There are many other possible causes of measurement error. A student can be having a bad day. Test-taking conditions often are not the same from place to place (they are not adequately "standardized"). Different versions of the same test are in fact not quite exactly the same. Sub-scores on tests are even less precise. This is mostly because there are often very few items on the sub-test. A score band for a Juanita's math sub-test might show that her score is between the 33rd and 99th percentile because only a handful of questions were asked. Scores for young children are much less reliable than for older students. This is because young children's moods and attention are more variable. Also, young children develop quickly and unevenly, so even an accurate score today could be wrong next month.

What do score increases mean?

If your child's or your school's score goes up on a norm-referenced test, does that mean she knows more or the school is better? Maybe yes, maybe not. Schools cannot teach everything. They teach some facts, some procedures, some concepts, some skills — but not others. Often, schools focus most on what is tested and stop teaching many things that are not tested. When scores go up, it does not mean the students know more, it means they know more of what is on that test. For example, history achievement test "A" could have a question on Bacon's Rebellion (a rebellion by Black slaves and White indentured servants against the plantation owners in colonial Virginia).

Once teachers know Bacon's Rebellion is covered on the exam, they are more likely to teach about it. But if those same students are given history test "B," which does not ask about

Bacon's Rebellion but does ask about Shay's Rebellion, which the teacher has not taught, the students will not score as well. Teaching to the test explains why scores usually go down when a new test is used. A district or state usually uses an NRT for five to ten years. Each year, the score goes up as teachers become familiar with what is on the test. When a new test is used, the scores suddenly drop. The students don't know less, it is just that different things are now being tested.

Can all the children score above average?

Politicians often call for all students to score above the national average. This is not possible. NRTs are constructed so that half the population is below the mid-point or average score. Expecting all students to be above the fiftieth percentile is like expecting all teams in a basketball league to win more than half their games. However, because the tests are used for years and because schools teach to them, there are times when far more than half the students score above average.

Why use norm-referenced tests?

To compare students, it is often easiest to use a norm-referenced test because they were created to rank test-takers. If there are limited places (such as in a "Gifted and Talented" program) and choices have to be made, it is tempting to use a test constructed to rank students, even if the ranking is not very meaningful and keeps out some qualified children.

NRT's are a quick snapshot of some of the things most people expect students to learn. They are relatively cheap and easy to administer. If they were only used as one additional piece of information and not much importance was put on them, they would not be much of a problem.

The dangers of using norm-referenced tests

Many mistakes can be made by relying on test scores to make

educational decisions. Every major maker of NRTs tells schools not to use them as the basis for making decisions about retention, graduation or replacement. The testmakers know that their tests are not good enough to use that way. The testing profession, in its Standards for Educational and Psychological Measurement, states, "In elementary or secondary education, a decision or characterization that will have a major impact on a test taker should not automatically be made on the basis of a single test score."

Any one test can only measure a limited part of a subject area or a limited range of important human abilities. A "reading" test may measure only some particular reading "skills," not a full range of the ability to understand and use texts. Multiple-choice math tests can measure skill in computation or solving routine problems, but they are not good for assessing whether students can reason mathematically and apply their knowledge to new, real-world problems. Most NRTs focus too heavily on memorization and routine procedures. Mutiple-choice and short-answer questions do not measure most knowledge that students need to do well in college, qualify for good jobs, or be active and informed citizens.

Tests like these cannot show whether a student can write a research paper, use history to help understand current events, understand the impact of science on society, or debate important issues. They don't test problem-solving, decision-making, judgement, or social skills. Tests often cause teachers to overemphasize memorization and de-emphasize thinking and application of knowledge. Since the tests are very limited, teaching to them narrows instruction and weakens curriculum. Making test score gains the definition of "improvement" often guarantees that schooling becomes test coaching. As a result, students are deprived of the quality education they deserve. Norm-referenced tests also can lower academic expectations. NRTs support the idea that learning or intelligence fits a bell curve. If educators believe it, they are more likely to have low expectations of students who score below average.

The damage caused by using NRTs is far greater than any possible benefits the tests provide. The main purpose of NRTs is to rank and sort students, not to determine whether students have learned the material they have been taught. They do not measure anywhere near enough of what students should learn. They have very harmful effects on curriculum and instruction. In the end, they provide a distorted view of learning that then causes damage to teaching and learning.

Criterion- and Standards- Referenced Tests

Criterion-referenced tests (CRTs) are intended to measure how well a person has learned a specific body of knowledge and skills. Multiple-choice tests most people take to get a driver's license and on-the-road driving tests are both examples of criterion-referenced tests. As on most other CRTs, it is possible for everyone to earn a passing score if they know about driving rules and if they drive reasonably well. In contrast, norm-referenced tests (NRTs) are made to compare test takers to each other. On an NRT driving test, test-takers would be compared as to who knew most or least about driving rules or who drove better or worse. Scores would be reported as a percentage rank with half scoring above and half below the mid-point.

In education, CRTs usually are made to determine whether a student has learned the material taught in a specific grade or course. An algebra CRT would include questions based on what was supposed to be taught in algebra classes. It would not include geometry questions or more advanced algebra than was in the curriculum. Most all students who took algebra could pass this test if they were taught well and they studied enough and the test was well-made. On a standardized CRT (one taken by students in many schools), the passing or "cut-off" score is usually set by a committee of experts, while in a classroom the teacher sets the passing score. In both cases, deciding the passing score is subjective, not objective.

Sometimes cut scores have been set in a way that maximizes the number of low income or minority students who fail the test. A small change in the cut score would not change the meaning of the test but would greatly increase minority pass rates. Some CRT's, such as many state tests, are not based on a specific curriculum, but on a more general idea of what students might be taught. Therefore, they may not match the curriculum. For example, a state grade 10 math test might include areas of math which some students have not studied.

Standards-Referenced Tests

A recent variation of criterion-referenced testing is "standards-referenced testing" or "standards based assessment." Many states and districts have adopted content standards (or "curriculum frameworks") which describe what students should know and be able to do in different subjects at various grade levels. They also have performance standards that define how much of the content standards students should know to reach the "basic" or "proficient" or "advanced" level in the subject area. Tests are then based on the standards and the results are reported in terms of these "levels," which, of course, represent human judgement. In some states, performance standards have been steadily increased, so that students continually have to know more to meet the same level.

Educators often disagree about the quality of a given set of standards. Standards are supposed to cover the important knowledge and skills students should learn — they define the "big picture." State standards should be well-written and reasonable. Some state standards have been criticized for including too much, for being too vague, for being ridiculously difficult, for undermining higher quality local curriculum and instruction, and for taking sides in educational and political controversies. If the standards are flawed or limited, tests based on them also will be. In any event, standards enforced by state tests will have — and are meant to have — a strong impact on local curriculum and instruction.

Even if standards are of high quality, it is important to know how well a particular test actually matches the standards. In particular, are all the important parts of the standards measured by the test? Often, many important topics or skills are not assessed. A major reason for this is that most state exams still rely almost entirely on multiple-choice and short-answer questions. Such tests cannot measure many important kinds of learning, such as the ability to conduct and report on a science experiment, to analyze and interpret information to present a reasonable explanation of the causes of the Civil War, to do an art project or a research paper, or to engage in serious discussion or make a public presentation. A few standards-based exams have gone beyond multiple-choice and short-answer, but even then they may not be balanced or complete measures of the standards.

CRTs and NRTs

Sometimes one kind of test is used for two purposes at the same time. *In addition* to ranking test takers in relation to a national sample of students, a NRT might be used to decide if students have learned the content they were taught. A CRT might be used to assess mastery *and* to rank students or schools based on their scores. In many states, students have to pass *either* an NRT or a CRT to obtain a diploma or be promoted. This is a serious misuse of tests. Because schools serving wealthier students usually score higher than other schools, ranking often just compares schools based on community wealth. This practice offers no real help for schools to improve.

NRTs are designed to sort and rank students "on the curve," not to see if they met a standard or criterion. Therefore, NRTs should not be used to assess whether students have met standards. However, in some states or districts a NRT is used to measure student learning in relation to standards. Specific cut-off scores on the NRT are then chosen (usually by a committee) to separate levels of achievement on the standards. In some cases, a CRT is made using technical procedures developed for NRTs, causing the CRT to sort students in ways that are inappropriate for standards-based decisions.

Sometimes the NRT is changed to more closely fit the state standards and to report standards- referenced scores. As a result, a state could report that 35 percent of its students were proficient according to state standards (depending, of course, on where the cut-off score is set), but that 60 percent of its students were above the national average score on the nörm-referenced test. Adapting an NRT also means that while everything on the test is in the standards, much of what is in the standards is not in the tests. If standardized tests are used at all, CRTs make more sense for schools than do NRTs.

However, they should be based on relevant, high-quality standards and curriculum and should make the least possible use of multiple-choice and short-answer questions. As with all tests, CRTs and NRTs, no matter what they are called, should not control curriculum and instruction, and important decisions about students, teachers or schools should not be based solely or automatically on test scores.

Guidelines for Test Design and Construction

Step 1: Defining the constructs you want to measure and outline the proposed content of the Test

Aptitude tests for job applicants

— First conduct a job analysis (task analysis) : listing the important components of the position you are trying to fill.

— The Job analysis will contain the critical incidents,

— A list of work related behaviors which are essential for successful completion of the job.

— A well designed aptitude test will contain items which measure the entire cross-section of critical incidents.

— To paraphrase, a properly constructed test will measure a representative sample of most critical incidents.

Test Planners must consider a variety of issues :

1. What are the topics and materials to be tested ?
2. What Kind of Questions should be constructed ?
3. What item and test formats should be used ?
4. When, where, and how is the test to be given ?
5. How should the tests be scored ?

1. *What are the topics and materials to be tested* ?

— For employment aptitude tests, this calls for the job analysis with special attention being paid to the critical incidents.

— For achievement tests, this calls for a content analysis in which the key subject areas are listed and the percentage of the test to be devoted to each individual subject area is decided.

— Content analysis for classroom achievement tests can be highly subjective if created by a single individual with no feedback by knowledgeable colleagues.

2. *What Kind of questions should be constructed* ?

The answer to this question is partially dependent upon the Educational Objectives you want to include in the test. Since the 1950's researchers have developed several taxonomies (or hierarchical categorization) of cognitive, affective, and psychomotor objectives to be addressed within testing situations.

The Taxonomy of Educational Objectives

The cognitive domain

Lists 6 categories which vary in difficulty with respect to cognitive abilities or level of understanding.

1. *Knowledge* : recall of specific facts. Knowledge questions can be identified by key verbs such as define, identify, list, and name.

2. *Comprehension* : understanding the purpose or meaning of something. Comprehension questions can be identified with key verbs such as convert, explain, and summarize.

3. *Application* : using information and ideas in novel situations. Application questions can be identified with key verbs such as compute, determine, and solve.

4. *Analysis* : Breaking down large pieces of information in order to examine the structure and interrelationships among its component parts. Analysis questions can be identified by key verbs such as analyze, differentiate, and relate.

5. *Synthesis* : Combining various elements or parts into a structural whole. Synthesis questions can be identified by key verbs such as design, devise, formulate, and plan.

6. *Evaluation* : making a judgement based upon reasoning. Evaluation questions can be identified by key verbs such as compare, critique, evaluate, and judge.

These 6 categories are progressively inclusive. In order for a test taker to succeed on questions from the higher categories, they must have the ability to answer the lower order categories. i.e. Critiquing a position or theory requires Knowledge, and the ability to analyze and synthesize the subject material to be evaluated.

The Gerlach & Sullivan taxonomy of Cognitive Objectives

Also has six levels of varying difficulty.

1. *Identifying* : consists of indicating which member of a set belongs in a particular category : Which of the following tests is considered a projective test of personality ?

   A. MMPI

B. The draw a person test

C. The 16PF

D. The Rorschach inkblot test

2. *Naming* : Supplying the proper verbal label for a referent, or a set of referents.

Collectively, the MMPI, the Rorschach, and the 16PF are considered tests of ____________.

3. *Describing* : consists of reporting relevant categories of objects, events, properties, or relationships. What are the ten scales of measurement associated with the MMPI-II and what do high scores on each of those scales indicate ?

4. *Constructing* : creating a product according to certain specifications. Give the outline of a treatment method for a fear of flying that combines Systematic Desensitization with the classic elements of Rogerian therapy.

5. *Ordering* : consists of arranging two or more referents in a specific ranking. List the following events in chronological order :

   A. Americans begin using civil service exams. B. Chinese begin using civil service exams.

   C. Wilhelm Wundt operates the first psychological laboratory.

   D. Sigmund Freud publishes "The interpretation of Dreams"

6. *Demonstrating* : Performing a certain behavior to accomplish a test relevant task. Give a clinical interview and develop a DSM-IV diagnosis on the next individual who enters the room. When the test developer has fully identified the content areas to be tested and the cognitive objective to be measured, she can create a table of specifications which will guide her through the test creation.

The table of specifications allows for a thorough analysis of content and difficulty, and provides a framework for specific test item construction. Test Developers also have to take into consideration time constraints when determining the length of tests. General Guidelines for timing deadlines :

Essay Tests : Five ½ page essays may be completed In an hour.

Multiple Choice Questions : 1 per minute.

True-False Questions : 2 per minute

Performance Tasks : task dependent

Constructing specific test items

Many decisions must be made by the test developers. Should the test be Objective (multiple choice, true false) or Subjective (essay tests) in nature. The answer to this depends upon the cognitive objectives being assessed. Some tests may have a combination of objective and subjective methods. Objectivity and Subjectivity refer to the standardization of the scoring procedures. If we decide on an objective test, we must decide whether or nct to supply the answer choices. This indicates the difference between testing recognition memory and testing recall memory

Also referred to as supply vs. selection or Constructed response vs. identification Free Recall is considered more difficult in most cases.

Essay Tests vs. Multiple Choice Tests

Advantages of essay tests

— Trivially Easy to construct an essay test, compared to the time required to construct a multiple choice test.

- Essay Tests allow for the examination of higher order cognitive objectives.
- Allows test takers to show the depth of knowledge they have of a particular subject area.
- Allows test takers to practice their writing skills.

Disadvantages of Essay Tests

- Subjectivity in grading means it is possible for two people evaluating the same essay to calculate different grades.
- Grading essays takes a significant amount of time (may not be feasible for tests of a large group of people).
- Because of time it takes to write essay, may not be able to survey a large portion of the subject material. (problem with representative sampling)
- Students may answer a different question than asked.

Advantages of multiple choice tests

- Objective scoring procedures means anyone can score a particular exam and come up with the same grade. (helps to increase reliability of the test)
- A representative sample of questions from all subject areas to be tested can be easily obtained.
- Exams can be scored relatively quickly, very suitable for large numbers of test takers.

Disadvantages of multiple choice tests

- Take considerable time to create, compared to essay tests.
- Much more difficult to assess higher order cognitive objectives such as analysis and evaluation.

— Can be made unintentionally more difficult by the use of : Negatives or (even worse) double negatives within the question and

— Interlocked Items : Where you must get the correct answer to a preceding question in order to get the right answer to the current question.

Standard Multiple Choice Formats

Short Answer Questions : Test taker must supply the answer.

Major guidelines

Questions are preferable to incomplete statements. If fill-in-the-blank format is used, the blank should come at the end of the statement. Avoid multiple blanks in the same item.

The ____________ is a good example of a __________ test.

True-False Items : Some of the most commonly used and simplest to create test items. True false items are sometimes criticized for encouraging rote memorization. True-False answers are affected by the use of specific determiners such as never, always, and only, indicating a statement which is usually false. Often, sometimes, and usually commonly indicate a true statement. Guidelines for constructing good True-False statements :

1. Ensure the statements deal with non-trivial information to discourage rote memorization.
2. Keep statements short in length and unambiguous.
3. Avoid negatively stated items, especially double negatives.
4. Avoid specific Determiners such as always, never, and only.
5. On Opinion statements, cite the source of the opinion.
6. Avoid tricky items.

7. Make true and false statements about equal length, and include an equal amount of both.
8. Make wrong answers more attractive by wording items in such a way that they are not obviously wrong.

Guidelines for matching items

Matching items are reasonably easy to construct. The drawback is that matching items primarily test lower order cognitive objectives, and thus encourage rote memorization.

1. Arrange the premise and response options in a clear logical column format, with question stem on left hand side and to be matched items on the right.
2. Number the question stems sequentially, and use letters to differentiate among response choices.
3. Use between 6 to 15 question stems, and two to three more response options than question stems.
4. Clearly specify whether the matching in one-to-one, one-to-many, and whether or not response choices can be used more than once.
5. Put the entire matching section of a single test page for clarity.

Ranking and rearrangement items are special type of matching questions in which order counts.

Multiple – Choice Questions

Are very versatile as you can measure the attainment of both lower and higher order cognitive objectives. Scores on Multiple choice questions are less affected by response bias (response set) than are true-false items. The key to constructing a high quality multiple choice question is to have good, plausible distractors. Shortcomings of multiple choice items :

1. Good items take time and thought to construct
2. Multiple choice stresses recognition over recall. Familiarity with an answer can lead to correct guessing.
3. Require more time to answer than true-false questions.

Guidelines for constructing multiple choice items

1. Question format preferred to incomplete statement. If incomplete statement is used, blank should be at end of statement.
2. State question clearly and at the appropriate reading level.
3. Place as much of the item is the stem as possible. Answer choices should be as short as possible.
4. Use opinion questions sparingly and cite the source or authority of the opinion.
5. Four to five choices are standard, but two or three choices can be used as well. How many choices appear is partially dependent on the ease of generating high quality distractors
6. If the answer choices have a natural order, arrange them in that fashion. (Dates, ages). Otherwise answer choices should be randomly arranged.
7. Try to make answer choices equal in length and complexity.
8. Try to make all answer choices plausible, but only one correct answer.
9. Formulate a logical reason why someone who doesn't know the correct answer would select from the distracter set.
10. Avoid the use of negatives, and in particular, double negatives.
11. Ambiguous and tricky options should be avoided.

12. Specific determiners should be avoided, and "all of the above" and 'none of the above' questions should be infrequent.
13. Place options in Stacked format, rather than row by row.
14. Make sure the amount of items tested is appropriate for the time constraints of the testing session.
15. Item difficulty should be such that overall performance is halfway between chance (pure guessing) and 100%. This will give your testing measure the maximum ability to separate according to performance.

Constructing Distractor Items

Usually, the question and the answer that you want to ask is relatively easy to develop. But what often takes the most time is coming up with plausible distracters. Two approaches can be taken :

— *The Rational Approach* : The test developers understanding of the subject material and their ability to organize that material leads them to adopt specific distracters for specific test items

— *The Empirical Approach* : You select distractors based on pre-test data.

You administer the test without any answer. Choices and have people complete the measure as a short answer test. Your test subjects should be similar in composition to the population you will actually be testing. You compile a list of incorrect answers for each question, and use the most popular (most frequent).

Evaluation is an important aspect of teaching and learning, and if done correctly can provide important information to both you and your students. Evaluation involves both *Testing* and *Grading*. In addition to evaluating how well your students are doing, you may gain valuable insights about your instruction by evaluating your own success in class.

CONSTRUCTING TESTS

Undoubtedly you will be called upon to construct or help to construct a quiz, midterm, or final during your career as a TA. Depending upon your discipline, the test that you create will generally be either an Objective test or an Essay test. Whichever type of test you need to construct, the planning phase of your test should be the same.

— *Review your instructional objectives*: Compare these written statements of what you expected your students to be able to do to the instruction which was presented to them. You need to be aware if an objective that you wrote was not covered in class, or implied a different process than what was taught before you write the test!

— *Delimit the content and skill areas tobe tested*: Decide on some way of selecting test items (a sampling scheme) to ensure that your quiz/test is representative of what was covered in class and to ensure that it gives an adequate sampling of student capabilities.

Objective Tests

Objective tests have the advantages of allowing an instructor to assess a large and potentially representative sample of course material, measure most types of learning, and allow for reliable and efficient test scoring. The disadvantages of objective tests include a tendency to emphasize only "recognition" skills, the ease with which correct answers can be guessed on many item types, and the inability to measure students' organization and synthesis of material. Suggestions for constructing high quality objective tests are offered below:

Does:

— Write the test items simply and clearly

— If an item represents a particular opinion, identify the author of the opinion.

— Write clear and unambiguous directions for the test as a whole and for each specific section of the test.

— Assemble items into a test according to some systematic plan, e.g., similar item-types grouped together.

— Devise a system to facilitate scoring the test (e.g., a separate answer sheet and an answer key in the same format).

Don'ts:

— Don't lift a statement verbatim from a textbook.

— Don't provide clues in one item for answers to other items.

— Don't intersperse item-types on the test.

— Avoid writing interdependent items such that the answer to one item is necessary to respond to the next item.

— Avoid items dealing with trivia.

— Avoid trick questions.

— Avoid ambiguity in items.

True/False Items

These items can assess student recognition of facts and definitions. To write good true/false items, following are some suggestions.

— Be sure a statement is unequivocally true or false.

— Avoid specific determiners such as "always" or "never"- they can be dead giveaways for false items.

— Beware of indefinite terms of degree or amount such as "in most cases" and "great".

— Beware of negative statements and double negatives.

— Beware of including more than one item in the same statement, especially if both are not equally true or false.

— Beware of giving clues to an answer by the length of an item.

Multiple- Choice Items

This is often the most effective of the objective-type items. Multiple-choice items can measure such things as acquisition of information or vocabulary, application of principles, or evaluation of sample data. Here are some tips to help to ensure high quality in the multiple-choice items.

— The item-stem should clearly formulate a problem.

— As much of the item as possible should be included in the stem.

— Randomize the occurrence of correct responses (i.e., you don't always want "C" to be the right answer).

— Be sure there is only one clearly correct answer (unless you are instructing students to select more than one).

— Make the wording in the response choices (distracters) consistent with the item stem.

— Don't load the stem down with irrelevant material.

— Beware of using answers such as "none of these" or "all of the above".

— Use negatives or double negatives sparingly in the question or stem.

— Beware of using sets of opposite answers unless more than one pair is presented (e.g., go to work, not go to work).

— Beware of providing irrelevant grammatical cues.

Completion and Short Answer Items

These are variation of the same thing. They are suitable for testing knowledge of facts (e.g., dates, vocabulary). Numerical problems are short answer items. The following suggestions should aid you in writing effective completion or short answer items.

— Don't leave too many blanks in a statement.

— Put blanks at the end rather than at the beginning of an item.

— Beware of indefinite items (many answers could be correct).

— Omit only key words for completion. Don't test for common words.

— In numerical problems indicate the type of units in which the answer is to be expressed if it doesn't give clues to the answer.

Matching Items

This is a variation of the multiple-choice item. Matching items are efficient for measuring associations of names, dates, etc. In addition, these items can be used to label charts, maps, and the like. Matching items are best when these guidelines are followed.

— Possible answers are homogeneous in nature (i.e., all choices are names, dates, body parts, etc.).

— The number of answer choices exceeds the number of problems.

— Sets of answers are kept short. Make more matching items rather than one items with 400 answers.

— Answers are put in a logical order (chronological, alphabetical (if one exists).

— Directions specify whether answers may be used more than once and specify the basis for matching.

Questions that you write should assess whether or not students CAN DO what you expect them to be able to do after an instructional sequence.

Essay Trests

The principal advantage of an essay test is that it requires the student to produce and organize an answer, select or create a pattern of ideas, and to demonstrate critical thinking. Its principal disadvantages are that it typically assesses only a small sample of course objectives. Again, the following are some suggestions which may enhance the quality of the essay tests that you produce.

— Have in mind the processes that you want measured (e.g., analysis, synthesis).

— Start questions with words such as "compare", "contrast", "explain why". Don't use "what", "who", "when", or "list". (These latter types of things are better measured with objective-type items).

— Write items so as to define the parameters of expected answers as clearly as possible.

— Don't have too many answers for the time available.

DETERMINING STUDENT GRADE

> "...a grade {is}...an inadequate report of an inaccurate judgment by a biased and variable judge of the extent to which a student has attained an undefined level of mastery of an unknown proportion of an indefinite amount of material."

As this quote indicates and many undergraduates claim, grading can be unjust, arbitrary, and just plain problematic. In conjunction with the instructor of record for a course, you can do much to alleviate the criticisms and barbs directed at the grading process. The following sections offer some useful suggestions for grading both essay and objective tests.

Grading Objectives

— *Prepare an answer key*: If you design the answer key to

follow the format of the students' answer sheets, the grading process will be much faster. If the test is based on your class objectives, you can also refer students to lecture notes and readings relevant to a given question on the answer key.

— *Determine if there is more than one correct response for any of your questions*: Decide, in advance, if certain incorrect answers merit partial credit.

— *Decide, in advance, the point-value of each question*: Ideally, you should give students this information on the test itself.

— *Post the answer key out side your office*: Students can then come by to check their performance against the key.

— *Distribute corrected tests in class or ask students to drop by your office to pick them up*: Don't leave corrected exams out in the hall near your office. Your "A" student may be delighted, but it's important to consider the feelings of those students who do poorly as well. (It is illegal to post test scores along with names, or even with alpha numbers.)

Grading Essay Tests

— *Read your students' exams with scrupulous care*: Your students have invested a good many hours in preparing for, and taking, examinations. Evaluating their responses deserves your undivided attention.

— *Prepare model answers in advance*: Whether you've written the test yourself or you're reading an exam prepared by someone else (e.g., the professor in charge of the course), preparing a key with model answers clarifies the major points that should be covered in student responses on the test.

— *Determine whether there is more than one acceptable answer or more than one possible solution to a problem.*

— *Prepare a list of common improper answers, together with the penalities for each.* This will help to ensure that your grading is consistent. If you do not hold to uniform grading standards, it is likely that at some point you'll be faced with at least one angry student presenting you with two nearly identical responses to which you have assigned different scores. That student will justifiably want you to account for your grading procedure.

— *Read all the answers to one question (By all students) before beginning to grade other questions.*

— *Grade papers as nearly anonymously as possible.* Oftentimes it is useful to ask students to record their alpha numbers on an exam rather than read their names. This means matching the numbers to their names after reading the exams, but it helps to remove biases you may have acquired toward students in your class.

— *Decide, in advance, how important such factors as spelling and grammer will be in grading the exams.* Decisions of this nature should not be arbitrary. What's right or wrong for one student's paper should be right or wrong for all students.

— *After you've graded the test, post or otherwise make available an examination key.* This allows your students to see the major points their essays were expected to cover or to see the correct method of solving problems on the exam. In addition, it is often useful to cite common errors that were made on the test and the points removed for such errors.

— *Establish the correspondence between point scores and letter grades before returing the exams.* Students tend to mark their progress in terms of grades and will want to know how they fared. Remember, you must be consistent in assigning grades based on test points.

— *Subjectivity should not enter into assigning grades.* If, however, you want to introduce some element of subjectivity into your grading (e.g., adding points for student participation in class discussion) make it clear to students that this is your intention. Students should be told at the outset of the course or prior to the exam the maximum and average number of points that you are allotting to this category of your evaluation.

— *If time allows, write comments about student responses.* Let your students know when they've really done an outstanding job as well as providing them with correct information (or a source to find it) when their responses are inaccurate.

Evaluating Teaching

As many TAs have already discovered, it is generally desirable to obtain some form of student input regarding their teaching and the course they are instructing while that course is still in progress. Such feedback can be used to make changes while a section is still going on and may be used in conjunction with end-of-term evaluation to plan for the next quarter.

You can gather *Mid-quarter feedback* by distributing a short questionnaire to your students around midterms. The intent of mid-quarter feedback is to provide you with information reflecting student opinion about specific aspects of your section, e.g., clarity of presentation, relevance of material, willingness to respond to questions. These brief surveys can also provide some global reactions to the course in general. By reviewing these questionnaires right away, you may be able to make changes that will affect the students from whom the feedback was obtained.

Another very different way to evaluate your success as a TA is to utilize the campus wide TA Development Program's *Videotape and consultation Service*. This service allows you to be videotaped while teaching. You can then gain a new perspective on your in-class performance by viewing your tape. By viewing your tape, you will be able to gain a "student's eye" view of your teaching and, at best, after receiving feedback on your tape you may be able to make changes in your teaching strategies. To arrange a videotaping, call TV Services x4346.

METHODS OF CONSTRUCTING HIGH QUALITY TESTS

In practice, the development and evaluation of any test to measure learning outcomes is a laborious but highly rewarding process requiring the collaborative effort of content and testing specialists. The methods used to construct high quality tests of academic knowledge and understanding for specific areas of academic instructions are given below.

Measurement Plan

The process of test construction comprises a number of rigorous steps.

1. Specify the domain of knowledge and understanding, such as elementary linear algebra, that the student is required to learn.
2. Identify the mental tasks or processes that the student must use in dealing with the particular subject matter; mental tasks such as recall, analysis, generalization, application, and discovery.
3. Write test questions or items that unambiguously assess the student's ability to deal with the knowledge domain as described by Steps 1 and 2.

4. Administer the test items written in Step 3 to a random sample of the population for which the test is intended.
5. Analyze the item response data collected in Step 4. This step is commonly referred to as the item analysis step.
6. Based upon the results of Step 5, select and, if necessary, revise the "best" items.
7. Administer the items selected in Step 6 to another random sample of the target population.
8. Repeat Steps 5 through 7, inclusive, until an optimal pool of items is identified.
9. Transform the raw scores of the optimal test to some meaningful metric.

Test Item Preparation

The first three steps of the measurement plan are the sole responsibility of the content specialist, i.e., the teacher and his or her colleagues. In most cases, Step 1 is rather straightforward. Not so for Steps 2 and 3, however, particularly test-item writing. Despite being governed by common sense, the writing of "good" test items is a difficult and time-consuming task that is best characterized as an art. Gronlund provides a practical and readable introduction to the "art" of designing a test and writing test questions. Another excellent and highly recommended reference for test design and item writing is Haladyna.

Item Format

An important consideration in test construction is the choice of how a particular test question should be asked and answered. A variety of item formats is available to the item writer even within the same test. Item formats for tests of learning outcomes fall into two broad classes: the free- or constructed-response format and the selected-response format. The free- or constructed-response item format requires the student to supply the correct response. The most familiar free-response item format is the essay. Essay questions differ in how much freedom is permitted the student in making a response. "Restricted" essays require brief and precise answers to specific questions. "Extended" essays, on the other hand, reflect more comprehensive questions that allow greater freedom in structuring a response.

A second type of free-response item format is the short-answer or completion item. The test item can be either a question, e.g., "If x = 2, then what does 2x + 5 equal?" or a statement with a missing element to be provided by the student. The selected-response item format requires the student to choose the correct response from within a set of possibly "correct" item responses or foils which accompanies the test item. The most common types of selected-response item formats are the true-false item, the multiple-choice item, and the matching item. For the true-false item format the choice is between the truth and falsity of a statement, e.g., "John F.

Kennedy was the 40th president of the United States." (False). The multiple-choice item format requires the student to select one of two or more possible answers to the question, e.g., "How many players make up the starting line-up of a major league baseball team?" {Seven, Eight, Nine, Ten, Eleven} (Nine). The matching item comprises two lists; a list of related questions, e.g., a set of quadratic equations, and a list of possible answers to the questions, e.g., a set of solutions to the equations. In this example the student's task is to "match" the solutions and equations.

Item Scoring

Scoring a test item can be either the assignment of a numerical value to a student's response or the placement of the response in one of two or more ordered categories. With selected-response items—i.e., true-false, multiple-choice, and matching items—and the free-response short-answer or completion item, scoring typically involves assigning a "+1" to the correct response and a "0" to each incorrect response. In particular, the item score is a Bernoulli random variable S_i having $S_i =$ 1 if item i is answered correctly and $S_i = 0$ if item i is answered incorrectly. A total test score, X, is typically computed by summing the item scores over all items, i.e.,

$$X = \sum_{i=1}^{k} S_i$$

for a test of k items. These item types are often referred to as objective items in the sense that personal judgment does not enter into the scoring. In most cases a computer program is used to score the items of the test. A serious threat to the precision of a selected-response item score is guessing. When a student does not know the correct answer to a test question but guesses correctly, the item score for that student is biased. In general, the smaller the number of response options the greater the bias associated with guessing.

Restricted and extended essays, on the other hand, require expert assessment or evaluation of the student's response. The simplest method of essay scoring is holistic scoring which requires the expert "reader" to place the student's response in one of several ordered categories of response quality. More complex methods of essay scoring can be and are used. All methods of essay scoring are susceptible to scoring bias stemming from differences among readers in judging the quality of the same response. Scoring bias is an obvious threat to the precision and usefulness of the measure.

ITEM ANALYSIS

How good is a test question or item in measuring a learning outcome? The answer depends upon the purpose of the test containing the item. A "good" test item is an item that is optimum relative to the purpose of the test, e.g., measuring knowledge or predicting success in a training program. Following are some of practical techniques for evaluating test items.

Item Difficulty

Item difficulty is defined as the probability of a correct response to the question, i.e., $P_r\{S_i=1\}=p_i$. The proportion of a random sample from the target population that correctly answers the test question is an estimator of P_i. For the i-th test item and a sample of size N,

$$p_i = \frac{n_c}{N}$$

n_c is the number of individuals in the sample that correctly answers the question. Items with p values close to zero (very "hard" items) or close to one (very "easy" items) do not, in general, contain much information about the performance of the target population, except for the tails of the distribution. For most applied measurement situations, tests having items with item difficulty values between 0.3 and 0.7, inclusive, will maximally differentiate students throughout the entire performance range. If, however, the intent is to discriminate at a specific level of performance—say for purposes of selection—then items with p values in the narrow interval consistent with that performance level are chosen.

Item Discrimination

Another important property of any test question is item discrimination. Item discrimination involves the strength of the relationship between a test item and the underlying (and unobservable) attribute being measured, e.g., knowledge or learning. Since the latent variable, Y, cannot be measured directly, we turn to a set of observable variables whose elements are related to Y. In most applications, this set turns out to be the set of item variables $\{S_i\}$. While it seems somewhat circular, the total score, X, is often taken as a measure of the underlying attribute, Y.

The stronger the relationship between the item score, S_i, and the total score, X, the greater the differentiation among examinees on Y due to the i-th item. The item score/total score point-biserial correlation, $\rho_{s,x}$, is a measure of item discrimination. In a sample of size N, the point-biserial correlation coefficient is

$$r_{s,x} = \frac{\bar{X}_i - \bar{X}}{s_x}\sqrt{\frac{p_i}{1-p_i}}.$$

In the formula, $\bar{X}_i$ is the mean total score of the $N_i=p_iN$ examinees who correctly answered the item, $\bar{X}$ is the mean total score of all the examinees, and s_x is the total score standard deviation. To avoid spurious correlation, is usually eliminated from the computation of the total score, X. Test items having $\bar{X}_i \leq \bar{X}$ are considered "poor" items in that $\rho_{s,x} \leq 0$. In this case, examinees that correctly answer the item tend, on average, to have the same or lower scores on Y than examinees giving an incorrect response to the item. Item difficulty, p_i, and item discrimination, $r_{s,x}$, are included in the "Item Analysis" section of each Examination Report prepared by University Testing Services.

Incorrect Choices

The incorrect choices or answers of a multiple-choice item are called distractors. Distractors of an item to be equally attractive to the student who does not know the correct answer. As such, the proportions of examinees selecting the distractors of an item should be approximately equal. Distractors having very high or very low p values relative to the other distractors of the item are of questionable usefulness and should either be replaced or modified. University Testing Services reports the response proportions of the distractors for each item.

Item-Characteristic Curve

A very attractive way of representing the information in an item is by plotting its item-characteristic curve (ICC). ICC's play a prominent role in Item Response Theory. The ICC of an item is a plot, over all values of Y, of the probability that an examinee at point y on the underlying Y continuum correctly answerstheitem,i.e., $ICC_i=P_r\{S_i=1|Y=y\}$ for all y. Formally, the ICC for the i-th item is considered to be a normal ogive function of Y (the familiar S-shaped curve). When plotted for a sample of size N, the ICC displays the proportion of examinees at each level of Y that correctly answers the item.

The item-characteristic curve of an item reflects both its difficulty (P_i) and discrimination ($r_{s,x}$)—as well as random guessing for selected-response item types such as multiple-choice items. Items with "steep" ICC's are very useful in differentiating examinees along the Y continuum. Items having horizontal or nearly horizontal ICC's, on the other hand, provide little or no information about Y regardless of their difficulty levels. Item ICC's should always be considered when evaluating and selecting items for a test.

Item-Item Correlation

The final item characteristic is the correlation coefficient for each pair of items. The correlation coefficient (phi coefficient) between dichotomous items g and h is defined as

$$\rho_{gh} = \frac{p_{gh} - p_g p_h}{\sqrt{p_g(1-p_g)}\sqrt{p_h(1-p_h)}},$$

where

$$p_{gh} = Pr\{S_g = 1, S_h = 1\}.$$

Our understanding of the item response process implies that each test item—certainly a "good" item—should be saturated with the underlying attribute represented by Y. As such, the correlation coefficients for distinct pairs of test items to be positive and generally high. Furthermore, for fixed Y = y,

$$p_{gh} = \Pr\{S_g = 1, S_h = 1\} = \Pr\{S_g = 1|y\}\Pr\{S_h = 1|y\},$$

$$\rho_{gh.Y} = 0$$

i.e., the partial correlation coefficient between item g and item h for fixed Y is zero. This result leads to $\rho_{gh} = \rho_{gx}\rho_{hx}$ which relates item correlation to item discrimination (recall that total score, X, is a proxy for Y). The quantity ρ_{gh} is fundamental to the measurement of the reliability of a test.

TEST RELIABILITY

Reliability, because it reflects the precision of a measurement, is an important property of a test. In the context of testing, precision refers to the stability of an examinee's score over repeated and identical administrations of the test. From Classical Test Theory the reliability of a test is measured by the correlation coefficient between the observed scores of two parallel forms of the test, $\rho_{xx'}$.

Test-Retest Reliability

One obvious method of estimating the reliability of a test is to administer the same test on two different occasions and compute the correlation coefficient for the total test scores. This method of reliability estimation is termed test-retest reliability. There are several problems associated with the test-retest method. Carry-over effects, changes in the individual's knowledge and skills, and other effects associated with time can lead to biased estimates of test reliability.

Parallel-Forms Reliability

If parallel forms of a test are available, then the reliability of the test is estimated by the correlation coefficient for the total scores of the two test forms, r_{xx}. This method of reliability estimation is termed parallel-forms reliability. In practice, only the largest of testing organizations have the resources to construct parallel forms of a test. Parallel-forms reliability estimates are subject to the same time-related threats associated with test-retest reliability.

Internal-Consistency Reliability

The most widely used method of reliability estimation is known as internal consistency reliability. Internal consistency reliability is attractive because it requires only one administration of the test. It is the method employed by University Testing Services in computing test reliability.

The easiest way to implement internal consistency reliability is to simply divide, in some way, the total test into two "parallel" halves denoted $Y_1$and Y_2, compute the correlation coefficient for the scores on the two halves, and then apply the Spearman-Brown formula to $\rho_{Y_1Y_2}$. This method of reliability estimation is known as split-half reliability. Obviously, there are many ways to divide a test into two parts, but none are likely to produce the parallel measures required by the Spearman-Brown formula.

There is no reason to limit division of the total test into halves. In fact, each item can be taken as a component of the test and the relationships among the items can be used to estimate the reliability of the test. If the k items of a test are highly inter-correlated, then the reliability of the test will be high. This result is consistent with the assumption that each item is saturated with a common underlying attribute of the examinees that is measured by X. Recall that $\rho_{gh} = \rho_{gx}\rho_{hx}$. It is in this sense that the test is said to be internally consistent.

The reliability coefficient computed and reported by University Testing Services depends only upon the number of items in the test and the variances and covariances of the items. For a test of k dichotomously scored items, reliability is defined as

$$\rho_{XX'} \geq KR20 = \left(\frac{k}{k-1}\right)\left(\frac{\sigma_X^2 - \sum_{i=1}^{k} p_i(1-p_i)}{\sigma_X^2}\right)$$

where σ_x^2 is the population variance of the total test score and p_i is the proportion of examinees that correctly answers the i-th item. The quantity KR20 is known as the Kuder-Richardson Formula 20. Another name for the formula is Coefficient α. If the test items are "essentially τ-equivalent" (a relaxed condition of parallel forms), then KR20 = $\rho_{xx'}$. Otherwise, KR20 underestimates the reliability of the test. When the KR20 estimate for a test is high, the reliability of the test is high. Low values of KR20, however, may or may not reflect low $\rho_{xx'}$ and should be interpreted with caution.

STANDARD ERROR OF MEASUREMENT

Another way of expressing the precision of a total test score that is derived from Classical Test Theory is the standard error of measurement. From CTT, an examinee's observed test score (X) has two unobserved components—a true score component (T) and an error component (E). These test scores are related as X = T + E. Obviously, the smaller the error the greater the precision in measuring the underlying attribute. Under the assumptions of CTT, the size of the error in a measurement X is given by the standard error of measurement

$$\sigma_E = \sigma_X \sqrt{1 - \rho_{XX'}}.$$

A sample estimate of σ_E is obtained by replacing σ_X and $\rho_{xx'}$ by their sample estimates s_X and $r_{xx'}$, respectively. The standard error of measurement is use to construct a 100(1–α)% confidence interval for the true score, T. Assuming normally distributed errors, a 100(1–α)% confidence interval for T is given by

$$\left(x - z_{\alpha} s_{E} \leq T \leq x + z_{\alpha} s_{E}\right),$$

where z_{α} is the upper α-point of the distribution of the standard normal variable. Before any samples are drawn, the probability that this interval contains the true score T is 1–α. As the reliability of the test increases, the confidence interval for T shortens and approaches T in the limit.

While error analysis is a powerful way of expressing the precision of a test score, s_E and the 100(1–α)% confidence interval for T are not included in the University Testing Services' Examination Report. Everyday experience indicates that many test users do not understand either the notion of true scores or the computation and meaning of standard errors and confidence intervals.

ITEM SELECTION

The selection of items for inclusion in a test designed to measure learning outcomes is guided by the content and statistical specifications contained in the Measurement Plan for that academic course. As a general rule it is recommended that items be chosen for a test that

1. meet the content requirements of the measurement plan,
2. have the "steepest" item-characteristic curves,
3. have item difficulty values consistent with the purposes of the test, and
4. are internally consistent.

TEST SCORE TRANSFORMATION

The raw or total test score [X = the sum of the (0-1) item scores], because it depends upon the number and type of items making up a test, is generally not very informative. The raw scores of tests of different lengths, for example, are not directly comparable. It is common practice to apply some form of transformation to the raw score of a test in an effort to make the test results more meaningful, particularly to the student.

Formula Scores

A major problem associated with multiple-choice tests is that of guessing, i.e., selecting the correct response to a test item in the absence of knowledge simply by chance. Under certain assumptions the effects of guessing can be estimated and the raw score adjusted. Assuming that the examinee randomly guesses whenever he or she does not know the answer to a test question, the number of items that the examinee would answer correctly without guessing is estimated as

$$X_c = \left(\frac{k}{k-1}\right)X - \frac{N}{k-1},$$

where X_c is the raw score corrected for guessing, X is the unadjusted raw score, N is the total number of items, and k is the number of response choices for each item. When the examinee answers all the test items, X_c is a linear of function of X. If examinees do not answer one or more test items, then a better formula for X_c is

$$X_c = \left(\frac{k-1}{k}\right)X + \frac{N-t}{k},$$

where t is the number of incorrect responses.

The assumption of random guessing in the absence of knowledge is a strong one and little is known of its effect upon X_c when it is violated. Adjusting total test scores for guessing should be done with care.

Percentage Scores

The simplest type of raw score transformation is to divide the raw score, X, by the total number of test items, N, and multiply the result by 100. This transformed score is called the percentage score. If the items of the test are a "good" representation of the material for this part of the course, then the percentage score can be viewed as a measure of the amount of course material the student has mastered. Obviously, interpretation of a percentage score is highly dependent upon the nature of the items making up the test, i.e. item content, item difficulty, and item discrimination. On the other hand, properties of the students taking the test do not enter into the interpretation of the percentage score.

Percentile Scores

Percentiles are transformed scores that are based upon the test performance of a specific group of individuals often called the norm group. The percentile score or rank is defined as the percentage of individuals in the norm group having a score equal to or less than a particular value. There are several ways of computing percentile scores. A typical method is to take one-half the number of individuals obtaining the specified score, add that number to the number of individuals obtaining a lower score, and divide the sum by the total number of individuals. However it is computed the percentile score is interpreted in reference to the norm group.

Change the norm group and the interpretation of the percentile score changes. While it is relatively easy to compute and interpret, the percentile score has its limitations. For one, the distribution of percentiles is rectangular and not amenable to many common statistical analyses. For another, differences among percentile scores can be misleading particularly when a large number of individuals in the norm group have the same or similar scores (as is the case with normally distributed raw scores).

Standardized Scores

Another very popular type of norm-referenced score is the standardized score. For a "norm" population having mean μ_x and variance σ_x^2, the standardized score of an examinee with score X_i is

$$Y_i = \sigma * \left(\frac{X_i - \mu_X}{\sigma_X} \right) + \mu * ,$$

where, $\mu*$ and $\sigma*$ are arbitrary. For example, the College Entrance Examination Board's SAT Verbal and Quantitative scores each have $\mu*=500$ and $\sigma*=100$. Since it is a linear transformation of X, Y has the same distribution as X. If that distribution is approximately normal, then the standardized score can be interpreted in reference to the standard normal deviate, i.e., interpreted as deviations about the mean. This may not be a useful interpretation for those unskilled in statistics.

Normalized Scores

As the name implies, the normalized score involves a transformation of the raw score such that the normalized score follows the normal distribution regardless of the distribution of X. While tedious to compute, the transformation is straightforward—first transforming X to percentiles and then finding the unit normal deviate corresponding to the each percentile. In most cases, the resulting normalized score is standardized to have mean $\mu*$ and standard deviation $\sigma*$. The two most common normalized scores are the T Score for which $\mu*=50$ and $\sigma*= 10$, and the Stanine having $\mu*= 5$ and $\sigma*$ approximately equal to 2.

5

TYPES OF TESTS AND EXAMS

Many teachers dislike preparing and grading exams, and most students dread taking them. Yet tests are powerful educational tools that serve at least four functions. First, tests help you evaluate students and assess whether they are learning what you are expecting them to learn. Second, well-designed tests serve to motivate and help students structure their academic efforts. Crooks, McKeachie, and Wergin report that students study in ways that reflect how they think they will be tested. If they expect an exam focused on facts, they will memorize details; if they expect a test that will require problem solving or integrating knowledge, they will work toward understanding and applying information. Third, tests can help you understand how successfully you are presenting the material. Finally, tests can reinforce learning by providing students with indicators of what topics or skills they have not yet mastered and should concentrate on. Despite these benefits, testing is also emotionally charged and anxiety producing. The following suggestions can enhance your ability to design tests that are effective in motivating, measuring, and reinforcing learning.

A note on terminology: instructors often use the terms *tests*, *exams*, and even *quizzes* interchangeably. Test experts Jacobs and Chase, however, make distinctions among them based on the scope of content covered and their weight or importance in calculating the final grade for the course. An examination is the most comprehensive form of testing, typically given at the end of the term (as a final) and one or two times during the semester (as midterms). A test is more limited in scope, focusing on particular aspects of the course material. A course might have three or four tests. A quiz is even more limited and usually is administered in fifteen minutes or less.

GENERAL STRATEGIES

Spend adequate amounts of time developing your tests: As you prepare a test, think carefully about the learning outcomes you wish to measure, the type of items best suited to those outcomes, the range of difficulty of items, the length and time limits for the test, the format and layout of the exam, and your scoring procedures.

Match your tests to the content you are teaching: Ideally, the tests you give will measure students' achievement of your educational goals for the course. Test items should be based on the content and skills that are most important for your students to learn. To keep track of how well your tests reflect your objectives, you can construct a grid, listing your course objectives along the side of the page and content areas along the top. For each test item, check off the objective and content it covers.

Try to make your tests valid, reliable, and balanced. A test is *valid* if its results are appropriate and useful for making decisions about an aspect of students' achievement. Technically, validity refers to the appropriateness of the interpretation of the results and not to the test itself, though colloquially we speak about a test being valid. Validity is a matter of degree and considered in relation to specific use or interpretation. For example, the results of a writing test may have a high degree of validity for indicating the level of a student's composition skills, a moderate degree of validity for predicting success in later composition courses, and essentially no validity for predicting success in mathematics or physics.

Validity can be difficult to determine. A practical approach is to focus on *content validity,* the extent to which the content of the test represents an adequate sampling of the knowledge and skills taught in the course. If you design the test to cover information in lectures and readings in proportion to their importance in the course, then the interpretations of test scores are likely to have greater validity An exam that consists of only a few difficult items, however, will not yield valid interpretations of what students know.

A test is *reliable* if it accurately and consistently evaluates a student's performance. The purest measure of reliability would entail having a group of students take the same test twice and get the same scores (assuming that we could erase their memories of test items from the first administration). This is impractical, of course, but there are technical procedures for determining reliability. In general, ambiguous questions, unclear directions, and vague scoring criteria threaten reliability. Very short tests are also unlikely to be highly reliable. It is also important for a test to be balanced: to cover most of the main ideas and important concepts in proportion to the emphasis they received in class.

Use a variety of testing methods: Research shows that students vary in their preferences for different formats, so using a variety of methods will help students do their best. Multiple-choice or shortanswer questions are appropriate for assessing students' mastery of details and specific knowledge, while essay questions assess comprehension, the ability to integrate and synthesize, and the ability to apply information to new situations. A single test can have several formats. Try to avoid introducing a new format on the final exam: if you have given all multiple-choice quizzes or midterms, don't ask students to write an all-essay final.

Write questions that test skills other than recall: Research shows that most tests administered by faculty rely too heavily on students' recall of information. Bloom argues that it is important for tests to measure higher-learning as well. Fuhrmann and Grasha have adapted Bloom's taxonomy for test development. Here is a condensation of their list:

— To measure *knowledge* (common terms, facts, principles, procedures), ask these kinds of questions: Define, Describe, Identify, Label, List, Match, Name, Outline, Reproduce, Select, State. Example: "List the steps involved in titration."

— To measure *comprehension* (understanding of facts and principles, interpretation of material), ask these kinds of questions: Convert, Defend, Distinguish, Estimate, Explain, Extend, Generalize, Give examples, Infer, Predict, Summarize. Example: "Summarize the basic tenets of deconstructionism."

— To measure *application* (solving problems, applying concepts and principles to new situations), ask these kinds of questions: Demonstrate, Modify, Operate, Prepare, Produce, Relate, Show, Solve, Use. Example: "Calculate the deflection of a beam under uniform loading."

— To measure *analysis* (recognition of unstated assumptions or logical fallacies, ability to distinguish between facts and inferences), ask these kinds of questions: Diagram, Differentiate, Distinguish, Illustrate, Infer, Point out, Relate, Select, Separate, Subdivide. Example: "In the president's State of the Union Address, which statements are based on facts and which are based on assumptions?"

— To measure *synthesis* (integrate learning from different areas or solve problems by creative thinking), ask these kinds of questions: Categorize, Combine, Compile, Devise, Design, Explain, Generate, Organize, Plan, Rearrange, Reconstruct, Revise, Tell. Example: "How would you restructure the school day to reflect children's developmental needs?"

— To measure *evaluation* (judging and assessing), ask these kinds of questions: Appraise, Compare, Conclude, Contrast, Criticize, Describe, Discriminate, Explain, Justify, Interpret, Support. Example: "Why is Bach's Mass in B Minor acknowledged as a classic?"

Many faculty members have found it difficult to apply this six-level taxonomy, and some educators have simplified and collapsed the taxonomy into three general levels: The first category knowledge (recall or recognition of specific information). The second category combines comprehension and application. The third category is described as "problem solving," transferring existing knowledge and skills to new situations.

If your course has graduate student instructors (GSIs), involve them in designing exams. At the least, ask your GSIs to read your draft of the exam and comment on it. Better still, involve them in creating the exam. Not only will they have useful suggestions, but their participation in designing an exam will help them grade the exam. *Take precautions to avoid cheating.*

Types of Tests

Multiple-choice tests: Multiple-choice items can be used to measure both simple knowledge and complex concepts. Since multiple-choice questions can be answered quickly, you can assess students' mastery of many topics on an hour exam. In addition, the items can be easily and reliably scored. Good multiple-choice questions are difficult to write.

True-false tests: Because random guessing will produce the correct answer half the time, true-false tests are less reliable than other types of exams. However, these items are appropriate for occasional use. Some faculty who use true-false questions add an "explain" column in which students write one or two sentences justifying their response.

Matching tests: The matching format is an effective way to test students' recognition of the relationships between words and definitions, events and dates, categories and examples, and so on.

Essay tests: Essay tests enable you to judge students' abilities to organize, integrate, interpret material, and express themselves in their own words. Research indicates that students study more efficiently for essay-type examinations than for selection (multiple-choice) tests: students preparing for essay tests focus on broad issues, general concepts, and interrelationships rather than on specific details, and this studying results in somewhat better student performance regardless of the type of exam they are given. Essay tests also give you an opportunity to comment on students' progress, the quality of their thinking, the depth of their understanding, and the difficulties they may be having. However, because essay tests pose only a few questions, their content validity may be low. In addition, the reliability of essay tests is compromised by subjectivity or inconsistencies in grading.

A variation of an essay test asks students to correct mock answers. One faculty member prepares a test that requires students to correct, expand, or refute mock essays. Two weeks before the exam date, he distributes ten to twelve essay questions, which he discusses with students in class. For the actual exam, he selects four of the questions and prepares well-written but intellectually flawed answers for the students to edit, correct, expand, and refute. The mock essays contain common misunderstandings, correct but incomplete responses, or absurd notions; in some cases the answer has only one or two flaws. He reports that students seem to enjoy this type of test more than traditional examinations.

Short-answer tests: Depending on your objectives, short-answer questions can call for one or two sentences or a long paragraph. Short-answer tests are easier to write, though they take longer to score, than multiple-choice tests. They also give you some opportunity to see how well students can express their thoughts, though they are not as useful as longer essay responses for this purpose.

Problem sets: In courses in mathematics and the sciences, your tests can include problem sets. As a rule of thumb, allow students ten minutes to solve a problem you can do in two minutes.

Oral exams: Though common at the graduate level, oral exams are rarely used for undergraduates except in foreign language classes. In other classes they are usually time-consuming, too anxiety provoking for students, and difficult to score unless the instructor tape-records the answers. However, a math professor has experimented with individual thirty-minute oral tests in a small seminar class. Students receive the questions in advance and are allowed to drop one of their choosing. During the oral exam, the professor probes students' level of understanding of the theory and principles behind the theorems. He reports that about eight students per day can be tested.

Performance tests: Performance tests ask students to demonstrate proficiency in conducting an experiment, executing a series of steps in a reasonable amount of time, following instructions, creating drawings, manipulating materials or equipment, or reacting to real or simulated situations. Performance tests can be administered individually or in groups. They are seldom used in colleges and universities because they are logistically difficult to set up, hard to score, and the content of most courses does not necessarily lend itself to this type of testing. However, performance tests can be useful in classes that require students to demonstrate their skills (for example, health fields, the sciences, education). If you use performance tests, Anderson recommends that you do the following:

— Specify the criteria to be used for rating or scoring (for example, the level of accuracy in performing the steps in sequence or completing the task within a specified time limit).

— State the problem so that students know exactly what they are supposed to do (if possible, conditions of a performance test should mirror a real-life situation).

— Give students a chance to perform the task more than once or to perform several task samples.

"Create-a-game" exams: For one midterm, ask students to create either a board game, word game, or trivia game that covers the range of information relevant to your course. Students must include the rules, game board, game pieces, and whatever else is needed to play. For example, students in a history of psychology class created "Freud's Inner Circle," in which students move tokens such as small cigars and toilet seats around a board each time they answer a question correctly, and "Psychogories," a card game in which players select and discard cards until they have a full hand of theoretically compatible psychological theories, beliefs, or assumptions.

Alternative Testing Modes

Take-home tests: Take-home tests allow students to work at their own pace with access to books and materials. Take-home tests also permit longer and more involved questions, without sacrificing valuable class time for exams. Problem sets, short answers, and essays are the most appropriate kinds of take-home exams. Be wary, though, of designing a take-home exam that is too difficult or an exam that does not include limits on the number of words or time spent (Jedrey, 1984). Also, be sure to give students explicit instructions on what they can and cannot do: for example, are they allowed to talk to other students about their answers? A variation of a take-home test is to give the topics in advance but ask the students to write their answers in class. Some faculty hand out ten or twelve questions the week before an exam and announce that three of those questions will appear on the exam.

Open-book tests: Open-book tests simulate the situations professionals face every day, when they use resources to solve problems, prepare reports, or write memos. Open-book tests tend to be inappropriate in introductory courses in which facts must be learned or skills thoroughly mastered if the student is to progress to more complicated concepts and techniques in advanced courses. On an open-book test, students who are lacking basic knowledge may waste too much of their time consulting their references rather than writing. Open-book tests appear to reduce stress, but research shows that students do not necessarily perform significantly better on open-book tests. Further, open-book tests seem to reduce students' motivation to study. A compromise between open- and closed-book testing is to let students bring an index card or one page of notes to the exam or to distribute appropriate reference material such as equations or formulas as part of the test.

Group exams: Some faculty have successfully experimented with group exams, either in class or as take-home projects. Faculty report that groups outperform individuals and that students respond positively to group exams. For example, for a fifty-minute in-class exam, use a multiple-choice test of about twenty to twenty-five items. For the first test, the groups can be randomly divided. Groups of three to five students seem to work best. For subsequent tests, you may want to assign students to groups in ways that minimize differences between group scores and balance talkative and quiet students. Or you might want to group students who are performing at or near the same level (based on students' performance on individual tests). Some faculty have students complete the test individually before meeting as a group. Others just let the groups discuss the test, item by item. In the first case, if the group score is higher than the individual score of any member, bonus points are added to each individual's score. In the second case, each student receives the score of the group. Faculty who use group exams offer the following tips:

— Ask students to discuss each question fully and weigh the merits of each answer rather than simply vote on an answer.

— If you assign problems, have each student work a problem and then compare results.

— If you want students to take the exam individually first, consider devoting two class periods to tests; one for individual work and the other for group.

— Show students the distribution of their scores as individuals and as groups; in most cases group scores will be higher than any single individual score.

A variation of this idea is to have students first work on an exam in groups outside of class. Students then complete the exam individually during class time and receive their own score. Some portion of the test items are derived from the group exam. The rest are new questions. Or let students know in advance you will be asking them to justify a few of their responses; this will keep students from blithely relying on their work group for all the answers.

Paired testing: For paired exams, pairs of students work on a single essay exam, and the two students turn in one paper. Some students may be reluctant to share a grade, but good students will most likely earn the same grade they would have working alone. Pairs can be self-selected or assigned. For example, pairing a student who is doing well in the course with one not doing well allows for some peer teaching. A variation is to have students work in teams but submit individual answer sheets.

Portfolios: A portfolio is not a specific test but rather a cumulative collection of a student's work. Students decide what examples to include that characterize their growth and accomplishment over the term. While most common in composition classes, portfolios are beginning to be used in other disciplines to provide a fuller picture of students' achievements. A student's portfolio might include sample papers (first drafts and revisions), journal entries, essay exams, and other work representative of the student's progress. You can assign portfolios a letter grade or a pass/not pass. If you do grade portfolios, you will need to establish clear criteria.

CONSTRUCTION OF EFFECTIVE EXAMS

— *Prepare new exams each time you teach a course*: Though it is timeconsuming to develop tests, a past exam may not reflect changes in how you have presented the material or which topics you have emphasized in the course. If you do write a new exam, you can make copies of the old exam available to students.

— *Make up test items throughout the term*: Don't wait until a week or so before the exam. One way to make sure the exam reflects the topics emphasized in the course is to write test questions at the end of each class session and place them on index cards or computer files for later sorting. Software that allows you to create test banks of items and generate exams from the pool is now available.

— *Ask students to submit test questions*: Faculty who use this technique limit the number of items a student can submit and receive credit for. Here is an example: You can submit up to two questions per exam. Each question must be typed or legibly printed on a separate 5" x 8" card. The correct answer and the source (that is, page of the text, date of lecture, and so on) must be provided for each question. Questions can be of the short-answer, multiple-choice, or essay type. Students receive a few points of additional credit for each question they submit that is judged appropriate. Not all students will take advantage of this opportunity. You can select or adapt student's test items for the exam. If you have a large lecture class, tell your students that you might not review all items but will draw randomly from the pool until you have enough questions for the exam.

— *Cull items from colleagues' exams*: Ask colleagues at other institutions for copies of their exams. Be careful, though, about using items from tests given by colleagues on your own campus. Some of your students may have previously seen those tests.

— *Consider making your tests cumulative*: Cumulative tests require students to review material they have already studied, thus reinforcing what they have learned. Cumulative tests also give students a chance to integrate and synthesize course content.

— *Prepare clear instructions*: Test your instructions by asking a colleague (or one of your graduate student instructors) to read them.

— *Include a few words of advice and encouragement on the exam*: For example, give students advice on how much time to spend on each section or offer a hint at the beginning of an essay question or wish students good luck.

— *Put some easy items first*: Place several questions all your students can answer near the beginning of the exam. Answering easier questions helps students overcome their nervousness and may help them feel confident that they can succeed on the exam. You can also use the first few questions to identify students in serious academic difficulty.

— *Challenge your best students*: Some instructors like to include at least one very difficult question — though not a trick question or a trivial one — to challenge the interest of the best students. They place that question at or near the end of the exam.

— *Try out the timing*: No purpose is served by creating a test too long for even well-prepared students to finish and review before turning it in. As a rule of thumb, allow about one-half minute per item for true-false tests, one minute per item for multiple-choice tests, two minutes per short-answer requiring a few sentences, ten or fifteen minutes for a limited essay question, and about thirty minutes for a broader essay question. Allow another five or ten minutes for students to review their work, and factor in time to distribute and collect the tests. Another rule of thumb is to allow students about four times as long as it takes you (or a graduate student instructor) to complete the test.

— *Give some thought to the layout of the test*: Use margins and line spacing that make the test easy to read. If items are worth different numbers of points, indicate the point value next to each item. Group similar types of items, such as all true-false questions, together. Keep in mind that the amount of space you leave for short-answer questions often signifies to the students the length of the answer expected of them. If students are to write on the exam rather than in a blue book, leave space at the top of each page for the student's name. If each page is identified, the exams can be separated so that each graduate student instructor can grade the same questions on every test paper, for courses that have GSIs.

ALLAYING STUDENTS' ANXIETIES ABOUT TESTS

Anxiety can interfere with students' performance on tests. You can reduce students' anxiety and enhance their performance by taking care in how you prepare students for an exam, how you administer and return the test, and how you handle makeup tests. All students, but especially freshmen and sophomores, can benefit from knowing what they will be asked to do on an exam and under what conditions. Students will also feel more relaxed and less intimidated if you provide reassurance and encouragement rather than dire warnings about a test's difficulty. The suggestions below are designed to help you prepare your students to do their best on tests.

Make the first exam relatively easy. Research on motivation indicates that early success in a course increases students' motivation and confidence. In particular, students who do well on the first test generally improve their grades on subsequent tests.

Give more than one examination. The length of the school term, the difficulty level of the course, and the amount of course material all determine the number of exams an instructor gives. Periodic testing during the term has been shown to improve students' performance on the final exam. Giving two or more midterm exams also spreads out the pressure, allows students to concentrate on one chunk of material at a time, and allows students and instructors to monitor progress.

Avoid "pop" quizzes. Unannounced or surprise quizzes may penalize students who are unable to prepare for every single class meeting.

Give students advice on how to study. Help students develop appropriate study strategies to organize and understand information from the assigned readings and class notes. Consult with your student learning center for information.

Encourage students to study in groups. According to researchers, students who study in groups recall more information than students working alone and are able to overcome their feelings of academic inadequacy and isolation.

Schedule extra office hours before a test. Some instructors schedule extra office hours for the week or so before an exam to give students a chance to ask questions and go over difficult aspects of the material. They especially encourage study groups to visit during office hours.

Schedule review sessions before major exams. Ask students how you can help them feel less anxious. Students often make requests that faculty can easily accommodate, such as providing information about the test format, offering a review session, or refraining from walking around during the exam.

PREPARING STUDENTS FOR AN EXAM

Give a diagnostic test early in the term. An early diagnostic test alerts students to the prerequisite skills and knowledge they need to succeed in your class. Some faculty give diagnostic tests throughout the term to identify which students are keeping up and which need help and to enable all students to identify the areas they need to work on. These diagnostic tests provide students with quick and frequent feedback and typically do not count heavily in the final grade. Attach a pool of final exam questions to the course syllabus and distribute both on the first day of class. A faculty member who uses this technique attaches to the syllabus fifty essay questions, all of which the class discusses during the term.

The final exam is composed of five essay questions from the list. Under this system, students need not spend the semester worrying about what will be on the final. If the exam is too long to be attached to the syllabus, bind it to the course reader so that every student has a copy at a small additional cost. Put old exams on file in the department office or library. Reviewing past exams gives students clues about what to study. Students can analyze old exams for format (length of test, number of points for each type of question), types of questions, and level of difficulty. If your campus is networked, you can enter exams onto a file server and students can retrieve them whenever they want.

Distribute practice exams. Practice tests with answers help students gauge what is expected of them. You can use practice exams as the basis for review sessions or student study groups. If you will be administering a multiple-choice test, you could distribute the stems of multiple-choice questions but not the response choices; for example, "Which of the following statements best characterizes Melanie Kleins view of the first year of life?" Before an exam, explain the format to students. Let students know the number of questions, whether the test will be multiple-choice or essay and open or closed book, and whether they can bring in notes.

Give students advice on how to prepare for an exam. For example, remind them to allocate their study time in proportion to the relative importance of various topics. See "Multiple-Choice and Matching Tests" and "Short-Answer and Essay Tests" for suggestions to give students for those types of exams. To lessen students' tension before a test, give the following recommendations:

— Avoid cramming by spreading studying over several weeks.

— Eat sensibly the night before a test and get a good night's sleep.

— Arrive early for the test.

— Take deep relaxing breaths as the test starts.

Administering Tests

— *Duplicate extra copies of the exam*: Have extra copies on hand to replace copies that have blank pages or are collated incorrectly.

— *Administer the test yourself*: You will want to be present to announce any corrections (of typographical errors, for example) or changes in the exam. Your presence can also motivate and reassure students and signal to them the importance of the test. Arrive early on the day of the test to answer questions and stay late to talk with students.

— *Read the instructions aloud at the beginning of class*: Even if you write the clearest of instructions, it is helpful to read them aloud to the class. Ask students whether they have any questions about what they are supposed to do. Be brief, however, since students want to use their time to show you what they know.

— *Plan for "what ifs"*: Decide how you will respond to questions such as "What if we don't finish?" or "What if we think two answers are correct?"

— *Minimize temptations for cheating*: Actively proctor exams, unless your institution is on the honor system. See "Preventing Academic Dishonesty" for advice on ways to reduce cheating during exams.

— *Don't hover over the class*: Bring a book or work that will occupy you so that you will not be looking over students' shoulders. But be watchful to discourage cheating.

If there is no clock in the room, keep students apprised of the time. At the start of the exam write on the board the beginning time, the finishing time, and the time remaining. Once or twice update the time remaining and announce the last segment ("You have five minutes left."). Some faculty give students prompts during the test ("If you are not yet on question 5, you need to work a little more quickly"). Keep to the finishing time -it is unfair to allow some students to go on working when others must leave to go to another class.

Devote part of the session to reviewing the answers with students. One faculty member gives a thirty-minute midterm in a fifty-minute class. Students turn in their answer sheets after thirty minutes, but they keep the question sheet. The remaining class time is devoted to going over the correct answers and answering questions. A variation on this technique is to divide the class into small groups and have them review answers and then reconvene as a class to discuss areas of disagreement or confusion.

Another option is to ask for student volunteers who will meet with you immediately after the test to identify any specific problems with the exam. Or you could set up a student exam review committee. Make one copy of the answer sheet available at the end of the test period. One faculty member described by Jacobs and Chase places a corrected test copy (multiple-choice items) on his desk so that students can review it after they have turned in their own exam. This is only possible, of course, in small classes.

Give students the opportunity to comment on the test. Researchers report that giving students space on the test itself to explain their responses to multiple-choice items helped relieve students' anxiety and reduced posttest complaints from students. Students were directed to write a short justification for any answer they felt needed more explanation or for questions they perceived to be tricky. The researchers noted that students averaged less than one explanation per test over four tests. The instructors added a point for a "good explanation of a wrong answer" and subtracted a point for "a bad explanation of a right answer". Or you can ignore the comments on those items for which a student selected the correct multiple-choice option. Some faculty offer students extra credit for rewriting multiple-choice items (limit two items per test).

Include a blank question on the exam. Ask students to write a question or pose a problem that they were well prepared to answer. Grade students on the quality of the question (level of difficulty, appropriateness) and their answer. Include one or more extra-credit questions on the exam. Give students the opportunity to answer additional questions for extra credit at the end of the test. Add these points to their scores and to offset items they answered incorrectly. Let students "buy" information from you during the exam. Tell students that midway through the exam (say, between twenty and thirty minutes of a sixty-minute test) they can ask you questions for a price. The price is losing points from their total score. For example, a student might ask whether an answer is right or wrong at a cost of one penalty point; an equation or formula may cost two penalty points; a diagram setup, four penalty points; and so on.

A faculty member in mathematics who uses this technique reports that half of a typical class takes advantage of this approach to help them "unfreeze" on difficult problems. A chemistry professor uses a similar strategy but makes the option available to all students. He distributes a "test insurance page," in a lottery scratch-off format, to students along with their exams. The page contains clues to answers; each time students scratch off a clue, points are deducted from their total score. Let students bring in "crib sheets." As reported in "Exams: Alternative Ideas and Approaches" and Janick, some faculty have had success by asking students to prepare one 5" x 8" index card that they can consult during the exam.

According to the faculty, this technique helps students make decisions about what material is most important, and it can alleviate pretest anxiety. Vessey and Woodbury report negative effects of using crib sheets. Students, they believe, become "crib sheet focused"; they fall to answer the exam questions appropriately and instead look for key words on the test question that they can match to key terms on their crib sheet. When a match is found, students simply end up transcribing their crib sheet to their test. Encourage students to evaluate the exam. If you want a sense of how students felt about the exam, ask them to complete an unsigned evaluation form that poses questions such as the following:

— Did the content you expected to see appear on this exam?

— Identify the questions you never expected to see.

— Were the questions clear enough that, even though you may not have known the answer, you knew what was being asked?

— What questions confused you?

— Or ask students to give a letter grade to the content, format, and fairness of the test.

Give students "a second chance to learn." After students turn in their in-class, closed-book exam, they receive a second copy to take home and complete as an open-book exam. Both exams are scored, and students can earn back up to one-half of the points lost on the in-class exam. A variation is not to give students a take-home test but instead to schedule, some days later, a repeat test containing equivalent items. Grading is handled by weighting the two exams differently: the lower score counts 25 percent and the higher score 75 percent.

Returning Examinations

Return test papers promptly. Most students are anxious to know how they have done, and a quick turnaround also encourages relearning or corrective learning. Most experts recommend that tests be returned within five days. Laws governing the privacy and confidentiality of student records forbid the posting of grades by name, initials, or student numbers; confidentiality and concerns about security also dictate that exams not be left in a pile in the department office for students to pick up. If you cannot return papers to your students during class or office hours (using photo IDs if necessary), arrange for a staff member in the department to return the tests. For example, let students know that they can pick up their own test from the department secretary between 3 and 5 p.m. in the department office.

Use some class time to discuss the overall results. After making some general comments on how the class performed as a whole, you can show the general distribution of scores, note items missed by many people, and correct widespread misunderstandings. For essay tests, describe what you expected in a good answer and the most common problems. Some faculty read or distribute unsigned excerpts from outstanding papers. Smith returns graded multiple-choice exams to students and then divides them into groups to discuss the answers among themselves. "Questionable" questions are referred to the instructor for discussion by the entire class. She reports that having students review exams in groups often takes less time than her own reviews and students report enjoying it more.

Schedule extra office hours after returning a test. Students who come to see you may be angry or may try to have their grades changed. Request that students wait twenty-four hours before coming to see you. This gives them a chance to reread the exam, cool down, and prepare specific questions. Let students know that if they request a review of the grading of their test, you reserve the right to change the grade either positively or negatively. Ask students to come with specific questions (not "Why is my grade so low?"). Some faculty request that students prepare a brief paragraph expressing their complaint and justifying the correctness of their answer.

When a student comes to see you, listen carefully. Do not interrupt the student to rebut each point. Try to shift the focus of the discussion from grades to problemsolving. Ask, "What can we do to help you do better next time?" Help the student shift his or her attitude from blaming you or the test toward gaining motivation to work more effectively. Don't change a grade out of sympathy or compassion but only because you have made a clerical error or mistakenly evaluated a response.

Avoid the need to arrange for makeup tests by giving frequent exams. Makeup tests are problematic. If you devise a new test, it might not be comparable to the original test. But if you use the same test, some students may have talked to others 11who took the original test. Scheduling a makeup test also poses logistical problems. One way to avoid using makeup tests is to give four exams, for example, and count the grades of only three. Students who take all four tests can drop their lowest score. Students who miss an exam will be graded on the three they have taken. Some faculty who give two midterms give double weight to one if a student misses the other.

Give students options on the number of tests they take. Buchanan and Rogers offer students the following options:

(1) four multiple-choice tests,

(2) four multiple-choice tests and a final, or

(3) three multiple-choice tests and a final.

In options one and three, each test is worth 25 percent of the course grade; in option two, each test is worth 20 percent. Students who miss one of the multiple-choice tests must elect option three. Students who miss two tests are handled on a case-by-case basis. The researchers report that about 5 percent of the students elect to miss any given test. Give an additional exam for the entire class at the end of the semester. The grade on this extra test can replace a missed exam or replace a lower grade. This procedure frees you from policing excuses and illness on exam days. This option also helps out the student who has an off day on a test. Hand out essay questions in advance. If you distribute in advance a list of essay questions from which the midterm questions will be taken, you will not have to write a makeup test.

Give a two-hour rather than a three-hour final exam and use the last hour for makeup tests. By administering makeup tests during the time block reserved for the final exam, you can avoid the complexities of special scheduling. Give an oral exam as a substitute. Oral exams are a practical alternative only in small classes and are more effective in advanced courses, where higher levels of learning can be assessed. Oral exams typically cover less material, but in more depth, than written exams.

Fast Feedback

The most widely used method for evaluating teaching is the end-of-course questionnaire. The questionnaires arrive too late, however, to benefit the students doing the evaluation. Nor do the questionnaires usually encourage students to give the specific comments an instructor might need either to identify how well students have been understanding the material or to spot weaknesses in classroom presentation, organization, pacing, and work load. Much more effective are fast feedback activities that take place during the semester. The term fast feedback is derived from management practices but can be applied to instruction. Informal sampling of students' comprehension of the subject matter will enable you to gauge how and what students are learning. And informal requests for constructive criticism will help you identify which teaching methods best contribute to your students' understanding of the material.

Decide what you want to assess. You can gather information on how well students are learning the material, on the effectiveness of your teaching strategies, or on other topics of interest to you. When looking at your instructional methods, focus on what can be changed during the semester--for example, the pace of the course, turnaround time on exams and assignments, or the level of difficulty of the material---and ask your students for specific responses about particular issues rather than a general evaluation of the course or your teaching.

Schedule fast feedback at times appropriate to the course. If you are teaching a course for the first time or have significantly revised a course you have taught previously, you may want to canvass students as early as three or four weeks after the semester begins. If you are teaching a course you have taught many times before, you may want to wait until midsemester before asking for student assessments. (If you solicit feedback immediately after a midterm, however, most of the comments will relate to the exam.) In addition, if you observe that students are having difficulty with the material or course requirements, you may want to probe the issue immediately.

Soliciting Students' Opinions

Distribute blank index cards during the last five or ten minutes of class. Pass out 3x5 cards to students and ask them to respond anonymously to two questions, one on the front of the card, the other on the back. You can pose general questions about what is going well in the course and what needs to be improved or changed. Other general questions: "What do you want more of? Less of?" "How are you finding the course?" "Any suggestions for improving the course?" "Any problems?" "What do you need before the end of the term?" You may prefer to ask more specific questions about aspects of the course, such as whether the problem sets are too difficult or whether the pace of the class is causing difficulties. Leave the room while students write their comments. Ask a student volunteer to collect the forms and return them to you or the department assistant.

Ask students to complete a brief informal questionnaire. During the last few minutes of class, distribute a short, simple questionnaire to students or to a random sample of students in a large lecture class. Limit the questionnaire to four to six short-answer or multiple-choice questions. The issues posed should be ones you can respond to during the term; otherwise your students may develop false expectations about the remainder of the course. You might ask about the level of difficulty of course content, the quality and quantity of assignments, the use of classtime, the nature of student preparation outside of class, or the pace of the class.

Consider asking students to list the one or two specific behaviors or incidents that weighed most heavily in their ratings. To assure that students respond candidly, leave the room while they complete the questionnaire anonymously, and ask a student volunteer to collect the forms and return them to you or the department assistant. Arrange for your students to be interviewed. Invite a colleague or staff member to conduct an oral evaluation with your students during the last ten or fifteen minutes of class. After you leave, the evaluator asks students to cluster into groups of five or six and to take several minutes to do the following:

— Select a spokesperson who will also write down the groups' comments.

— Name something in the course that they find helpful or worthwhile or that has helped their learning.

— Name something that has hindered their learning and that they would like to see changed.

— Suggest how the course could be improved.

The evaluator circulates among the groups as they work to remind them how much time they have left and to make certain that they are staying with the task. The evaluator then asks each spokesperson to report the group's findings, and the evaluator records the results on the board. After all groups have reported, the evaluator summarizes for the class the points of consensus and asks for clarification on points of disagreement. The evaluator collects the written comments from the spokespersons and prepares an oral or written summary for you.

Respond quickly to students' comments. Ideally, you will want to respond to your students' comments at the next class meeting. So schedule fast feedback activities at those times during the semester when you will have the opportunity to immediately review the class's comments. Consider carefully what students say. First, look over the positive things your students have said about the course. This is important because it is too easy to get swayed by negative comments. Then read their suggestions for improvement and group them into three categories:

— Those you can change this semester (for example, the turnaround time on homework assignments)

— Those that must wait until the next time the course is offered (for example, the textbook)

— Those that you either cannot or, for pedagogical reasons, will not change (for example, the number of quizzes or tests)

— You may want to ask a colleague or a teaching consultant to help you identify options for making changes.

Let students know what, if anything, will change as a result of their feedback. Thank your students for their comments and invite their ongoing participation in helping you improve the course. Students appreciate knowing that an instructor has carefully considered what they have said. Clarify any confusions or misunderstandings about your goals and their expectations. Then give a brief account of which of their suggestions you will act upon this term, which must wait until the course is next offered, and which you will not act upon and why. Let students know what they can do as well. For example, if students report that they are often confused, invite them to ask questions more often. Keep your tone and attitude neutral; avoid being defensive, indignant, or unduly apologetic.

Checking Students' Understanding of the Material

Ask students to write a "minute paper." Davis, Wood, and Wilson describe a Berkeley physics professor who, in the late 70s, developed this technique, which can be used in any discipline. At the end of a class period, ask your students to write for a minute or two on the following two questions: "What is the most significant thing you learned today?" and "What question is uppermost in your mind at the end of today's class?" The resulting minute papers, submitted anonymously, will enable you to evaluate how well you have conveyed the material and how to structure topics for the next class meeting. Angelo and Mosteller describe a Harvard statistics professor who asks students "What was the 'muddiest point' in my lecture today?"

Ask students to list key concepts or ideas. At the conclusion of a series of lectures or readings about a particular topic, ask students to write short phrases summarizing the three to five key concepts or main ideas about the topic. You can review these lists to verify whether your students have grasped the important ideas. Students can also use their lists to review for exams. You may want to initiate a class discussion that asks students to compare and contrast their entries or define and apply the concepts.

Ask students whether they are understanding you or not. But avoid the generic "Any questions?" Instead ask, "How many are following me?" or "How many are with me on this point?" Also refrain from posing general questions that might put students on the spot: "Who is lost?" Have students briefly paraphrase a lecture or a reading assignment. At the beginning of the class period, you can request oral or written paraphrases and then judge whether students have understood the assigned reading or the last lecture. Or you can request paraphrases at the end of the period to check on whether students understood the material you presented.

Ask students to provide a closing summary. At the end of a class session, ask students, individually or in pairs, to write a very brief summary of the main ideas you covered in class. Have students turn in their summaries--making sure they understand this is not a quiz. Or at the beginning of class, ask students to summarize the main ideas from the previous class or the reading and to write one question they expect to be answered during class.

Student Rating Forms

Student rating forms, also called student end-of-course questionnaires or student evaluation forms, are traditionally administered at the end of the term to solicit student evaluations of a course. Typically such end- of-course information is used by faculty committees and administrators to make personnel decisions regarding an instructor: merit increases, promotion, tenure. At one time, it was considered controversial to administer student rating forms. Now such forms have become commonplace because it makes sense to survey students to find out what they think about their experiences in the class over the term and also because a substantial body of research has concluded that administering questionnaires to students is both valid and reliable. Here is some of what we know about student rating forms from the research:

Ratings of overall teaching effectiveness are moderately correlated with independent measures of student learning and achievement. Students of highly rated teachers achieve higher final exam scores, can better apply course material, and are more inclined to pursue the subject subsequently. An instructor's ratings for a given course tend to be relatively consistent over successive years; there is not much variation in student ratings for an individual instructor regardless of whether the form is administered to current students or to alumni.

There is little or no relationship between the following characteristics of students and their ratings of instruction: age, grade point average, year in college, and academic ability No consistent relationships have been found between student ratings and such variables as the amount of homework assigned or grading standards. Researchers do report the following relationships:

— Students tend to rate courses in their major fields and elective courses higher than required courses outside their majors.

— Faculty tend to receive more positive ratings than graduate student instructors.

— The gender of a student has little effect on ratings. The gender of an instructor, however, may have an impact. Though some studies report no relationship between a professor's gender and student ratings, others show that adhering to a gender-appropriate teaching style may be rewarded by higher evaluations.

— Ratings can be influenced by class size (very small classes tend to receive higher ratings), by discipline (humanities instructors tend to receive higher ratings than instructors in the physical sciences), and by type (discussion courses tend to receive higher ratings than lecture courses).

— Students' expectations affect their ratings: students who expect a course or teacher to be good generally find their expectations confirmed.

— Many campuses have standard rating forms that all faculty administer and centralized procedures for analyzing the data. Check with your department to find out what policies exist on your campus. If you are free to design and administer your own questionnaire, the suggestions below will help you make the most of student rating forms. If you use the standard campus questionnaire, these suggestions can improve the way you administer the forms and interpret the results.

Designing the Questionnaire

Use forms that give students the opportunity to provide quantitative ratings and to comment narratively on an instructor's performance. Forms that include both quantitative and narrative data are the most useful for getting the broadest picture of students' reactions. Davis presents sample student rating forms and items that can be used in end-of-course questionnaires, grouped by such categories as accessibility, organization and preparation, and interaction. Kulik describes the catalogue of items for instructor-designed questionnaires (IDQs), grouped by categories such as student development, course elements, and student responsibility. Theall and Franklin offer cautions in developing your own questionnaire: it is a time-consuming process to produce a valid and reliable form. They recommend using specific, unambiguous items. For example: "instructor defines new or unfamiliar terms," "repeats difficult concepts," "provides frequent examples." Especially if you are using these forms for your own improvement, the items you select or develop should capture specific behaviors that are amenable to change.

Select items that reflect your department's and institution's criteria of effective teaching and that are within students' range of judgment. For example, current students can judge how well prepared instructors are, how effectively they make use of class time, how well they explain things and with what level of enthusiasm, and how responsive they are to difficulties the students may be having in the course. Students can also comment on whether the instructor promotes original thinking and critical evaluation of ideas. In contrast, current students are not qualified to judge whether instructors are up-to-date in their field or to rate how adequately a course prepares them for advanced course work in the field.

State each item clearly. For example, "The instructor routinely summarizes major points" is unambiguous, while "The instructor is well prepared and gives fair exams" confounds two different issues. For at least some of the key items, provide a numerical rating scale. The use of quantifiable items enables you to calculate a class's average response and to note the distribution of responses, both of which are useful in interpreting the results of the evaluation. Use either a 5-point or 7-point scale, with 1 representing "not at all descriptive" and 5 (or 7) "very descriptive." Also provide a "Don't know or doesn't apply" option that students can check.

Include at least one item that asks students about the effects of the course. For example, ask students to describe or rate the knowledge, appreciation, or skills they acquired in the course or their intellectual, personal, or professional growth as a result of the instructor's teaching.

Include at least one quantitative measure on the overall effectiveness of the instructor.

Include at least one open-ended item that asks about the overall effectiveness of the instructor. For example, "Please identify what you perceive to be the greatest strengths and weaknesses of this instructor's teaching."

Limit the number of questions about student characteristics. Student characteristics have relatively little influence on ratings of overall effectiveness. You might want to know, however, whether students are taking the course as an elective or to fulfill a requirement.

Keep the form short. Since students may fill out evaluation forms for all their instructors, questionnaires should be brief.

Administering the Questionnaire

Announce in advance the date on which rating forms will be handed out. Schedule the time sometime during the last two weeks of the term; allow ten to fifteen minutes for this activity. Encourage students to attend that day and complete the form. Do not distribute forms at the final exam, when students are preoccupied with other matters. Inform the students about the purpose of the questionnaire. It is helpful to stress to students that their ratings and comments are important and will be used by both you and your department. Students may want to know how the completed forms will be handled. Here are some sample 'instructions that can be placed on the rating forms and read aloud:

Designate a student from the class (or a department staff member) to supervise questionnaire administration. You may hand out the forms (always bring several more than the official number of students enrolled), but you should not be present while students complete the questionnaires; and you should not collect the forms. Ask the designated collector to place the forms in a large manilla envelope, noting on the outside your name, the course number, the total number of students present, the total number of forms collected, and the date. The sealed envelope should be delivered to the department office. Do not look at the forms until after you have submitted final grades for the course. Some campuses provide the faculty with summaries of their rating forms, including computer printouts that show trends and comparative data. If your campus does not provide such a service, you will want to analyze and summarize the data yourself.

Summarizing Responses

Look at the number of students who completed forms and the total class enrollment. Ideally, you would like a response rate (number of completed forms divided by number of enrolled students) of 80 percent or higher. When less than two-thirds of the enrolled students in classes of one hundred or fewer students or less than one-half of the enrolled students in classes of more than a hundred students have submitted forms, the data should be interpreted cautiously if the questionnaires are being used for personnel decisions, such as merit, tenure, or promotion.

Keep the data separate for each course offering. Aggregating data for several different courses may obscure differences in teaching effectiveness for various kinds of instruction and may raise questions of proper weighting of the responses in each course. Aggregating data for several offerings of the same course may obscure long-term trends toward increased or decreased student satisfaction. Do not summarize data if there are fewer than ten questionnaires. Student questionnaires from independent reading courses or seminars with very small enrollments may be accumulated over several terms and summarized when their numbers are sufficiently large.

If your department does not already do so, prepare summary statistics for the quantifiable questions. The summary should include the following:

— The frequency distribution of student ratings for each item (the number and percentage of students selecting each response)

— The average response, either the mean (calculated to one decimal point), mode, or median

— The standard deviation (an index of agreement or disagreement among respondents)

— Departmental norms (averages) or comparison norms, if available, on key items for courses of a similar size, level, and type of instruction (for example, laboratory, seminar, studio, lecture)

The summary should reflect the entire range of comments as well as their preponderance. To prepare such a summary, read all the students' comments about a single question, develop categories or headings that meaningfully group most of the comments, and record the number of comments made in each category. In deciding what to ignore and what to consider, take into account your goals for the course, your values and emphases, and your teaching style. Also remember that it is human nature to focus on that piercing negative comment to the exclusion of the positive remarks from most of the class. An outside teaching consultant or supportive colleague can help you put students' comments in perspective.

Interpreting Responses

For quantifiable questions, determine the percentage of omitted responses. Some items may be left blank because they do not apply. Items with low response rates should be interpreted cautiously. Look at the average ratings for the quantifiable questions. Average ratings can be interpreted on an absolute scale and in relation to the ratings of other similar courses and instructors. For example, a mean rating of 4 on a 7-point scale for overall course evaluation may be labeled "moderately effective." However, if half of all similar courses receive mean ratings above 4, then this 4 rating falls in the lower half. There is some debate within the field on whether such comparisons are meaningful, even among courses similar in level (lower division, upper division, graduate), size, format (lecture, laboratory, and so on), and student demographics.

Cashin argues for using comparative data, pointing out that because students tend to rate most items high, a score of 3.5 on a 7-point scale is not really an indicator of "average" effectiveness. In using student ratings to improve your teaching, try to incorporate some comparative information to better understand your own strengths, weaknesses, and accomplishments. Perhaps the best comparative information, as Kulik suggests, comes from noticing changes in the ratings of a course you have taught several times. Look at the range of student responses for the quantifiable questions.

The range provides important information. For example, the average of all ratings for your course may be 5 on a 7-point scale. But notice whether all students rated the course as 4, S, or 6 or whether some 2 and 3 ratings were balanced out by some 7s. If ratings cluster at the two ends of the scale, then some aspects of your teaching work for one group of students but not for another--an area to explore. The standard deviation also provides useful information. A standard deviation of less than 1.0 (on a 5-point scale) indicates relatively good agreement among the respondents. Deviations above 1.2 indicate a divided class on that item.

Note your highest and lowest rated items. One way to analyze student ratings is to calculate the averages for individual questions and note your highest and lowest rated items. See whether your strengths and weaknesses cluster in patterns on any of the following topics: organization and clarity, enthusiasm and stimulation of student interest, teacher-student rapport, teaching and communication skills, course work load and difficulty, fairness of exams and grading, classroom climate. As a rule of thumb, it is usually cause for concern when a third of the students give low ratings to some aspect of a course. In looking at your highest and lowest rated items, try to identify specific behaviors of yours that might have caused students to give you those ratings. If you do this exercise with a colleague who has administered the same form to his or her students, you can exchange examples of behaviors that lead to high ratings.

From the open-ended comments, identify specific problems. Lunde recommends reading the comments to pinpoint specific complaints--for example, student anxiety about the degree of structure in the course or your expectations for students. Then determine whether the complaint is justified (in this case by looking at the syllabus and handouts). If the worry is legitimate, identify specific steps you can take to address the weakness. Keep in mind that students give few detailed suggestions on how to improve a course; they are better at spotting problems. If you have the time or can prevail upon an experienced teaching consultant, you could analyze open-ended comments using a grid technique, a method for determining whether students who rate a course highly are saying the same things as those who rate the course lower.

Consider how characteristics of courses can influence ratings. Small classes, electives, and courses in the humanities tend to receive more favorable ratings. For each characteristic the differences are minimal, but together they may be meaningful. It may also be helpful, in interpreting the results, to take into account whether this course is your favorite, one you frequently teach, or a course that you are teaching at the request of the department chair. Ask a knowledgeable consultant or a colleague for assistance. Some teachers can read their students' ratings and map out strategies to improve teaching. Others find it helpful to review the ratings with a knowledgeable colleague or teaching consultant, available on some campuses.

Consultants can help you interpret the results and explore strategies for improvement. Consider making your ratings available to students. Several departments on campuses around the country--and some entire institutions-- have a tradition of making their course ratings public. Many faculty members in these departments or on these campuses believe that because faculty members work harder at their teaching when they know the results are on view to their peers and to students, teaching is of higher quality when the rating forms are publicly available.

6

Reporting Student's Achievement

International research provides evidence for the view that parental encouragement and support for learning activities at home, and parental involvement in schools and classrooms, have a positive impact on children's learning. To be active partners with schools, parents must have relevant information to enable them to support the learning of their children. The most common sources of information for parents are newsletters, parent evenings, conversations with teachers, and direct inquiries to schools.

Schools are more effective at providing information about 'social events' and 'activities' within the school and less effective in informing parents about teaching and learning processes and the curriculum. Reports on student progress provide parents with information they require in order to support the education of their children. Written reports and parent-teacher meetings are the most common means through which parents receive this information.

Parents are very clear and consistent about what they want in student reports. They want to be:

— kept well informed about their children's progress;

— given information about achievement and progress in both academic and non-academic areas of learning;

— informed about both strengths and weaknesses of their children; and

— provided with pertinent and constructive advice about how they can support their children's learning.

The rationale for encouraging parents to be active partners in the education of their children is built on research findings that show parental encouragement and support for learning activities at home, and parental involvement in schools and classrooms, have a positive impact on children's learning. High levels of parental involvement have also been shown to be strongly related to increased student motivation. Parent involvement is a term used to describe the various processes of parental and community input to schooling.

Fullan distinguished between parent involvement in instructional and non-instructional contexts. Instructional involvement relates to parent activities that provide assistance in the classroom or with learning activities at home, such as homework. Non-instructional involvement refers to participation in decision making, governance and community-school relations. Instructional involvement by parents has direct benefits on the learning outcomes for their children.

Epstein has disaggregated the processes involved in effective parent involvement into the following components:

— parenting practices and home conditions that support the learning of children in school;

— assistance with learning activities at home;

— monitoring student progress and student programs;

— involvement at the school - including assisting with and attending school activities; and

— contributing to decision making and advocacy through organisations such as parent associations, and school councils.

Parents indicated the following roles, in order of importance:

— taking an active interest in the learning of their children;

— being actively involved in schools;

— communicating with schools; and

— participating in school decision making.

Research on the participation of parents in governance and decision making provides no evidence of a direct relationship between the degree of parent involvement and student learning outcomes. It does, however, provide evidence of a number of indirect benefits, such as increasing the resources for the school as well as individual benefits for the parents who participate through the enhancement of their planning and management skills.

A particular aspect of parent involvement that is explored in a number of recent studies is the concept of parents as complementary educators or partners, with teachers, in the learning process. Parents as partners, with a shared sense of purpose, with teachers, provide the basis for improving student learning. Drawing on the work of Pugh and Wolfendale, Bastiani lists the central characteristics of effective parent-teacher partnerships in education as follows:

— sharing of power, responsibility and ownership, though with each party having different roles;

— a degree of mutuality, that begins with the process of listening to each other and that incorporates responsive dialogue and 'give and take' on both sides;

— shared aims and goals based on a common understanding of the educational needs of children; and

— commitment to joint action, in which parents, students and teachers work together.

STUDENT PROGRESS

Parents require reports on their children's progress to provide fundamental information that supports parents in making decisions about the education of their children. In particular, they want information that will assist them in supporting their child's learning at home and will reassure them of the educational progress of their child. Written reports and parent-teacher meetings are the most common means through which parents receive information on their children's progress.

Broadfoot's research in New Zealand found that parents strongly support this aspect of reporting. Informal meetings and telephone calls from teachers, student diaries, examination results, samples of work annotated with teacher comments and corrections, and the examination of their child's workbooks and homework are other ways that parents gain information about progress at school.

Parents want regular and more frequent written reports than they currently receive. They also want flexibility in arrangements for making formal and informal contact with teachers. Parents express a clear need to be advised immediately if their child's learning or behaviour becomes a concern. They do not want to wait to be advised through the next formal report, if they can take action at an earlier time.

The format, structure and clarity of written reports is a source of dissatisfaction for some parents, especially when there is a lack of consistency within a school or across different years as to how and when information is presented or reported. Parents indicate that they need help to interpret the information contained in reports.

Parents are very clear and consistent about what they want in terms of the substance of reports on their children's progress. They want to be:

— kept well informed about their child's progress;

— given information about a range of different aspects of achievement covering all curriculum areas as well as information on social development and behaviour;

— informed about strengths and weaknesses; and

— provided with diagnostic assessments and constructive advice about how they can provide support for their children's learning.

Parent Views on Reporting Children's Progress

— Methods of assessing and reporting on student achievement are contentious matters among parents. Two distinct forms of reporting are common, narrative reporting, and reporting using grades and marks.

— Parents indicate the following areas of satisfaction and dissatisfaction with narrative reporting of student progress:

— They are satisfied with the detail of narrative reports. They believe they receive more information about their child from narrative reports than from other types of reporting.

— They are dissatisfied with narrative reporting when it is uninformative, vague, and ambiguous.

— They view narrative reporting as informative when it not only describes what the student has achieved, but includes evaluative comments about the level of achievement and expected levels of achievement.

Other aspects of reporting provide marks or grades to indicate the level of a student's achievement. Parents indicate that this form of reporting:

— is more reliable than narrative forms of reporting because it is less dependent on individual teacher skill;

— enables parents to understand the level of achievement of their child in a comparative sense;

— is not useful where parents are unsure what the grades refer to or do not mean the same thing in different contexts;

— can be a motivating factor for students, especially older students; and

— is not appropriate for students who are constantly failing and may be less useful in the early primary years.

Parents express a desire for objective benchmarks or standards against which they can make judgements about their child's progress. They believe independent standards would provide relevant information in forming a judgement about how well their child is achieving. Whilst some parents believe that grades, such as 'A', 'B', 'C', etc., can meet this need, others prefer alternative reporting strategies such as those based on a common set of clearly defined descriptors of levels of achievement.

STUDENT ACHIEVEMENT IN INDIVIDUAL SCHOOLS

The achievement level of students at individual schools is the main type of school performance information reported to parents. In many countries such reporting focuses on the achievement of students on the basis of tests and examinations of learning outcomes in the cognitive domain with considerably less focus on the affective and social outcomes.

In England the average achievement score in each school is provided to parents. Further, the Parents' Charter requires that comparative performance tables of examination and national curriculum test results be published for schools. In addition to the information on student performance, other information on the improvement of schools and the rank of schools is published for various categories of schools.

Public reporting of test results is a common occurrence in the United States (US) where more than twenty-eight States include school-level test scores in public reporting on school performance. The Stanford Achievement Test, a normed multiple choice test, is commonly used across the US, but some systems have designed more complex assessment standards, such as those linked to state curricula. In Kentucky, schools are held accountable for specified performance standards in the areas of reading, writing, mathematics, science, social studies, arts and humanities, practical living and vocational studies. The standards are aligned with the state curriculum.

Student achievement is assessed against these standards through examinations that require students to provide complex open-ended responses to questions and portfolio assessments of collections of student work. Similar assessment methods are used in Maryland to test reading, writing, language usage, mathematics, science and social studies. No student is assessed on all six parts of the examination system, as the purpose is to evaluate school rather than student performance.

School review reports

Another form of reporting about schools has also been in place at various times since the inception of schooling in many countries. This has been based on the professional assessments of one or more experienced educators who have been required to make a judgment about the quality of each school. Inspections, or school reviews, in various forms take a holistic view of the school and examine and report on school processes as well as student achievement data.

School inspections in England and Scotland and school reviews in New Zealand assess the performance of schools against a range of performance indicators. These include standards of achievement, quality of learning, school efficiency, behaviour and discipline, and student development in non-academic areas; student attainment, the quality of teaching and learning, school development planning, and responsiveness to parents; school administration, curriculum management, student support, the achievement of sub-groups, personnel management and financial management.

Parents in England are encouraged to use the reports to compare the performance of schools in their local area. In Scotland all parents receive a summary of the published report and may obtain the full report on request.

Prospectuses and annual reports

Each year every school in England is required to publish a prospectus that describes its achievements and the courses it provides. The prospectus must present information on the school's results in public examinations and National Curriculum tests and compare them with national and local results. Schools are also encouraged to explain the aims and values of the school, their approach to teaching, and arrangements for programs such as sex or careers education. Free copies of the prospectus are available to parents.

Additionally, parents in England are provided with an annual report from the governing body. Legislation requires these reports to include specified information on student achievement, truancy, post-school destinations of students, and school budget. Many schools issue prospectuses and annual reports to their parents and communities. No system mandates that schools must issue a comprehensive prospectus of the type described above for England. Many systems require schools to produce an annual report, although there is significant variation in the required content and the quality and accuracy of the information reported.

Key Issues in Reporting about Schools

Capturing the complexity of schools

Research indicates that performance indicators of school performance, such as test results and retention/ attendance data needs to be interpreted carefully in making reliable judgements about the quality of learning. Simple summary information cannot describe the complexity of school performance. Public reporting systems need to focus on the broad objectives of schooling and the multi-dimensional nature of school performance.

Parents possess a clear and distinctive model of a 'good school', which is based on wide-ranging criteria. This model of a 'good school' includes a high level of teacher professionalism, a broad curriculum, a safe and secure environment, strong leadership, parental involvement, effective communication, well-maintained facilities and adequate resources.

Research findings about the variation in student achievement indicate that about half of the variation is attributable to differences in the achievement-related capacities and dispositions of students. Of the remaining half, approximately four-fifths is attributable to differences due to the effectiveness of classrooms - teaching programs, etc. - within schools, and the remaining fifth to differences between schools.

The challenge in developing strategies for reporting on the achievements of schools is to describe the substantial variation that is attributable to educational processes within schools, in addition to the variation in achievements between schools. The core issue is how to capture both the multi-dimensional nature of achievement and the variation in the impact of individual schools in reports on school performance.

School inspections and review models based on qualitative and quantitative data provide the most common mechanism for reporting that takes account of the complexity of schools. The English and Scottish inspection systems assess both school processes and student outcomes in a number of areas. The professional judgements of school performance in such processes draw on information from a range of sources, usually including interviews, classroom observations, and data on student achievement.

The advantage of standardised testing is that results can be compared nationally and the testing process is relatively straightforward. A disadvantage in using standardised tests for assessing school performance is that they may not be designed to assess the particular curriculum which is taught in the schools concerned. The most common non-cognitive indicators used in school reporting in the US include attendance, drop-out, and truancy rates and post-school destinations. The methodology for assessing school performance in terms of more substantive non-cognitive aspects of school performance such as affective and social development of students is not as well developed as that for cognitive development.

Secondary schools in England view the independence of inspectors as essential to the aim of public accountability. Observations of schools were considered anecdotal information.

Ensuring fairness

Two approaches can be used to maximise fairness in the use of school performance information. The first is to explicitly take account of contextual information to adjust student test results for pre-existing social and educational differences among students. One approach to assessing the contribution schools make to the achievement of students - value-added' - is to use statistically complex models to estimate the effect of individual schools.

Understanding the difference between school effectiveness and school performance is critical to assessing schools fairly. School performance is defined as the average level of achievement of students in the school in the particular domain assessed, [eg. mathematics]... School effectiveness is defined as the relative level of performance of a school [for students of different backgrounds and levels of prior achievement] in a particular area of assessment.

Concerns have been expressed that the publication of information about the performance and effectiveness of schools will be misused because the public will not understand the difference between 'performance' and 'effectiveness'. Models of reporting on schools that provide information for each individual school and allow a comparison of achievement for 'like' groups of students across a system or groups of schools provide the basis to evaluate both performance and effectiveness. Alternatively, 'value-added' measures can be used as indicators of the effectiveness of schools.

The 'like-school' groupings used in some States are based on socio-cultural characteristics of students (eg. social disadvantage, non-English speaking background), which are relatively weak determinants of student achievement. Hence they represent only a small part of the impact of student characteristics on achievement. A much stronger impact is found for prior levels of achievement. The validity of grouping students and schools into 'like-groups' is highest when the student characteristics that have the most impact on student learning outcomes are the basis for allocating schools to comparable groups.

Public confidence in reporting

School performance information needs to be presented in a form that parents can easily understand. The public reporting of school performance information which is both valid and fair is technically complex, yet if the public does not understand how performance measures are determined, it will affect their confidence in the system. Systems have a responsibility to disseminate information about the procedures used to determine school performance.

Accountability systems use formulas and calculations that are not clearly understood by parents. Elmore and his colleagues noted that confusion was particularly strong among parents who had difficulty in adjusting from norm-referenced standardised tests to criterion-based outcomes assessments. Parents found it difficult to understand the new assessment terminologies and expressed the need for some linkage to past systems to assist their understanding of the new developments. The clarity, integrity and rigour of reporting is of paramount importance if the public is to have confidence in them.

In England, Parents' Charter states that the purpose of performance tables is to help parents choose schools and colleges for attendance by their children. With the increased role of market models in the public sector, the provision of information to support efficient and effective choices is of greater importance.

There are indications that parents are influenced more by information about discipline and the general reputation of the school than by educational considerations. The choice of school may involve finding a satisfactory alternative to the 'local school' rather than making an optimal choice from a wide range of possible schools. Information about schools must address a broad and diverse range of aspects of provision and performance if it is to satisfy the wide range of needs of parents in choosing a school.

Reporting as pressure for school improvement

Most education systems that report on school performance, for example England, Scotland, Kentucky and Mississippi, have school improvement as an explicit goal of reporting. Public reporting about schools provides pressure for schools to improve. Public reporting energizes parents and other community members to pressure schools for higher performance, particularly when data show differences in performance among schools that are roughly comparable in the public's eye.

Pressure from parents is part of a broad approach to school improvement in which systems and schools set improvement targets established on the basis of performance information. For example, in Scotland, a follow-up inspection is held within 18 months of the original inspection and the subsequent report made available to parents. The follow-up report is a "powerful motivator" for schools to achieve their improvement targets.

The English inspection process, by identifying strengths and weaknesses and assisting schools to tackle their weaknesses, has twin functions of improvement and accountability. There is much evidence that school inspections in England have a direct impact with schools establishing action plans and achieving improvement targets within months of the inspection. The improvement targets focus on school processes (such as revising syllabuses, improving management, or raising teaching standards. Schools are also required to set annual improvement targets for student learning outcomes.

School performance information as a form of assurance and accountability

Public information on school performance is required if the process of accountability for the use of public funds is to be transparent. In Australia, all but a small number of non-government schools, in addition to government schools, receive a significant proportion of their recurrent income through State/ Territory and Commonwealth government funding.

Governments, business, and community leaders are more willing to ease regulations and leave decisions in the hands of teachers and principals when schools report regularly and clearly on results. As well, the public needs such information as assurance to monitor their investment in public education. Parents also require performance and effectiveness information to assure themselves that they have made an appropriate choice of school. Parents consider that they have a right to access information relevant to the education of their children.

Variation in what is reported to parents

There is considerable variation in the type of information that parents and the public receive about school performance. In England, The Parents Charter requires that all parents receive:

— regular reports from independent inspectors;

— performance tables for all local schools;

— a prospectus for all local schools; and

— an annual report from the school their children attend.

This information is considerably more comprehensive than that available in most other systems. Within Australian education systems there is substantial variation in what parents receive in the way of reports on school performance. In most systems they have access to an annual report produced by each school and in many instances to a prospectus. Very few systems provide parents with school reports based on independent review or inspection and only one requires schools to report student outcome information in a way that provides a valid assessment of the performance and effectiveness of schools.

POLICIES AND PRACTICES OF EDUCATION SYSTEMS

The Curriculum Statements and Profiles for Schools are generally organised around a learning continuum for primary and secondary schooling. The key concepts of the various approaches adopted by State/ Territory systems are:

— curricula defined for each Key Learning Area (KLA) and based on outcomes rather than content;

— a continuum of learning across grades; and curricula divided into a number of levels, each of which approximates to two years of schooling.

Key Learning Area (KLA)

The Key Learning Area (KLA) concept is evident in most state/ territory curricula. For example, the framework includes English, Mathematics, Science, Technology, Studies of Society and Environment, The Arts, Health and Physical Education, and Languages Other Than English, and in Western Australia they are basically the same but Technology is called Technology and Enterprise. Most States/ Territories have Key Learning Areas that are the same or similar to these. The number of KLAs used in various systems range between six and eight. In some States/ Territories the KLA approach is not applied to the last two years of schooling.

Standardised Testing

A second major trend that has emerged over the last decade is the introduction of systemic standardised testing. Such tests are conducted most frequently in Years 3 and 5 in literacy and numeracy, but also occur in other years.

Quality Assurance Systems

These processes chiefly revolve around schools establishing goals and targets and then reporting publicly on their achievement through an annual reporting process. In a small number of cases the quality assurance component involves some form of external independent verification of the school's evaluation and limited general public or local reporting, but most systems fall short of these standards.

Current Policies and Practices

There is a pattern for government school systems to have publicly declared curriculum standards established from the first to the twelth year of schooling . In most States/ Territories, a statutory body responsible for curriculum development, such as a Board of Studies, sets such standards. The standards are in most cases derived from the nationally developed statements and profiles referred to earlier. The standards are expressed as criterion-based outcomes standards expected at each 'stage' of schooling.

All government education systems have adopted criterion-based curriculum outcomes, founded generally on either the national statements and profiles or State/ Territory variations of them. There is variation across systems, however, in the extent to which criterion-based outcome approaches have been implemented, particularly in the extent to which the outcome statements and standards have been made explicit across all KLAs. Some systems have had criterion-based outcomes in place for all KLAs for three years or more. Others have a longer time frame for the completion of this process and are still in the early stages of implementation.

In some instances the 'learning outcomes' are being expressed through individual syllabus documents rather than through KLAs. In some States/ Territories schools report to parents against these standards and in other States/ Territories reporting does not relate to such standards. The linking of criterion-based outcomes to specific stages of schooling makes the standards explicit. Some systems have also been able to, or are in the process of, establishing external benchmarks of achievement against the standards. These allow student achievement levels to be compared with the learning outcomes appropriate to the age and the achievement levels of other students across the State/ Territory.

At their most sophisticated, such benchmarks - which are currently only established in English literacy and Mathematics - allow schools, parents and students to evaluate their performance overall, and the performance of sub-groups of students, against an external indicator. Systems consider that their standardised testing and reporting programs also provide information about standards. They use the results, at school and system level, to determine whether the level of student performance is improving. Some States use this information to identify students requiring additional support.

Catholic systems have adopted one of two approaches to the specification of educational standards and the assessment of achievement. Either they have linked student outcomes directly to the curriculum standards approach of the statutory curriculum body in their State/ Territory, which is common, or they have linked directly to the nationally developed Statements and Profiles. A small number of Catholic systems also participate in standardised testing programs conducted by the States/ Territories. The information on curriculum and standards in each system is available to parents, but in most cases parents must either explicitly request the information or rely on schools to conduct appropriate information sessions.

There are differences among school systems as to whether systemic policies and guidelines inform such school practices or whether decisions about reporting policies are at the discretion of the school. Government school systems typically publish policies and guidelines for assessment and reporting. Common principles espoused in these documents indicate that practices should:

— be integrated into teaching and learning practices;

— be aligned with relevant curriculum documents - usually through a focus on reporting against specified curriculum outcomes;

— be fair, valid and comprehensive;

— value teacher judgements;

— be based on an appropriate range of assessment methods and strategies; and

— convey useful and meaningful information.

Students are frequently involved in assessing and reporting on their own achievement. No system provides any guidance on this policy, but a number of systems encourage the practice. Whilst student involvement in self-assessment is more common than in reporting, some schools have advanced practices in which students report to parents on their own self-assessment, select work samples to be part of the report to parents and, more commonly, take part in parent-teacher meetings.

Criterion-based outcomes approaches vary in their complexity and rigour and in the extent to which they are mandated as policy. In its most complex manifestation there is a requirement that schools report to parents on the attainment level of each student against specified curriculum outcomes. Such approaches may also report student achievement against the state/ territory average or state/ territory benchmarks.

Some systems encourage schools to use an outcomes approach based on curriculum documents for the State/ Territory or, in some instances, directly on the nationally developed Statements and Profiles.

Systems that do not require schools to report against criterion-based outcomes indicated that individual schools decide such policy. In a small number of instances, systems reported that schools use a 'subject and content-covered' reporting process whereby individual achievement levels in various subjects are indicated by comments or letter grades. A small number of systems made specific mention of the practices of schools in reporting on the achievements of students with special learning needs. Such reporting was usually against the specific program developed for each individual student.

It is common practice in many systems for student work samples to form part of the formal report to parents. The teacher may annotate these samples. The work samples are used to provide tangible evidence of the student's achievement of certain outcomes or skill development. Systems generally acknowledge that non-academic outcomes, such as social skills and behaviour, may be included in written reports to parents, but such reporting is likely to be the initiative of individual schools.

Parent-Teacher meetings

Most systems encourage schools to provide opportunities for teachers to discuss written reports with parents in a face-to-face meeting. These meetings are held at least once a year but are usually conducted more often. One system that was more specific reported that the parent teacher meetingn enables parents to provide teachers with information about their child.

It also allows teacher's to discuss issues of importance about students and the learning outcomes they intend to cover.

Systems report that it is a common practice for teachers and parents to discuss the progress of individual students at times other than the formal parent-teacher meeting. Parents can make a formal meeting appointment or may discuss their children informally with teachers in the course of their interaction with the school. Many systems indicate that schools are to advise parents that they can seek an meeting at any time to discuss the progress of their child.

Schools may instigate an meeting with a parent outside of the formal reporting processes. This practice is less common and is usually an urgent response to a student not progressing at the rate expected or not behaving satisfactorily.

Reporting to parents on the outcomes of annual standardised tests is becoming increasingly widespread. Such tests are mainly in literacy and numeracy and at specified Year levels. Five out of the eight government systems require schools to report to parents on the literacy test results of students sitting an external test in Years 3 & 5, or the equivalent grade level for the system. In a smaller number of States/ Territories the standardised test includes mathematics/ numeracy and can include an additional curriculum area. There are also examples of similar tests being conducted at the secondary school level, though this occurs in only a minority of systems.

Information on individual student exam results in end of secondary schooling credentialling processes is reported directly to students by statutory bodies in each State/ Territory. Students are generally provided with their results in individual subjects. Assessment is typically based on a combination of school and external testing, with a moderation process to ensure comparability of standards between school and external marking.

Systems that make information on school achievement publicly available indicated that they do so to:

— inform parents and the public;

— enable schools to compare their results with the state/ territory-wide profile;

— monitor standards and plan interventions where appropriate;

— provide valid information on which to base resource decisions;

— provide an informed basis for improvement initiatives;

— build public confidence; and

— meet accountability requirements.

Catholic systems generally do not intervene in determining how schools report to their communities. Most systems have an expectation that schools will report against the specific aims and objectives set out in their school development plan, school charter or similar documents. Across systems, however, there is a wide range of approaches by which schools report on their own performance and effectiveness. Some systems leave it entirely to the discretion of schools, the case in most non-government systems; some report against targets that individual schools establish for themselves, the most common State/ Territory system model; and others report against established standards and benchmarks, in addition to their own locally developed goals.

The audience for the planning and reporting documents is the school community. The school plans with and for its community and accounts to them via an annual report. In essence, such annual reports provide an evaluation of how well the school is achieving its academic and non-academic goals for students. In practice the reports from schools serve a dual purpose of accountability to both the school system and the school community. About half the school systems have an integrated planning and reporting framework. Most are quite specific about what is to be included in the planning and what is to be reported in the school's annual report. In addition to providing contextual information, the annual report is expected to provide an assessment of the school's success in achieving the goals, objectives and targets identified in the linked planning document.

Some State/Territory systems prescribe areas of achievement that schools are required to report on. For example, one system requires its schools to report on the following: improving student performance, teaching and learning, leadership, managing staff, the learning environment, and interaction with the school community. Another requires reporting on occupational health, safety and welfare, performance management, skills of staff using technology, and literacy and numeracy initiatives. A third system mandates reporting on literacy, numeracy, behaviour management and information technology.

At its most rigorous, such reporting covers prescribed areas with transparent standards or benchmarks against which schools are required to make judgements about their performance. Approximately half the State/ Territory systems use external verifiers to assess the validity and accuracy of the information published by schools.

There is significant variation in rigour among systems in school-based reporting of student learning outcomes. Catholic systems all indicated that the overall profile of learning achievements of students in individual schools was either not reported or the method of reporting was at the discretion of the school. Only one Catholic system indicated that it has issued guidelines to its schools on school-level reporting of student outcomes.

Government school systems generally have more prescribed systems of reporting on the performance and effectiveness of schools. Few systems, however, require schools to report learning outcomes in a way that would allow parents to evaluate the performance or effectiveness of the school. It is more common for schools to provide selective information that focuses on highlights only, with no explicit information provided on the range and level of achievement of the school as a whole.

Most Government systems that require schools to report on the profile of student achievement do so only in the context of the school's own goals or targets. In a small number of systems this includes information on student achievement in external tests or progress in achieving benchmarks against criterion-referenced outcomes. Very few systems systematically report school profiles of achievement, either in standardised tests or in relation to criterion-based outcomes, against externally established benchmarks or state/ territory means.

The most sophisticated of these approaches not only encourages schools to assess students against curriculum outcomes on a continuum across the compulsory years of schooling, but also provides state/ territory and other relevant benchmarks6 against which schools can assess their achievements and progress. Such benchmarks may be disaggregated for various sub groups of the student population, eg. boys/ girls, students from a non-English speaking background, and disadvantaged students. A refinement, which is critical to enabling fairness in the interpretation of performance data, provides schools with benchmarks to assess their achievements against other schools that serve comparable populations.

No system in India directly disseminates reports on the profile of learning outcomes in individual schools to individual parents. However, in some systems this information is available to individual parents should they seek it. Some systems have specific education policies or regulations that prohibit the release of achievement data that is necessary for any assessment of the effectiveness and performance of schools. The issues most frequently mentioned by school systems in the information they provided for this research related to 'fairness' and 'equity'. There was particular concern in reporting on student learning outcomes.

A small number of State/ Territory systems have addressed, or are planning to address, these issues by providing achievement profiles for 'like-schools'. Individual schools will be able to make fair assessments of their effectiveness and performance against other schools serving similar populations.

Reporting to Parents on School Programs

In general schools provide public information that serves marketing purposes, communicates about on-going programs, and reports on achievement and progress.

Marketing information

Schools control both the content and the format by which parents receive information about their educational programs. In both government and non-government systems schools use a prospectus as a marketing tool to attract new student enrolments and provide information about their educational programs. Many schools also actively seek to publish articles in the local media to provide information to parents and the wider community and to create a positive impression of the school in the community.

Many systems indicated that schools also issue a booklet or school handbook to inform parents about the educational offerings of the school and, in particular, the courses available. Whilst it could be presumed that there may be marked differences between the type of information reported to parents of primary and secondary aged students, systems indicated little such differentiation except in relation to subject choice.

Not all marketing information is provided to parents in printed form. Many schools have open days and provide targeted information sessions for parents whose children are about to enter their first year of primary or secondary schooling. Marketing is clearly a significant purpose of these sessions, but they also play an important role in facilitating the transition from pre-school to primary schooling and primary to secondary schooling.

Schools in all systems provide information to parents about ongoing programs and initiatives. The main forms of communication are school newsletters and parent-teacher information sessions. Some teachers also write to parents about their programs, though systems did not report this to be a common practice.

Systems, and curriculum bodies such as Boards of Studies, also occasionally place information about school programs into the wider public domain. This is particularly the case where programs are provided across a number of schools, the topics relate to schools generally or the program is a special initiative of the system. Such information is provided through publications such as system newspapers or through booklets issued by systems about programs and opportunities in particular curriculum areas, such as vocational education for example.

Most systems that have information on the performance of students report publicly about the performance of students, but provide little information about the performance of schools. Systems ensure that such reporting does not allow the identification of individual students. Statutory bodies in some States/ Territories provide public information on students whose performance in Year 12 has been meritorious in some way.

Most government systems aggregate student achievement information for each school. A number of them have policies or regulations that specifically restrict the publications of data that can be used to compare schools. No system currently reports publicly on the performance of individual schools on standardised tests or criterion-based outcomes across K-12. A small number of States/ Territories publish the achievements of schools in end of schooling examinations such as tertiary entrance examinations.

Most government school systems across Australia publish sparse information on the performance of specific sub-groups of students. These sub-groups are typically boys, girls, Aboriginal and Torres Strait Islander (ATSI) students, students from a non-English speaking background (NESB) and students from economically disadvantaged backgrounds. Some States/ Territories also provide public information on the achievements of students with high mobility, isolated students and students with a disability. Catholic systems indicate that they report on sub-groups as required for Commonwealth accountability purposes or for internal monitoring purposes, but do not report in the public domain.

Where information about the achievement of sub-groups of students is published at system level it is generally based on the performance of students in standardised tests at specific year-levels, most commonly Years 3 and 5, in literacy and numeracy. Some systems also report results against tests in other KLAs. A number of systems plan further developments in reporting on school performance and effectiveness based on student achievement. Developments being planned include 'value-added' reporting and improvement in the capacity of the relevant databases to support reporting of longitudinal data.

Systems use the term "public" in reference to the publication of school performance information in a number of different ways. In some cases it means that information is relatively inaccessible but can be made available to individual members of the public if they make an explicit inquiry, in other instances the term indicates that information is available through the media or other outlets.

DEVELOPING AND IMPLEMENTING REPORTING POLICIES

All education systems across Australia report that it is the practice at system and school level for parents to be consulted over the development, implementation and improvement of school level reporting policies. Not all systems have policies formally requiring or encouraging this participation.

School Councils or Boards, where they exist, are either consulted over school policies for reporting to parents or have responsibility for determining school policy in this area. Parents and Friends Associations, or similar parent bodies, may also have input to the development of school reporting polices and practices.

There is considerable variation in the way the general parent body participates in developing school-level reporting policies. When schools are reviewing their assessment and reporting policies they often seek parent views through surveys, request feedback via the school newsletter or call special meetings of parents to discuss proposed changes.

All systems reported that relevant parent bodies are consulted in the development of system level policies. Boards of Studies, or their equivalents in each State/ Territory that determine the reporting policies for achievement in external examinations, in particular the end of schooling credential, normally have parent and community representatives on their boards.

Reporting to Parents on Children's Progress

Parents place a higher priority on receiving information about their children's progress than any other type of information they receive from schools. Their interest is first and foremost in the development of their children and they use the information they receive to more effectively support their children's learning. Parents glean information about their children's progress from a range of sources, both formal and informal.

Reports from parents suggest that there is variability across the nation in the satisfaction of parents with the information they receive. The difference in satisfaction is not due to the State/ Territory or the type of education system in which children are educated, but to differences between schools. Parents in all States/ Territories, and in both government and non-government schools, provided evidence about the need to improve practices in reporting. The majority of parents are satisfied, in general, with the information that they currently receive. A substantial minority of parents, however, detailed aspects of the reporting process and access to information about schools that did not meet their needs. A large proportion of parents overall indicated areas in which they seek improvement.

The most common way in which student academic progress is reported to parents is through some form of rating of achievement in each subject area, usually in coded form. Examples of the codes reported to parents are:

— 'A', 'B', 'C', 'D', etc., sometimes with + or -attached to the letter grades. In this type, there may be some advice to parents about what an 'A' etc. means, such as 'excellent' or 'outstanding'.

— 1, 2, 3, 4 or 5 - usually with an explanation of what the numbers mean.

— Other letters, such as 'E' (excellent); 'A' (above average); 'S' (satisfactory); 'U' (unsatisfactory), etc.

— A variation of this type of report is where schools record next to each subject the students' marks in the end of year exams for that subject. Schools that record exam results often also note where the student came in class in the subject. For example, a student may be recorded as being ranked 5 of 25 students in his/ her class in Science. A variation is to record students' test scores and the average scores for the class.

Gradings or ratings are usually complemented by teachers' comments on students' achievements. Teachers' comments are valued more than the grade or mark in a subject by many parents because they provide more specific and personal information about their children. Such comments also inform parents about how well teachers really know the children. Many parents read the comments before reading other sections of reports.

The interpretative nature of teacher comments appeals to parents. After recording the marks or grades, the comment provides an interpretation of the child's progress and achievement, either overall or in a particular subject. Grades themselves merely signify a level of achievement, while comments provide parents with a basis for action.

The value parents place on teachers' interpretations of student performance possibly explains why they are so critical of what they term 'meaningless' comments. Parents don't like cliched phrases in reports such as 'working well', or 'satisfactory'. They either don't know what these terms really mean, or they find them too imprecise and unhelpful, or trite and irrelevant. They don't inform parents about their child.

Parents report an increased use of computer-generated comments. Parents understand the desire for more efficient methods of preparing reports, but believe the effort is wasted if the resultant information is of little value to them and not directly relevant to their children. If comments are generated from a computer list they lose their impact because parents don't believe that they are really about their children.

Many parents receive descriptive reports on student progress, as distinct from the rating or ranking approach described above. Descriptive reporting systems are more common in some systems than others, and are mostly linked to criterion-based outcomes approaches to curriculum. They are a relatively recent initiative. Reports based on outcomes-based curricula usually list a range of outcomes in each subject or Key Learning Area and note whether, or to what extent, the student has achieved that outcome.

Often a code is attached to each outcome to indicate level of mastery of the outcome. Most commonly 'B' = beginning; 'C'= consolidating; and 'E' = established. Other variations are either of the form 'NE' (not in evidence); 'E' (emerging); 'F' (frequently); and 'WE' (well established) or 'achieves consistently' 'achieves sometimes' or 'cannot yet achieve'. These reports may also include teacher comments. Reporting against learning outcomes sometimes includes student self-evaluations of how well they are achieving curriculum outcomes.

Some schools also report to parents on the number of assignments not completed and some secondary schools include a comment from the pastoral care or year coordinator - or equivalent. This is usually a summary comment on the child and parents value these comments in the same way that they value interpretative comments on academic achievement. Parents reported that they want information on the whole child, including academic, social, and emotional development as well as progress in extra-curricula activities. They are particularly interested in knowing how their child is 'fitting in' or developing as a person. However, schools report relatively little of this information.

One very satisfied parent received the following report (edited) on how her child is developing. This level of detail on non-academic achievement is rare.

Parents in schools with significant numbers of students from non-English speaking backgrounds (NESB) commented that their schools translated the reports for parents and provided interpreters at parent-teacher meetings. They indicated that criterion-based outcomes reporting had added to the workload of schools and were impressed with this support. English speaking parents also expressed concern in some instances, given their own difficulties with understanding reports, about how much NESB parents understood.

Most parents from non-English speaking backgrounds do not receive translated reports or have access to interpreters. Some parents with poor English language skills indicated that they would appreciate greater provision of translating and interpreting services.

Frequency

Parents most commonly receive written reports twice a year, at the end of each semester. Many receive a report at the end of each term. Some receive a written report only once a year.

Termly reporting is more common in some systems or sectors than in others. Parents appreciate receiving more frequent reports. Such reports, often called 'interim reports', - with the end of semester reports typically more detailed than those at the end of Terms 1 and 3.

Interim reports often address matters that are broader than academic achievement alone. In many instances they function to provide an assurance to parents that all is going well, or in the case of Term 1 reports, that a child is settling into the grade, or new school. Given that most reporting is at the end of each semester, the interim reports enable schools and parents to keep in touch in the 5 Ð6 months between semester reports.

Parents want reporting to provide them with a basis for monitoring and supporting their children's learning and they clearly indicated that mid-year is too late for the first report of the year. Parents consider earlier reporting on how well students are progressing and areas where they would benefit from further development to be a vital part of an effective reporting process. Those who receive reports, written or oral, at the end of Term 1 are extremely appreciative of the early feedback.

Parents view the parent-teacher meeting as a complement to the written report. It enables them to clarify information in the written reports and discuss how their children's learning might be improved. If the timing allows, they also use the meeting as an opportunity to give feedback to the teacher about their children, and to raise any concerns they might have.

To be able to achieve this level of interaction requires a high degree of confidence on the part of parents, and many reported that they feel too intimidated in most meeting situations to be more than relatively passive participants.

Some parents attend the meetings to let the teachers know that they are committed and interested parents. These parents indicated that if teachers believe they are uninterested in their children's progress, they (teachers) might be less rigorous in monitoring the quality of the children's work.

Types of meetings

In some systems the most common approach is for a time (an evening, or afternoon/ evening) to be set aside and parents who wish to avail themselves of the opportunity make an appointment. These meetings are generally linked to the written report and scheduled shortly after they are forwarded to parents. Often students are responsible for conveying notices about these meetings to their parents.

In this approach, schools that have concerns about the progress of individual students usually write, specifically to parents asking them to make an appointment. In many of these instances parents take a negative view of attendance at a parent-teacher meeting, particularly if the school only contacts them when there is 'bad' news. Participation of other parents is optional.

Some schools create a context by believing that parents have to be particularly keen or have a 'problem' child to want to attend and conveying a message that indicates that where there are no concerns there is no need for a meeting. Reporting processes in such schools make it harder for less assertive parents, because they place a greater emphasis on the parent taking the initiative to make an appointment.

Some parents are satisfied with this type of reporting arrangement if they are confident that teachers will initiate contact if there is a need for a meeting. If parents in this context do not receive a request to attend a meeting they then interpret it as 'good news'. Some parents receive advice with the written report that "no meeting is required". While this provides some reassurance to parents, it can also have the effect of discouraging them from making an appointment to meet with the teacher, even if they really want to discuss their children's progress.

The alternative to asking parents to make an appointment for a meeting on a scheduled night is to set the evening or night aside and make an open invitation for parents to attend. Some parents feel more comfortable with this approach as there is less formality associated with their attendance. Parent-teacher meetings are generally linked to the written report, but are usually brief, often no more than 5-10 minutes. Some parents view these meetings as being ceremonial only, and feel that they are conducted, particularly in secondary schools, using an assembly line or supermarket queue approach.

Many schools and teachers include examples of student work and classroom tests as part of parent-teacher meetings. These are used to illustrate what is being discussed. Parents appreciate and value the opportunity to have work samples and tests used in this way. The examples assist parents to more readily understand the points teachers are making. Often parents want a meeting with their children's teacher outside of the formal parent-teacher meeting. Parents find that most schools are approachable and co-operative if they want to arrange a meeting. Primary schools are most likely to be co-operative.

Parents reported that some secondary schools do not make it easy for them to arrange these meetings. most positive comments about parent-teacher meetings came from parents who felt that their meetings with teachers had been constructive and useful and focussed on both academic and non-academic development, including the future development of the child. When the meetings focus on what the report might mean to parents and teachers, parents indicated that they have far more value to them than the written report.

Parents often believe they get a more truthful report from their meetings with teachers than from the written report. This is because they believe teachers are cautious about what they commit to paper, and therefore will say face-to-face a number of things that they will not write in a report.

Work Samples and Classroom Tests

Work samples and completed tests are popular with parents as a form of reporting on student progress. As mentioned above, they are sometimes used illustratively in parent-teacher meetings but have a function throughout the year in keeping parents informed. The use of work samples was reported more commonly in some systems than others and more often in States/ Territories that have a curriculum and reporting framework that includes a statement of criterion-based outcomes. In many schools, marked classroom tests are sent home. This provides parents with a 'snapshot' of how learning is progressing.

There is wide variation in the types of samples sent home and the form in which they are presented. In some schools, work sample packages are sent home at regular intervals, such as the end of Terms 1 and 3. In other cases the samples are forwarded on the initiative of individual teachers.

Students often assess their own work samples - an approach supported by parents. A number of parents commented that students appear to set higher standards for themselves in their self-assessments than they would have expected.

External Tests

A majority of parents support standardised testing because it currently provides them with the only external indicator they have of how their children compare with other students across the State/ Territory.

For many parents - and in some States/ Territories more than others - it provides them with diagnostic information to identify areas where their children require further support and assistance. Parents also support standardised testing because it provides additional information for monitoring school and teacher standards, not just the performance of their children.

Parents find information from state/ territory-wide testing most useful when the reports provide specific information, often of a diagnostic nature, which is beyond that provided by the child's teachers. For some parent s, test results at Year 3 or 5 were the first indication they had received that their child had a learning problem. In many cases it was the catalyst for the parent to take action to remediate the problem.

Parents who are less enthusiastic about standardised testing indicated that this is, in part, due to the fact that they cannot interpret the results. Parents find systemic standardised testing programs that provide diagnostic information to be particularly useful. However, diagnostic information is of little use if schools do not know how to accurately interpret test results or fail to act to remediate any problems that are identified. Parents reported instances of learning problems identified in later years, which they subsequently discovered had been, or should have been, apparent from earlier test results.

Parents believe that standardised tests provide pressure for teachers and schools to maintain quality. They see teacher quality as integral to their children's progress and improvements in teaching as associated with improvement in student learning.

Many parents, including those who support standardised testing, however, sounded a note of caution about their use. They clearly do not want the tests to lead to unnecessary or excessive performance pressures being placed on students, particularly primary aged students, and they want safeguards to ensure that testing does not lead teachers away from a focus on teaching to a focus on testing.

INFORMAL SOURCES OF INFORMATION ON STUDENT PROGRESS

Parents are information bowerbirds when it comes to knowing how their children are progressing. They use any information source, some not intended as formal reporting mechanisms, and sift and analyse the information to glean what may be useful to them. They build up a picture from multiple sources of information that give the same message.

Classroom visits

Parents who visit the school frequently, particularly if they are classroom helpers, gain much information about their children's progress through those visits. As classroom helpers they are able to assess the standards of work in the classroom and make judgements about their child's achievements compared with other students and compared with specified standards.

Some parents use school open days (or nights) to learn about their children's achievements. These are scheduled occasions when parents are invited to the school and into classrooms to view children's work. Parents find these occasions useful for comparing their child's work with that of other students.

Homework

Homework is very useful in informing parents about how their children are progressing. Homework that is returned marked by teachers is even more useful. For many parents, homework provides an insight into what is being taught in classrooms. Homework is the only means that many have to assess on a regular basis how their children are achieving and progressing in the months prior to the first written report of the year.

Parents of secondary school students also find that homework tells them about how their children are progressing. They report, however, that secondary students are less forthcoming in showing them work. Homework assignments, particularly when the child involves the parents or discusses the work with them, is a common way that parents of secondary students learn about their progress.

Many parents report that teachers involve them formally in their children's homework practices. This most commonly involves having them sign off on their children's homework and has the effect of requiring parents to monitor the completion of homework. Most parents who reported this practice like it not only because it provides them with an entr...e that they might not otherwise get to their children's work, but also because it tells them that the school is organised about homework and monitors it. Parents mentioned that a weekly plan for homework is appreciated because it enables them to plan homework completion around family commitments.

Parents prefer to see homework that is relevant to the learning program. They do not like to see homework that they find meaningless 'busy work'. Parents use homework much like they use information from tests, to provide an insight into teacher and school quality. Planned, meaningful and relevant homework practices send positive messages about school and teacher quality.

Parents find informal conversations with their children and with teachers a good source of information about their children's progress. They like to chat with their children, usually at the end of each day, about the day and what they did and what they learned.

Parents also often find that visiting the school regularly puts them in a position to gather teacher comments in a less formal way. If they are regular visitors to the school and are known by teachers they find that they often have 'classroom door ' or 'canteen' conversations with teachers. Parent organisation members, in particular, say that their position and profile in the school enables them to access more frequent information about their children.

Parents noted a tendency, particularly among primary schools, to avoid facing or telling hard truths. They feel that teachers often couch negative comments in unclear or misleading language, or put comments on learning difficulties in a warm, encouraging and positive tone. Nevertheless parents really want a "fair and honest" assessment of how their children are progressing. They do not want to find out in later years that a child has "a problem because he didn't have the fundamentals." Parents believe that advice can be 'honest' without being negative. Many considered that written reports are too often 'politically correct' at the expense of 'honesty'.

Where ratings or codes are used, parents need to understand not only what the codes mean, but also how the assessments are arrived at. They believe that knowledge of assessment processes is essential if they are to fully understand the report.

Objective standards

The lack of clarity and vagueness noted by many parents in reports was considered by others to be due to a lack of objective standards through which they could really see where their child 'was at'. The term 'where he (or she) is at' was used repeatedly by parents. It denotes a need for a sense of precision and 'positioning' that many parents do not feel that they get from what they call 'vague' reports.

These parents do not believe that the reports they now receive enable them to understand how their children are achieving. Many were more explicit and asked for information that would enable them to compare their children's progress with other students or with some agreed state/ territory-wide standard.

In discussions with parents the need for comparative information on student achievement was raised more frequently than any other issue relating to reporting on children's progress. Parents, who had previously been exposed to a system whereby students were ranked in class, often asked for this form of reporting to be reintroduced because they felt that under a ranking system they could see how their child compared with other children.

Parents also expressed concern about how a system of standards reporting would affect the selfÐ esteem of lower achieving students. Others indicated that competition is a 'fact of life' and that students should get used to it.

Many parents believe that students already know the 'pecking order' in their classes. Others were uncomfortable about not being able to reconcile their need for an objective statement about the attainment level of their children with a strong dislike of competition and 'labelling'. This view is more common among primary school parents.

Some parents suggested that a system of recording students' results in tests (marks) would enable parents to see how their children were performing without them being ranked. Others were against any system of reporting based on standards established by individual schools, as they believed it could be inadequate or misleading for their needs, as one school's standard might not be high enough.

The comparability of school standards is critical when students change schools, move from primary to secondary school, or are preparing for post secondary schooling. Parents reported examples of students who believed they were high achievers - 'A-level' students in their primary school - and discovered that in secondary school they were only getting 'C's. Parents of these students did not believe that this reflected their children's ability but rather the standard of learning at the primary school.

Whilst the issue of standards was noted more at critical stages of transition in schooling, it was considered important at all stages. Reporting against standards enables parents to know when they need to get their children to 'pull their socks up' and it enables students themselves to monitor their own progress more easily.

Parents also believe that a system based on state/ territory level standards would expose under-performing teachers and put pressure on them to improve. The current situation enabled too much leeway for the teacher to set the standard, and that even when students were graded, it was only against the class-level standard. Under these conditions parents had no way of knowing whether the teaching standard at their school, and therefore the achievements of their children, were 'up to scratch'.

Reporting based on objective standards is likely to be more effective at detecting students who require additional support or referral to a specialist. A number of parents reported that too frequently student problems went undetected and 'slipped through the net' because there was little to alert teachers or parents to the problem.

Interpretative and constructive reporting

Parents who are highly engaged with their children's learning often find considerable frustration when they receive a bland report, especially if it mainly features ticks or letter codes. They want something more substantial. They want reports that not only tell them what their children have achieved, but what they face next or need to do to improve. Importantly, they also want advice on how they, as parents, can help.

Parents find that if they ask or push for specific information they usually get it. However, they want written reports to routinely include interpretative and constructive comments, so that they do not have to ask for it. They are dissatisfied at having to seek out the implications of their children's reports rather than having it provided to them. Parents directly and indirectly expressed interest in the development of all facets of their children. They believe that schools have a role in much more than academic development. They want reports to express that.

Many expressed disappointment that student reports have little focus on development in non-academic areas. The development of social and relationship skills are particularly important, possibly reflecting a recognition that interpersonal skills are important to happiness, which is what parents most want for their children, and to future career success.

Some States/ Territories and education systems are introducing changes from letter grades and similar assessment approaches to a criterion-based outcomes reporting approach. Many parents are finding it difficult to adjust to this form of reporting, not because they don't like this approach to curriculum, but because the reporting format used is not easily understood. Parents are critical of the current methods of outcomes reporting, although they are not critical of the use of an outcomes approach per se.

Parents find it difficult to adjust to assessment reports that apply to learning levels across two years of schooling and the lack of a direct match between grades and levels. Parents who have had this system of outcomes reporting explained to them and understand how their children have been assessed find the reports useful. When too much detail is provided to parents about the outcomes achieved by their children, especially when the outcomes are described in jargon, parents find the information overwhelming and the detail can obscure the overall picture of the child's performance. Some parents find the descriptions "too long and too wordy" and "hard to understand".

In systems where work samples are sent home as part of the process of reporting on the achievement of outcomes, parents need an explanation of what the expected learning outcomes are for a particular piece of work. Parents value teachers who annotate the sample and explain the relevance of the learning. Sometimes samples are sent home without any comment at all. In these cases parents are unable to make use of the sample to inform them about how well the child is progressing.

Overall, it is evident that the assessment of outcomes for teaching purposes needs to be a separate process from that for purposes of reporting to parents. If parents are ultimately to support criterion-based outcomes approaches to curriculum then they must be reported to parents in a way that is useful, meaningful and clearly understood.

Timeliness of information

The timing of the distribution of student reports is important to parents. They consider written reports to be a catalyst for continuing engagement in their children's learning as they respond to the information reported.

Parents prefer not to receive reports on the last day of a term. They then have to wait through the holidays, sometimes feeling anxious, before they can discuss the report with the teacher. In these cases they also believe that they lose valuable time in which they could be providing learning support to their children over the holidays.

Computer-generated reports

Parents express a degree of mistrust of computer-generated reports. They appreciate that teachers may find that they save time, but if the outcome is information that is of inferior use to parents, then the time spent generating reports is wasted. This criticism by parents is particularly aimed at the 'select a comment' type report, not those for which teachers use a computer as a word processor to prepare the sort of comments that they previously wrote by hand.

Parents indicate that they find computer reports to be more impersonal and limited. Parents like to think that each report is tailored to their children. Parents reported instances of schools withdrawing computer-generated reports after parent backlash.

— Parent-Teacher Meetings

— Organisation of meetings

Parents generally make favourable comments about parent-teacher meetings. However, parents are dissatisfied when such meetings are poorly organised and planned and when they are insensitive to the needs of parents. When the meetings lack focus and purpose parents see them as ceremonial only, ie. that they are useful only as an exercise in 'waving the flag'. Meetings of 5-10 minutes are limited in their usefulness and provide parents with an opportunity to do little more than make contact with the teacher. In the secondary context, the numbers of parents waiting for meetings, and number of teachers that parents wish to meet in a short space of time, means that it is sometimes impossible for parents to see more than a few teachers at a parent-teacher session.

Some schools advise parents of the meetings via students, some of whom discourage their parents from attending the meetings, or fail to pass on notices. Parents believe that some schools do not take the meetings seriously and view them only as an obligation. In some instances, not all teachers make themselves available or are disinterested in reporting to parents.

Parents who are dissatisfied with parent-teacher meetings believe that they could be more focussed. These parents indicated that they:

— do not find a general chit chat about the child constructive;

— often find the discussion vague and unhelpful; and

— sometimes come away from parent-teacher meeting wondering if the teacher really knows their children.

Some parents counter this by attending the scheduled meeting to show they are interested in their children's education, but then look for other opportunities to have a substantive discussion about their children's progress. Parents who know what their children are learning are able to use their knowledge to provide a context for the meeting and find the discussion focussed and helpful as a result.

Many parents also view these meetings as opportunities for two-way communication, not just the teacher telling parents about the child, but parents telling the teacher of their perceptions. Parents want the outcomes of such discussions integrated into decisions about how school and home might jointly support student learning. Teachers do not always take notice of parents' advice in meetings, or are slow to respond. Not all parents feel confident about a more active role in parent-teacher meetings and need to be supported in that role.

Parents believe that their children are an integral part of the reporting process, part of the 'loop'. The whole cycle of assessment, reporting, responding, etc. involves the child. It is common for students to report to parents after self-assessment of their work, parents usually discuss the written report and its implications with their children, and frequently the parent-teacher meeting is a three-way discussion with parents, teachers and students participating.

Parents are surprised at how seriously children assess themselves. A more common role for students in the reporting process is to discuss the report with their parents. There is considerable variation in the depth of the discussion, from fairly perfunctory engagement to more in-depth discussions. Reports which provide more written detail, particularly in the form of learning outcomes or thoughtful written comments from the teacher, give parents a better basis for constructive discussion with their children. Annotated work samples often provide a more accessible basis for a discussion about student learning than 'formula' reports.

It is relatively common for students to be present and have a role in parent-teacher meetings. Many parents believe that because the meeting is about the child and their progress, they should be part of the discussion. In particular, parents believe that students will be encouraged to be more involved in their own learning. This belief in an active role for students was reported more commonly by secondary school parents - some of whom mentioned that there was an expectation in some schools for children to be present.

Parents of primary school students also support the involvement of their children in such meetings. Student involvement in meetings is not just about students responding to the report, but also contributing through an on the spot self-assessment. Some parents, however, are not in favour of having their children present at parent-teacher meetings. They feel that it would constrain the discussion and prevent the parents and teacher from being as open as they would like in discussing children's progress. Some parents who are in favour of having their children participating in the discussion also want an arrangement that provides an opportunity where some part of the meeting can be restricted to them and the teacher.

Newsletters

School newsletters are the usual and most common means by which parents find out what is happening at their schools. The frequency and regularity with which they are published means that they link parents with the school on a continuous basis. Newsletters are almost universally appreciated and liked for providing the sort of information that parents expect from them.

Newsletters don't provide much information in the way of student learning programs. Parents do not necessarily expect this to be detailed in newsletters. They do expect them to provide a broad coverage of what is occurring or being planned to occur in the school. When newsletters do provide brief outlines of the learning program and activities- often by profiling a different class or activity in selected editions- parents find the information interesting and useful. A small number expect to receive at least some curriculum information in newsletters.

Newsletters are mostly about politics and funding etc. There is not enough curriculum information. Many schools make a great effort to ensure that their newsletters are understood by parents as they view them as the primary means of communication with parents. Some go to considerable trouble to ensure the widest possible readership, including translations into other languages.

Homework, Student Diaries and Communication Sheets

Parents use their children's homework, and other school-work that the children bring home, to learn about and monitor the educational programs of the school. They value the insights they get from homework because it is specific to their child. Where parents are provided with the overall learning framework for the class, such as

— through an information session or information sheet, they find the homework particularly meaningful to them, as they can then place the homework in the context of their children's overall learning program.

— Student diaries or journals fulfil a similar role for parents. That is, they enable an ongoing and regular interaction between children's schoolwork and work at home, thus providing an avenue for parents to become informed about their progress and a basis for monitoring the learning program of the school.

— The term 'communication sheet' is used to cover communications from individual teachers to the parents of students in their classes. Where this mechanism for communicating with parents is used, it is most often the initiative of an individual teacher, rather than a school-wide practice. The use of communication sheets is not very widespread, but is very popular with parents who receive them. Where provided, parents find them to be both regular and informative.

— The communication sheet is used by teachers to provide regular updates to parents about what is happening in their classes, what the students are learning and what parents could do to help. It is different from the student diary in that it is direct teacher to parent communication, rather than communication through students' work.

School Publications

School publications such as the student diaries noted above, yearly calendars, prospectuses and annual reports provide parents with information about the school, but parents did not cite them as particularly common sources of information. Parents receive the school calendar. A term calendar with a lot of the things all ready and set up. That's quite a useful tool to have on the fridge. It highlights parent evenings, school assemblies and excursions that might be happening. And all of these things really are seen by parents as an opportunity for contact with the class teacher.

Parents want schools to have events planned, programmed and communicated to them well in advance. This assists them to manage their own diaries and conveys to parents a sense that the school is well organised and operates in an orderly fashion. Parents particularly dislike being advised at short notice about school excursions. One emerging source of information is the website being developed by many schools. A small number of parents mentioned these websites as a potential source of information, but they did not view them at present as being a substitute for printed publications or meetings with teachers.

Parent Organisations

Meetings of parent organisations are considered an excellent source of general information for those parents who attend. The information may be provided through formal parts of the meeting, including input from the principal, but is just as likely to be gained from the informal conversations held before or after the meeting.

Some school newsletters include reports from parents organisations or from the School Council, but, unless this is the case, parents who do not attend meetings of their school parent organisation miss out on a lot of incidental information. Parents consider that the information flow should be a two-way street, and should be more interactive so that parents can offer comment and feedback on the information provided. Members of parent organisations overwhelmingly believe that the extent to which this occurs is dependent on the willingness of the school's principal.

The principal also influences the extent to which parents, and parents organisations in particular, are able to be informed about and contribute to discussions about the school's teaching and learning programs. Whilst some principals involve parents fully, others restrict parents' engagement in what is happening and tightly control the opportunities for parents to provide advice. Often parents are asked for advice on peripheral aspects of a school's program.

Some parent organisations hold seminars and invite guest speakers to talk on various issues. The guest speakers may be school staff members, such as counsellors or heads of faculties, who discuss their roles in the school. The speaker may be from outside the school and talk on a subject, such as a drug education program, that provides contextual information for parents to consider in discussing school policies and practices. The seminar may be part of the regular parent organisation meeting or may be hosted by the parent organisation as a separate event. The use of guest speakers is not a common practice in schools, but when the topic is of relevance to parents they appreciate them.

For some parents, membership of their school's parent organisation can provide an entree to school committees, which in turn provide parents with access to valuable knowledge. Parents who are members of a parent organisation are able to more readily access valuable information that would not otherwise be available. The parents who were in this position were very enthusiastic in endorsing their active membership for this reason, and expressed some regret that more parents were not active in parent organisations and able to gain this bonus from their membership.

Informal Opportunities

Learning through informal opportunities contributes considerably to parents' understanding about school programs and the learning activities of their children. Their main 'informal' source is their own children. Each day parents like to talk with their children about what has happened and how the day has gone. This keeps them in touch with their children and over time a store of knowledge accumulates. Parents with more than one child find that they build on what they learn through the first child's schooling experiences, so that they are much wiser and better informed for the schooling of subsequent children.

Parents find that younger children are more open about what happens at school than secondary students. Children who are not experiencing success or satisfaction with their schooling are less forthcoming in telling parents of their experiences than are those who are happy and feeling successful. Parents are aware that learning about schools through the filter of their children is flawed, but it is nonetheless valuable to them.

Parent involvement in schools as classroom helpers or in other volunteer roles such as helping in the canteen enables them to informally gather information. Some schools have an open invitation for parents to come up to the school at any time and visit classrooms and view school assemblies. Taking part in the daily life of the school in this way gives parents access to different information. They observe the school functioning and the programs students are learning, gain a 'feel' for the school and its students, and see the programs and practices their children tell them about in action. Parents consider that 'in-school' experiences of this kind give them a different and richer form of knowledge about the school. However, only a minority of parents access knowledge about the school through this type of involvement.

Many parents also look for informal chats with teachers to gain general information about school activities or knowledge about their children's learning program. Teachers are generally regarded as being open and approachable and responsive to parent inquiries, although some parents find secondary schools less welcoming.

Parents frequently commented that they wish they did not have to go searching for information. Secondary school structures, in particular, can sometimes be bewildering to parents who are trying to find out how or where to get information.

A small number of schools provide advice to parents on how they can access inform-ation, make an inquiry or lodge a grievance. They tell parents how they can find out information. The rationale in such schools is that they would rather have parents deal with them directly than air their grievances or concerns among other parents.

By closing that gap we feel that we're going to start promoting the whole feeling that it is a community and that parents need to be as comfortable in the school as their kids are.

Parent networks are a valuable source of information to parents. Information is shared, traded, discussed and passed on through these networks. Parents with less access to information, such as those in full time employment, are able to link up with a parent in a network. Sometimes a parent who is less confident about approaching a school directly will ask another parent with good links to the school to get information on their behalf.

School Curriculum

Parents want information that provides a comprehensive overview of what students will be learning in the coming term or year. Formal parent information programs such as information days and evenings and some publications aim to provide information for parents about schools' teaching programs and the relevant curriculum. The information should also cover excursions and expectations regarding homework.

How the curriculum is translated into teaching and learning strategies and classroom organisation is a major focus of information evenings and sometimes this subject is also included in school newsletters. Parents understand that the purpose of the school in providing this information is to seek their support for the initiatives, and/ or to provide them with the knowledge and skills to more effectively assist with their children's learning. Parents of students in the primary years are more likely to be offered the opportunity to learn about teaching strategies than parents of students in secondary schooling.

Primary school parents, in particular, express a desire for more education in specific teaching strategies in reading and mathematics. They want to support their children's learning, but many report that when they try to assist, their children say they are teaching the wrong way and not the way the teacher does it. These parents would appreciate having more up-to-date knowledge of teaching practices so that at home they can support and reinforce the work that the teacher is doing during the school day.

Few schools have a formal communication policy so that parents know exactly what they can expect to receive or how to get an answer to their question. Information is mostly provided in a piecemeal fashion. Parents who are familiar with a school know what they can expect.

Parents of secondary school students often feel as if they are being kept at arms length and do not feel that they have the same accessibility to information that they had in primary schools. Lack of accessibility is a particular concern for parents from non-English speaking backgrounds or those with less education themselves. Some schools have liaison officers who work to improve communication and information flow between the school and specific communities. The róle of these officers is strongly supported by parents.

Parents also expressed a desire for more school information to be translated. Another group with access problems is parents of secondary students. Information sent home via students often does not reach parents. Parents rarely describe information only in terms of what is being communicated, they also describe it in terms of how it makes them feel as parents. They see school-to-home communication as an indicator of their relationship with schools.

The information and how it is communicated signal schools' understanding of their relationships with parents. Parents' involvement in their children's education is a deeply emotional one. This is evident in the language parents use when talking about schools. They are not just interested third parties. They see themselves, not just their children, as having an integral personal relationship with the school. The issue for schools in formulating communication policies is to understand and respond to this emotional engagement, to understand that anything that affects children is likely to have meaning for parents too.

Children are central to their parents' lives. Many schools recognise this, but in the eyes of parents others appear not to do so, and are dismissive of the parent role. Schools have particular challenges in regard to communication with parents from different cultural or educational backgrounds.

Teaching and Learning Information

The area where parents express the strongest need for further information is in improving their knowledge of curriculum, learning programs and teaching methodology. They want this knowledge to reinforce their understanding of at-school learning so they can assist their children at home, particularly if they are having difficulties. Information nights are the main source of this information, however the timing of these sessions does not suit all parents, and they would like alternative times to be offered. Information nights also vary in quality. Whilst parents indicate some are excellent, others are said to be boring, repetitive and not specific enough to provide the information that parents find most useful.

There are some information needs that cannot be satisfied in information sessions. Many parents do not feel that they have the confidence, or knowledge to be able to assist students at home, especially where new teaching methods are involved, and would like practical training sessions. Mathematics and reading are the skill areas where primary parents, particularly, would like more knowledge of teaching strategies. Secondary parents are much less satisfied than primary parents with the information they receive about teaching and learning. They receive little information about teaching methods and learning expectations.

Parents often have difficulty in accessing sufficient information to enable them to adequately understand the implications of particular subject choices. Many feel that schools have had little regard for the parent role in making subject choice decisions. Secondary parents feel, in some cases, that they have been excluded from, or are given inadequate information relating to decisions about their children's subject choice. Subject choice is the area where secondary parents express strongest dissatisfaction.

Parents prefer to receive information through face-to-face meetings such as information evenings, meetings with teachers and training sessions. This format allows parents to interact and ask questions or seek clarification. They view written communication as being best suited for providing either supplementary information - such as handouts that can be taken away from information or training sessions - or for communicating incidental factual information, such as that contained in school newsletters.

To better prepare them to help with their children's learning, parents want to be able to access classes or training sessions on teaching methods and curriculum content. Models of effective parent training programs exist among primary schools but relatively few programs of this type are offered to parents of secondary school students.

Not all parents are able to attend scheduled meetings at schools. They express a desire for more flexibility in scheduling and other ways to access information that they may have missed. Parents are often faced with a situation of "show up on such and such a night or miss out". They do not want to be too demanding of teachers' time, as they recognise the time commitments already being made by school staff, but they seek more flexibility than that currently provided in the arrangements offered by many schools. Related to this issue of flexibility is one in which parents often realise a need for information at times between scheduled information sessions. They would like to be able to access this information, in some form, without having to wait until scheduled sessions.

Parents want schools to be approachable and to be positive and responsive to their need for information. They want schools to understand the role of parents as partners in the education of their children. For this reason they also want teachers, both primary and secondary, to acknowledge that classroom programs and teaching strategies are legitimate areas for parent interest. They do not want the parent role in schools to be restricted to the more ephemeral activities associated with uniforms, fundraising, working bees and monitoring homework.

Most schools now provide opportunities, with varying degrees of openness, for parents to provide feedback on school policies. Parent involvement in curriculum policies and teaching programs is not as extensive as in other areas of the schools' operations. Many parents are disappointed that so few parents take up opportunities to contribute to policy development. Others are frustrated that they sometimes provide input and then nothing changes. Some schools limit parent participation to a small group only or to token parent representatives, while other schools make only limited acknowledgment of parental contributions to decision making.

Parents in all schools want the opportunity to be consulted and to share in decision making about how parents are informed and what they are informed about. They recognise that they may not always be able to contribute, but they want recognition of the fact that they have a role in school decision making and that they, not the school, are ultimately responsible for managing the education of their children.

Parent judgements about the schools that their children currently attend are based chiefly on their own interactions with schools and comments from their children and other parents. The majority of parents indicate that they are able to access the information they need on school achievement, but a large minority would like more, particularly more objective, information about the achievements of schools.

Parents generally have little knowledge or understanding of the terms 'school performance' and 'school effectiveness'. Only a small proportion of parents understand the notion that systematic and structured assessments of schools against specified criteria can be and often are undertaken by systems.

Most parents conceived public reporting about school achievement to be solely in terms of the ranking of schools based on the academic performance of their students in external examinations. Parents do not want public ranking of schools, because it leads to high levels of competition which could have negative results for some schools.

How Parents Use Information about School Achievement

Choosing Schools

The primary purpose that parents cite for wanting to know about school achievement is to assist them to select schools for their children. Parents actively choose from among schools, particularly at entry to primary schooling and at the point of transition from primary to secondary school. Parents are less likely to compare schools when selecting primary schools if they are satisfied with the school in which their children are currently enrolled. In government school systems where schools have been 'dezoned', parents are more likely to make an active choice of primary school, but the pool from which parents select is geographically narrower than the secondary pool.

Having made a choice of school parents rarely change unless there are very compelling reasons to do so. Pressure to change comes mostly from extreme dissatisfaction with how their children are progressing, a change of home location, or a need to change in Years 11 and 12 - in cases where the previous school caters only to Year 10.

A school can change from year-to-year depending on the teachers and the principal in the school and it's a big decision to make up your mind where you're going to send your children. Once you make that first decision, nine times out of ten you'll stay with [the school]. But if it's not working for a particular child - all children can be different in the family - then you have to be able to [seek out information on other schools].

Monitoring Schools

Parents try to use information on school achievement to evaluate how well schools are meeting the needs of other children like their children and to seek assurance that schools are doing a 'good job'. Once their children have enrolled, parents judge the effectiveness of their school almost entirely on how the school is meeting their expectations for their own children's progress. That is, if their own children are happy and achieving according to parental expectations, they are less interested in the schools' achievements overall.

Those who ask for more accountability, a large minority of parents, want more information on how effective schools are in achieving their goals for students and want to know how well schools are meeting expected standards.

Perhaps it would be good to find out at the end of the year if the teachers have done what they set out to do.

Some kind of common benchmarks for all schools would be helpful to parents. [It would] allow them to make informed comparisons.

Schools should be assessed and monitored as to teaching quality, teacher competence. The schools shouldn't just focus on [Year 12] results, but feedback that reports on the broad scope of a school.

Parents express concern that the information they currently receive is not objective, that is it is made available for self-promotion purposes, or that it is inadequate.

There is no way to know about the real academic performance in comparison to other schools. The only way is to test and compare and analyse the results and publish them. We need a quality assurance system for education. This is the way to deliver consistent quality. ... A QA system would give you benchmarks and assurances. A QA system [should be] for all state and private schools.

Improving Schools

Parents do not generally use overall school achievement information to apply pressure for school improvement, preferring instead to choose a different school if they are extremely dissatisfied. Before reaching this stage, however, parents are likely to seek improvement in relation to the specific issue.

The issue about which parents are most likely to seek improvement is that of teacher quality. Despite some parents citing examples where they had been influential in removing a teacher or ensuring that a particular teacher did not teach their child, most parents indicated that they feel quite powerless in tackling issues of teacher quality. Parents believe that only a very small minority of teachers are ineffective, but that one poor teacher can have a devastating and some times lasting effect on a child.

Parents view written information provided by schools as a form of marketing or as being provided for public relations purposes and view it with some caution. They do not completely disregard written information, but attempt to use it to complement information from other sources. Some parents look to written information to confirm their own impressions of a school.

Parents value personal experiences more than any other source of information. They believe that first-hand impressions are the most reliable form of information about a school. Direct interaction with the school gives parents a feel for the climate of the school. Parents often use the words 'school climate' or 'school ethos' to describe what is important to them. These experiences may be very subjective as a way of judging the effectiveness of a school, but parents trust their impressions, and indicate that they rarely misjudge a school.

The type of personal contact and experience of schools that parents talk about in this context are school open days, formal visits to schools - usually comprising an appointment with the principal, but sometimes also including a guided walk around the school - and informal visits when parents visit schools unannounced and request to look around.

At school open days parents judge schools on how well the sessions are organised, how friendly, warm and approachable the staff are, how principals project the school, and how the schools' values, as espoused by principals, match their own expectations of a school. They also make judgements based on the behaviour of the students at the school.

In some States/ Territories more than others, primary schools market themselves to parents of students at local pre-schools. Parents apply the same criteria on these occasions as they do when judging schools on their open days.

During individual visits to a school, often accompanied by their children, parents judge schools on the principal's demeanour, what they have to say, and, if their children are present, how the principal relates to and speaks about students. Parents value these meetings with principals more for the opportunity to gather these sorts of impressions than to receive information - as useful as the latter might be. If taken on the tour of a school they will also make judgements on how well the school is presented and how well it is cared for. They look for tidiness, absence of litter and graffiti, and for the quality and attractiveness of the facilities and grounds. They look for signs of 'pride in the school'. These criteria are a basis for parent judgements regardless of the wealth of the school.

If they have an opportunity, parents will observe how students relate to each other, and how the staff relate to students. They will also assess the school by the behaviour and manner of any student they come across. Parents often visit schools without an appointment, so they can observe the schools and their students when they are not 'on show'.

If the visit is to assist in choosing from among schools, parents often also consider the impression that the schools make on their children. In many cases the children's preference has priority, though parents indicate that the views of both themselves and their children usually coincide.

Parents who have children currently enrolled in a school frequently judge the school by how happy their children are, by the quality of work the child is doing, including homework assignments, and by the quality of the schools' interactions with them as parents. Whilst personal contact is the source of information that parents most value, they rarely rely entirely on the sort of information and impressions described above.

Networks

Family networks, their own children included, and other parents provide parents with information about schools. Informal parent networks are the most utilised source of information for parents with students already in the school. If parents do not visit the school on a regular basis, they can tap into their networks to find out how the school is going and what the issues are at the school. This information is extremely anecdotal and subjective but, nonetheless, parents value the information and store it away in their minds. They rarely make a firm judgement on one incident, issue, or successful experience but over time build up a store of impressions.

Parent and family networks are accessed for opinions about schools when parents are looking to choose a school. Parents do not always consider information from these sources reliable, but they trust them more than information from any other source, their own experiences excepted. The family network is considered more reliable in choosing a school if there has been a previous family association with the school. For example, if siblings or cousins have attended the school.

A large proportion of parents are quite systematic about monitoring schools through family, neighbour and parent networks. They actively seek the opinions and experiences of other parents whose children attend or have attended the school. Parents also judge the school their children are attending by how happy the children are at school and how well they are achieving their parents' expectations for them. If their own children are satisfied with the school and are achieving adequately, parents are not overly concerned with the schools' performance relative to other schools. They will only consider changing to a 'better' school if they or their children are dissatisfied with the current one.

When parents are choosing a secondary school their children often visit potential schools with them and their children's preferences are often the deciding factor. Parents report that their children usually have the same criteria that they do, although school uniform and the school their peers are likely to attend are especially important to children. Parent and family networks are largely responsible for the creation and maintenance of the concept of a school's 'reputation'.

A school's reputation, deserved or otherwise, is an important currency to parents. They choose schools on reputation, and then fight to maintain the reputation. Parents like principals who, through newsletters and local press articles, seek to reaffirm and promote the good reputation of a school. A good reputation is closely related to the image of a school. For some parents the reputation of the school is all they need to know.

Parents consider school success rates in standardised tests, external examinations and the profile of tertiary entrance scores, or equivalent, when assessing schools. They value this sort of information but rarely make judgements about schools on the basis of this information alone. Parents have a number of reasons for not placing too much emphasis on student performance in examinations. They have a much more complex idea of what a 'good' school is and of the school that is most appropriate for their child. They consider performance in examinations as just one facet of what a school should be achieving for their children. For example, a school in which students do well in examinations at the expense of developing the social and discipline skills would not be viewed favourably by many parents.

Many parents in schools with formal annual reporting systems, such as reporting against the school's goals and objectives, were unaware that such reports existed. Parents who were aware of them, or vaguely aware in many instances, often did not know how they could access the reports. Parents in systems with external school reviews were generally unaware that they existed, and therefore did not know whether and how they could access the findings.

QUALITY OF TEACHING AND LEARNING

Academic reputation, while not the sole reason that most parents have for choosing a school, is important. Most parents quickly learn, usually through parents' networks, what the reputation of a school is for academic rigour. They find it difficult to assess the validity and reliability of the information about a school's reputation.

The subjects and specialist programs on offer, particularly in secondary schools, are important to parents, as is the quality of teaching in them. How well the school performs in tertiary entrance results overall might be irrelevant to a parent looking for a school with a good art program for a child gifted in this area. The quality of the art program and art teaching may be a factor of paramount importance in this case.

Parents usually learn about the effectiveness of different faculties and their teachers through anecdotal comments, other students and the school's 'reputation' in each area. Parents are interested to know whether the teaching and learning styles used by the school will meet their child's learning needs. They believe that a teaching or learning style appropriate for some students may not be effective for others. For example, parents noted that while a competitive environment can challenge and motivate some students, it may not be the best environment for others.

School policies

Parents often reported that they sought specific school policies when choosing a school. These policies are usually ones that are important to the goals they have for their children. Some polices are more important to some parents than to others. For example, parents with a child who has a disability may want to know about the school's integration policy and a parent whose child has a learning difficulty will be interested to know about its 'special needs' policy.

Policy areas that are of interest to a large number of parents are student welfare, pastoral care, discipline and behaviour management, and, in secondary schools, the drugs policy. Other important policy areas are the integration of special needs students. Some parents have a very specific policy interest and they will seek out school practice in this area to determine whether it matches their expectations. For example, a parent might specifically choose a school that fosters and encourages an inclusive multicultural environment. Some parents have learned that there is often a gap between what schools say they do and what they actually deliver.

Types

Some parents have very specific requirements about the type of school that their children will attend. In these instances there is often not a lot that an individual school can do about its 'type', other than capitalise on its positive attributes. For example, parents may have a strong preference for schools in a specific sector - Catholic, independent or government. For other parents the first requirement may be that the school is single-sex.

Parents have quite strong views about their preferred size of school. Many value large schools, but others prefer their children to attend small schools. Parents who value larger schools choose them because they have more resources and expertise and are more likely to provide their children with a wider range of opportunities, such as extra-curricula programs. Parents who choose small schools do so because they provide a friendlier and more secure environment.

Location

The location of a school is a consideration for parents when choosing a school. Rural parents regret that they have little choice, but report that they are generally satisfied with the local school. Parents of primary school students usually consider the local school as their first option. It is usually the closest and most convenient school for parents and many believe through anecdotal evidence or previous experience of the school that the local school will be satisfactory for their children.

Provided local primary schools have a good reputation, parents will generally not look further afield. In this context, parents may choose among three or four local schools, where more than one school is viewed as serving the local area. By 'good' reputation, parents mean good student discipline, perceived high academic standards and a friendly environment. However, if children do not thrive in the local school, parents will seek an alternative. Parents cast their net much wider geographically when choosing a secondary school. The location of the school is less important than for primary schools, but the availability of transport is an important consideration.

Parents who 'know' their way around schools and education systems use what knowledge they can acquire about schools to make good educational decisions for their children. Many of these parents indicated they are concerned that not all parents have access to similar information. They do not believe that parents should have to "chase " information and would greatly appreciate access to information from sources which do not have a vested interest in what it says about individual schools.

Parents compare schools when "shopping around" and accept that ultimately if they are to secure the best school for their children then all schools must be evaluated against the needs of the child, which may involve direct comparisons between alternative schools. However, there is a significant force of opinion against the public comparison of schools through ranking in the media.

Many parents were, however, familiar with the 'league table' concept of reporting on school performance. Ranking schools on their performance in end of schooling examinations was the most common experience that parents had of this form of comparison. They do not find this information provides particularly useful information about schools, although many parents do take some notice of such sources of information. The major criticisms that parents had of simplistic measures of school performance is that they do not take account of differences in student ability and they do not tell them how effective a school would be for average students, students from disadvantaged backgrounds or students not aiming for university.

Some parents were critical of schools for using questionable practices to ensure their exam averages 'improve', such those whose practice was to evict - or not enrol in the first place - potentially low achieving students. Parents indicated that it was easier for them to identify schools that were successful for getting students into university than it was to find out how effective school were at getting students into other post-secondary courses or into jobs. Whilst some schools market themselves as being equally successful for all students, parents overall do not believe this. Parents know that some schools concentrate on the highest achieving students to the detriment of others.

Many parents receive school achievement information directly from schools. They question the use of student achievement data that is currently available, especially Year 12 examination data, not only for the reasons noted earlier, but because the information presented applies to only a relatively small proportion of students, usually high achievers. They want useful information about the achievements of schools for all types of students, across all years of schooling, and across all aspects of student development. Parents often receive information from schools, such as through principals' reports or articles in the local media about how a school performs in certain tests, but they believe that such information is released selectively to show each schools in its best light.

Where school accountability systems are in place parents are generally unaware of the processes and how they could access achievement reports. Often only a 'select' grouping of parents is informed that a report exists, or parents have to ask specifically for a report. It is evident from this that current accountability processes focus on accountability to the particular school system with little regard as to the needs of parents. In other cases, the official reports prepared for parent consumption simply lose credibility and integrity when parents compare them with the other data they collect to make a choice among schools.

Some parents believe that the current 'market' environment in which schools compete for students presents an obstacle to current accountability practices because it pressures schools to present themselves in a positive light and to hide rather than address their problems.

Parents have their own ideas about what a 'good' school might be, but indicated they would appreciate further research-based guidance and advice on what makes schools more or less effective. They would like to build a better informed, balanced, comprehensive and structured framework for making judgements about schools.

The following are some of the characteristics that parents who identify as characteristics of effective schools:

— a warm, friendly and secure environment for their children;

— a broad curriculum - including opportunities for students to choose extra-curricula options;

— high academic standards;

— continuity in the provision of programs;

— a focus on the social, physical and emotional development of children;

— effective discipline and student welfare policies;

— parents viewed as partners in the education of their children, and

— students treated as responsible participants in their own education.

7

Grading Practices

There are no hard-and-fast rules about the best ways to grade. In fact, as Erickson and Strommer point out, how you grade depends a great deal on your values, assumptions, and educational philosophy: if you view introductory courses as "weeder" classes — to separate out students who lack potential for future success in the field — you are likely to take a different grading approach than someone who views introductory courses as teaching important skills that all students need to master.

All faculty agree, however, that grades provide information on how well students are learning. But grades also serve other purposes. Scriven has identified at least six functions of grading:

— To describe unambiguously the worth, merit, or value of the work accomplished

— To improve the capacity of students to identify good work, that is, to improve their self-evaluation or discrimination skills with respect to work submitted

— To stimulate and encourage good work by students

— To communicate the teacher's judgment of the student's progress

— To inform the teacher about what students have and haven't learned

— To select people for rewards or continued education

For some students, grades are also a sign of approval or disapproval; they take them very personally. Because of the importance of grades, faculty need to communicate to students a clear rationale and policy on grading. If you devise clear guidelines from which to assess performance, you will find the grading process more efficient, and the essential function of grades — communicating the student's level of knowledge — will be easier. Further, if you grade carefully and consistently, you can reduce the number of students who complain and ask you to defend a grade. The suggestions below are designed to help you develop clear and fair grading policies. For tips on calculating final grades, see "Calculating and Assigning Grades."

GENERAL STRATEGIES

Grade on the basis of students' mastery of knowledge and skills: Restrict your evaluations to academic performance. Eliminate other considerations, such as classroom behavior, effort, classroom participation, attendance, punctuality, attitude, personality traits, or student interest in the course material, as the basis of course grades. If you count these non-academic factors, you obscure the primary meaning of the grade, as an indicator of what students have learned. For a discussion on why not to count class participation, see "Encouraging Student Participation in Discussion."

Avoid grading systems that put students in competition with their classmates and limit the number of high grades: These normative systems, such as grading on the curve, work against collaborative learning strategies that have been shown to be effective in promoting student learning. Normative grading produces undesirable consequences for many students, such as reduced motivation to learn, debilitating evaluation anxiety, decreased ability to use feedback to improve learning, and poor social relationships.

Try not to overemphasize grades. Explain to your class the meaning of and basis for grades and the procedures you use in grading. At the beginning of the term, inform students, in writing how much tests, papers, homework, and the final exam will count toward their final grade. Once you have explained your policies, avoid stressing grades or excessive talk about grades, which only increases students' anxieties and decreases their motivation to do something for its own sake rather than to obtain an external reward such as a grade.

Keep students informed of their progress throughout the term. For each paper, assignment, midterm, or project that you grade, give students a sense of what their score means. Try to give a point total rather than a letter grade. Letter grades tend to have emotional associations that point totals lack. Do show the range and distribution of point scores, and indicate what level of performance is satisfactory. Such information can motivate students to improve if they are doing poorly or to maintain their performance if they are doing well. By keeping students informed throughout the term, you also prevent unpleasant surprises at the end.

MINIMIZING STUDENTS' COMPLAINTS ABOUT GRADING

Clearly state grading procedures in your course syllabus, and go over this information in class: Students want to know how their grades will be determined, the weights of various tests and assignments, and the model of grading you will be using to calculate their grades: will the class be graded on a curve or by absolute standards? If you intend to make allowances for extra credit, late assignments, or revision of papers, clearly state your policies.

Set policies on late work: Will you refuse to accept any late work? Deduct points according to how late the work is submitted? Handle late work on a case-by-case basis? Offer a grace period? See "Preparing or Revising a Course."

Avoid modifying your grading policies during the term: Midcourse changes may erode students' confidence in your fairness, consistency, objectivity, and organizational skills. If you must make a change, give your students a complete explanation.

Provide enough opportunities for students to show you what they know: By giving students many opportunities to show you what they know, you will have a more accurate picture of their abilities and will avoid penalizing a student who has an off day at the time of a test. So in addition to a final exam, give one or two midterms and one or two short papers. For lower-division courses, Erickson and Strommer recommend giving shorter tests or written assignments and scheduling some form of evaluation every two or three weeks.

Consider allowing students to choose among alternative assignments: One instructor presents a list of activities with assigned points for each that take into account the assignments' educational and motivational value, difficulty, and probable amount of effort required. Students are told how many points are needed for an A, a B, or a C, and they choose a combination of assignments that meets the grade they desire for that portion of the course. Here are some possible activities:

— Writing a case study

— Engaging in and reporting on a fieldwork experience

— Leading a discussion panel

— Serving on a discussion panel

— Keeping a journal or log of course-related ideas

— Writing up thoughtful evaluations of several lectures

— Creating instructional materials for the course (study guides, exam questions, or audiovisual materials) on a particular concept or theme

— Undertaking an original research project or research paper

— Reviewing the current research literature on a course-related topic

— Keeping a reading log that includes brief abstracts of the readings and comments, applications, and critiques

— Completing problem-solving assignments (such as designing an experiment to test a hypothesis or creating a test to measure something)

Stress to students that grades reflect work on a specific task and are not judgments about people: Remind students that a teacher grades only a piece of paper. You might also let students know, if appropriate, that research shows that grades bear little or no relationship to measures of adult accomplishment.

Give encouragement to students who are performing poorly: If students are having difficulty, do what you can to help them improve on the next assignment or exam. If they do perform well, take this into account when averaging the early low score with the later higher one.

Deal directly with students who are angry or upset about their grade: Ask an upset student to take a day or more to cool off. It is also helpful to ask the student to prepare in writing the complaint or justification for a grade change. When you meet with the student in your office, have all the relevant materials at hand: the test questions, answer key or criteria, and examples of good answers. Listen to the student's concerns or read the memo with an open mind and respond in a calm manner. Don't allow yourself to become antagonized, and don't antagonize the student. Describe the key elements of a good answer, and point out how the student's response was incomplete or incorrect. Help the student understand your reasons for assigning the grade that you did. Take time to think about the student's request or to reread the exam if you need to, but resist pressures to change a grade because of a student's personal needs (to get into graduate school or maintain status on the dean's list). If appropriate, for final course grades, offer to write a letter to the student's adviser or to others, describing the student's work in detail and indicating any extenuating circumstances that may have hurt the grade.

Keep accurate records of students' grades: Your department may keep copies of final grade reports, but it is important for you to keep a record of all grades assigned throughout the semester, in case a student wishes to contest a grade, finish an incomplete, or ask for a letter of recommendation.

EFFECTIVE USE OF GRADING TACTICS

Return the first graded assignment or test before the add/drop deadline: Early assignments help students decide whether they are prepared to take the class. Some faculty members give students the option of throwing out this first test. Students may receive a low score because they did not know what the instructor required or because they underestimated the level of preparation needed to succeed.

Record results numerically rather than as letter grades, whenever possible: Tests, problem sets, homework, and so on are best recorded by their point value to assure greater accuracy when calculating final grades.

Give students a chance to improve their grades by rewriting their papers: Many faculty encourage rewriting but do not count the grades on rewritten papers as equivalent to those of papers that have not been rewritten. See "Helping Students Write Better in All Courses."

If many students do poorly on an exam, schedule another one on the same material a week or so later: Devote one or more classes to reviewing the troublesome material. Provide in-class exercises, homework problems or questions, practice quizzes, study group opportunities, and extra office hours before you administer the new exam. Though reviewing and retesting may seem burdensome and time-consuming, there is usually little point in proceeding to new topics when many of your students are still struggling.

Evaluating Grading Policies

Compare your grade distributions with those for similar courses in your department: Differences between your grade distributions and those of your colleagues do not necessarily mean that your methods are faulty. But glaring discrepancies should prompt you to reexamine your practices.

Ask students about your grading policies on end-of-course questionnaires: Here are some sample questions:

To what extent:

- Were the grading procedures for the course fair?
- Were the grading procedures for the course clearly explained?
- Did you receive adequate feedback on your performance?
- Were requests for regrading or review handled fairly?
- Did the instructor evaluate your work in a meaningful and conscientious manner?

STRATEGIES OF STRUDENT'S GRADING

Integrate Grading

The writing process is recursive and includes various stages of revision. In integrating grading into the writing process, professors must consider the relationship between the grading process and a grade. The grading process results in a grade, the final evaluation professors give either to an individual assignment or to a series of assignments that included grades for individual writing assignments within the series. The grade is one part of the grading process, not the focus of the process. Indeed, the grading process extends from the development of a writing assignment to the administration of a final grade. When the grade is abstracted from the grading process, students may be left wondering how a grade was derived, professors may be put in the awkward position of explaining and defending a grade after the fact, and evaluation may be severed from the process of writing.

Nevertheless, integrating grading and the writing process is not without difficulties, including tension between the professor's roles as mentor and judge. The dual roles of mentor and judge raise ethical issues about the grading process and the grade and, in some quarters, undercut the writing process in favor of the grade. Such undercutting is unfortunate because the writing process can help students learn not only how to approach a writing task effectively but also how to evaluate their own and their peers' writing.

Why do Professors Need to Construct Effective Writing Assignments?

Because the writing assignment specifies what students are expected to do and how students' written products will be evaluated, the writing assignment should include necessary information about audience and purpose, the two pillars of writing. The writing assignment also is the appropriate occasion for discussing discipline-specific norms and conventions for writing. Writing assignments, like most written products, should go through a process that includes peer review, so professors can enlist colleagues and students to critique writing assignments before the assignments are formally introduced.

How Can Professors Ensure That Their Professional Judgements Are Fair?

Although answers to the question of fairness are often discussed in terms of reliability and validity, the application of statistical requirements for reliability and validity are probably impractical in grading classroom writing. Grading methods that include the use of a rubric or some other tangible expression of grading criteria can promote greater fairness in grading, however.

Nevertheless, fairness in classroom assessment is complicated by a variety of issues. In fact, fairness is inextricably linked with professional judgment, because the professor is the grading authority in the classroom. Thus, professors need to be sensitive to their responsibility for fairness when they grade students' papers.

How Can Professors Use Their Authority to Promote Students' Learning?

A powerful way to promote students' learning is to involve them in the grading process. To do so, professors should consider training students to function effectively as peer reviewers, modeling for them the integration of formal, subject matter, and teaching authority into the grading process so that students have examples of professional evaluators they can emulate when they serve as peer reviewers. When students are given the opportunity to function as professionals in the classroom, they can learn how to make informed decisions about writing quality, a task many students will be required to do in their vocations in nonacademic settings. Students' involvement also includes self-assessments.

How Can the Professors Help Students to Learn How to Respond Effectively to Writing?

Providing effective feedback to students will help them learn to revise their writing. Unfortunately, the literature on professors' feedback to students' writing includes numerous examples of how not to provide feedback. Three common inappropriate responses are cryptic responses, negative responses, and too much response. These forms of response are predicated on views of grading that are not commensurate with the writing process, primarily because they focus on errors. Fortunately, negative examples can serve a cautionary note, suggesting that professors need to learn how to provide effective feedback.

Professors can take a step toward providing useful feedback by recognizing the perils they face when they read students' writing.

When professors are sensitive to those perils, they can take a more cautious and more positive approach to reading and responding to students' writing. In particular, professors can provide written comments on students' writing by creating a dialogue when writing responses, pointing out writing, refraining from making unprofessional c successful omments, summarizing the gist of marginal comments at the end of a paper, giving students options for revising the paper, writing comments that model good writing, and deferring the assignment of a grade as long as possible. Positive, well written responses perfect the art of providing effective feedback to students and serve as models of desirable writing.

What Support is Available to Help Professors Effectively Grade Students' Writing?

Effective grading of students' writing is hard work that requires a great deal of time and a commitment to reading the literature on grading classroom writing. Without administrative support, including appropriate class sizes and teaching loads, professors need to consider just how much time and energy they should devote to promoting the intertwining of the writing and grading processes. To the extent that professors do elect to use these intertwining processes, they might consider establishing a plan to integrate the processes in their classes over an extended period of time and to consult the literature on the grading of classroom writing for detailed information about effectively promoting the writing and grading processes.

Computerized Testing

Despite many unresolved technical and equity-related problems, test-makers are plunging headlong into new computerized methods of administering multiple-choice exams. Unfortunately, simply automating bad tests does nothing to solve their long-standing problems and may actually compound them.

The Educational Testing Service (ETS), for example, introduced its computerized Graduate Record Exam in October 1992, and has begun working on a computerized SAT. The National Council of Architectural Registration Boards already uses an ETS manufactured computerized test as part of its professional licensing process. Computerized tests are also part of ETS new generation of teacher tests, the Praxis Series, and the National Council Licensure Examination for nurses is only available on computer. In addition, many colleges, universities, and public school districts are using computerized placement tests.

Proponents of computerized testing praise its ability to provide immediate score reporting and faster and more flexible test scheduling (a test can be offered several times a week rather than a few times per year). They also point to the efficiency of Computerized Adaptive Testing (CAT), which provides a final score with fewer items in a shorter period of time than conventional paper-and-pencil, multiple-choice tests. In the future, computerized testing may also offer a greater scope of types of items through the use of graphics and video. But the new tests are being rushed into operation before adequate evidence of either their comparability to current exams or their fairness have been collected.

Unresolved Problems

Test-makers claims that the scores of computerized and pencil-and-paper tests are equivalent are inadequately supported. In fact, research studies find there usually is a difference. Most studies show higher scores for paper-and-pencil exams, but a few have found advantages for those who take computerized tests. These averages may mask individual variations. Some respondents may still get lower scores even if the average score increases. Also, some types of questions perform differently on the two types of tests.

Computerized tests constrain test-takers compared to paper-and-pencil tests. With computerized versions, test-takers are unable to underline text, scratch out eliminated choices and work out math problems — all commonly-used strategies. Studies also suggest that computer screens take longer to read than printed materials, and that it is more difficult to detect errors on computer screens.1

Most computerized tests show only one item on the screen at a time, preventing test-takers from easily checking previous items and the pattern of their responses, two other practices known to help test-takers. Scrolling through multiple screens does not allow side-by-side comparisons.

Test-takers with the ability to manipulate computer keys rapidly may be favored by long passages that require reading through many screens.

Test-makers may try to use computerizd exams to circumvent Truth-in-Testing disclosure requirements. ETS has not revealed how it intends to continue making test questions and answers available to university admissions test-takers.

Computers may worsen test bias. The performance gap which already exists on multiple-choice tests between men and women, ethnic groups, and persons from different socioeconomic backgrounds could widen as a result of computerized testing.

Schools with large minority or low-income populations are far less likely to have computers, and poor and minority children are much less likely to have computers at home. White students are more likely to have earned computer science credit than either African American or Hispanic students.

The additional cost of computerized tests is certain to have a large effect on who chooses to take them. Poorer students are unlikely to take the computerized GRE, for example, because it costs nearly twice as much as the paper-and-pencil version.

Girls may be adversely affected by computerized tests. A much greater number of females than males report no school access to computers, no computer learning experiences, and limited knowledge about computers3. In addition, computer anxiety is much more prevalent among females than males4, with Black females reporting the greatest anxiety5.

USING COMPUTER IN SCIENCE ASSESSMENT

Research and development efforts in alternative forms of assessment are on the rise in science education, along with growing interest in using computers in science assessment. A review of technological applications in science assessment was provided by Helgeson and Kumar, recent developments in computer scorable, large scale tests were reported by Martinez and Bennett, and a theme issue on computer-based science assessment was prepared by the Journal of Science Education and Technology.

Types of Computer Applications

Assessment applications for computers can be broadly classified into two categories: traditional and contemporary. In traditional applications the infrastructure is rigidly algorithmic. Examples include forced-choice and multiple-choice testing, grading, and record keeping. In more contemporary applications the infrastructure is quasi-algorithmic or non-linear in nature. Examples include constructed response testing, adaptive testing, figural response testing, simulations, and solution pathway analysis.

Forced-choice and multiple-choice testing are the most traditional applications of computers in testing and are often used to test low level knowledge acquisition. Considering the need for aligning testing with education reform efforts underway, the focus of researchers should be the contemporary rather than traditional approaches to computer-based assessment. Contemporary computer applications would allow for better analysis of the new kinds of process-oriented science instruction suggested by the science education reform efforts.

Among contemporary computer applications, simulations appear to hold promises for large scale assessment. A comparative study of computer simulations and hands-on tasks such as the classic "batteries and bulbs" activities shows that student outcomes are not much different between computer-based and hands-on assessments. Gorrell reported a computer simulation-based assessment for collecting process information in learning among undergraduates in behavior analysis.

In figural response testing students manipulate pictorial tasks on a computer screen using a mouse to solve problems. According to Martinez this approach has been found suitable for science assessment involving extensive graphics in disciplines such as stereochemistry and molecular biology. Constructed response testing gives students the option of presenting their answers or solutions to a problem on a computerized grid sheet. The computer also grades student responses with a preset standard deviation range, thereby reducing the chances of students losing all credit for a question because they picked the wrong answer from a multiple response. Students receive partial credit for partially correct answers.

Braun, Bennett, Frye and Soloway reported using expert systems for scoring constructed responses of high school students in Advanced Placement computer science courses. They found the expert system was able to score between 82% and 95% of the responses successfully and show a high correlation with a human grader on correctness. In computerized adaptive testing the computer tailors a test according to an examinee's level of achievement and ability. For example, based upon the kind of response made to a question on a particular topic, the computer will decide whether to stay on the same topic to ask another question that will help the student review or clarify background knowledge, or proceed to a higher level question and to a different topic.

Using computers for analyzing solution pathways is another emerging trend. Gong, Venezky and Mioduser used a computer-based learning progress map incorporating a database for biology testing leading to valuable and interesting analyses of student performance. Young also reported an anchored assessment approach involving a videodisc anchor and interacting computer software. The software functions as a ledger for recording the kinds of information the student searches and uses for problem solving using the videodisc. According to Young this anchored assessment technique has provided information on student performance in the solution space which otherwise would be obtainable only through verbal protocols and extensive transcription of data. In another study a Pen-Point computer was used to study solution pathway procedures in solving classical multiple step modularity problems.

The computer applications described here have several underlying assumptions that guide their roles in assessment. First, computers are information management tools and they provide enormous opportunities for gathering and managing a variety of assessment data. Second, computers provide a less obtrusive medium for students to express their thought processes in a problem solving task. Third, computers function as an extended working memory thereby reducing the cognitive load on the problem solver and adding considerably to "logical/mathematical intelligence". Fourth, hypermedia computer systems provide a flexible non-linear environment whereby the moves and steps a problem solver takes during an interaction with the computer could be recorded for assessment. Fifth, human computer interaction is not just a mechanical relationship. It is mediated by a hypothetical interface, the "computer technology-cognitive psychology interface", which is a complex interaction between human cognition and the computer environment.

While computer applications and the underlying assumptions of the role of computers in assessment open up doors of opportunity for the development of innovative computer-based tools, they also raise serious issues. Some of the key issues relate to validity, gender equity, instructional delivery, the mode of user interface, and responsibility to the public. Developing computer-based assessment tasks in science that are valid for large groups is an issue that has yet to be fully resolved. Establishing the validity of computer tests by comparing them against traditional pencil-and-paper tests is a double-edged sword.

The main purpose for bringing computers into assessment is to develop tasks that will provide more information about thinking processes that are difficult to obtain through standardized multiple-choice tests. On the other hand, for public accountability, it is very difficult to compare and justify computer-based assessment results that are aimed at individual or small groups against large scale traditional standardized tests. Also, public pressure to disclose the questions and answers of large scale examinations, such as the computerized adaptive tests, has raised concerns about maintaining test validity over a large period of time. Therefore, more research is needed in the development and evaluation of computer-based assessment applications that are valid on a large scale.

Computer-based learning has been shown to raise gender equity issues. Considering testing as a part of learning in science, gender equity is a serious issue in computer-based testing. Assessment tasks that are more appealing to female students ought to be taken into account in developing computer-based tests in science. If computers are to be used for science assessment they must also be used as an integral part of science teaching and learning. Research and development efforts should focus on computer technology applications and instruction as well as assessment in science.

Using computers for performance assessment is an interactive experience, and it depends upon the mode of user interface that links the person and the computer. User interface devices such as keyboards, mice, light pens, and induction pens all have different effects on the performance of the individual at the computer. Due to progress in computer technology, using virtual reality to simulate hands-on assessment tasks may be useful for designing more effective computer-based performance assessment applications in te rms of less obtrusive user interface and an increased sense of realism.

Research efforts in computer-based assessment need to take into account the effects of user interfaces on student performance in order to develop more valid assessment tools using computers. Considering the developments in contemporary approaches to computer-based science assessment, it is evident that computers are viable tools for assessment. However, the inherent issues discussed earlier should be addressed in order to make computer-based testing an acceptable practice for large scale assessment.

Continued research and development efforts are needed in order to shape computers into tools that are unquestionably effective on a large scale for performance assessment in science education. Computer-based assessment remains a fertile field for research and development in science.

Grading Students

Some instructors record letter grades for tests and assignments, and others record numerical values, often the percent correct on tests. Later, under either method, the grades are averaged, often employing a weighting process designed to make some grades count more heavily than others. Discussion of the merits of different approaches usually centers around the question of whether it is better to average letter or numerical grades or around some feature of the weighting process. Following are the several aspects of assigning grades:

First, an issue that underlies for both approaches, variability of test scores, is discussed. The use of standardized scores is presented as a solution to the variability problem, ideas on assigning letter grades, and recommendations are then presented.

Variability

An important characteristic of the grades as initially recorded is seldom questioned, namely the variability of the scores of each test or assignment. Indeed, it is ironic that instructors may go to considerable trouble to weight grades according to their perceived importance when, in fact, the result may be quite different from what was intended, due to failure to account for differences in score variability from one test to another.

Standardised scores

The best approach to avoiding situations like the one just presented is to record and average standardized test scores. In order to calculate standardized scores it is necessary to know the standard deviation of the scores prior to standardization. This statistic is a measure of how "spread out" the scores are and is explained in any elementary statistics text. Though nearly any program reporting test results will include this statistic, a fair approximation for most classroom tests may be obtained by subtracting the lowest score from the highest and dividing by 4. In the example above, the standard deviations are about 15 and 3 percentage points respectively for the midterm and final examinations.

A standard score is then the number of standard deviations the number-right or percentage score is above or below average. Commonly called a z-score, its formula is: z score equals (observed score minus average score) divided by standard deviation. Then scores of 80% and 97% on the midterm and final respectively would each yield z-scores of 1.0, because both are one standard deviation above average. Similarly, scores of 50% and 91% would correspond to z-scores of -1.0. It may be difficult to work with z-scores, because half of them will be negative and all will probably lie between -3 and 3.

Therefore, it is convenient to transform the z-scores into T-scores as follows: $T = 50 + 10z$. T-scores will have a mean (average) of 50 and a standard deviation of 10. Thus, a T-score of 60 represents a number-right score one standard deviation above the average. If the distribution of scores approximates the shape of the normal curve, about 16% of the T-scores will be above 60 and about 10% above 63. Similarly, about 16% of T-scores will be below 40 and about 10% below 37. If T-scores are computed for every test, averaging them will provide a composite score from which the influence of the variability of the scores has been eliminated. (Strictly speaking, if more than two scores are to be averaged, the intercorrelations among the scores should be taken into consideration in order to control for the degree of "overlap." However, simple averaging of T-scores should produce a good approximation of the more precise result.)

T-scores are typically provided for multiple-choice tests processed by measurement services offices at universities. Moreover, T-scores can be calculated for any numerically evaluated non-test assignments you may wish to include in the course composite. Like other scores, T-scores may be weighted differentially. For example, if you wish to weight the final exam twice as much as the midterm, multiply the T-scores from the final by 2, add the midterm T-scores and divide by 3. It should be noted at this point that T-scores report only a student's relative position in the class and not an absolute measure of achievement. However, the difficulty level of nearly all academic tests is arbitrary and that, regardless of the scoring method, they provide nothing more than ranking information.

Assigning letter grades

Finally, when the T-scores have been averaged, there is the problem of assigning letter grades for the course. Until this point, we have been able to speak with conviction, deducing conclusions logically through arguments based on statistical principles. However, when it is necessary to determine the dividing line between As and Bs or Ds and Fs, there is no such clear-cut approach available. Of course, if student X's average is higher than student Y's, student Y's letter grade must not be higher than student X's, but beyond this recommendation, the best advice is to inspect the distribution of average T-scores with the following questions in mind:

- What is a typical letter grade distribution for a course of this type with this kind of student?
- Are there any circumstances which might warrant altering this "typical" distribution, e.g., did the course progress especially well or poorly?
- Where in the distribution are key students whose work you know especially well, students you believe might deserve especially good or poor grades for reasons other than test performance?
- Where are naturally occurring "breaks" in the distribution of average T-scores? (There is no "scientific" reason for letting these points determine letter grades, but if their use is not inconsistent with other considerations, it will help to prevent hard feelings on the part of students who otherwise might miss a better grade by one T-score point.)

Two ideas to be avoided or at least questioned in determining letter grades are:

- That the T-score spread should be the same for each letter grade.
- That an equal number of As and Fs, Bs and Ds, should necessarily be awarded.

Finally, it must be remembered that assignment of letter grades across a range of average scores is essentially arbitrary and a matter of professional judgment.

Recommendations

1. Do not prescribe percent-correct score ranges for letter grades in your course syllabus. Instead, indicate that you will exercise your professional judgment as to what constitutes A, B, C, etc., only after reviewing the test scores.

You may wish to indicate only tentative letter grades for any given test and base final test grades on the average of standardized scores from several tests.

2. When testing higher level cognitive skills, vary the difficulty of the questions so as to discriminate among all skill levels. Include items sufficiently difficult to challenge even the most talented students and a few items sufficiently easy that most will answer correctly. The latter may include a disproportionate number of lower level cognitive skills. The average percent-correct score should be somewhere in the range between 50% and 70% in order to maximize discrimination among achievement levels.

3. Alert students to the fact that the test may be more difficult than what they are accustomed to, but that the percent-correct scores will be interpreted in a relative, rather than an absolute sense.

4. Determine the minimum passing score on each test by identifying items that you (and/or your colleagues) judge to represent essential knowledge, or that you (or they) believe should be correctly answered by any student deserving of a passing grade. Base the passing score on the percentage of the total points these questions contribute. You may wish to compute a separate score for items so identified, but it is probably sufficient to use this percentage regardless of which items are answered correctly.

5. Use your professional judgment to determine cut points between grades. You might consider the test performance of students about whom you have independent knowledge of achievement via other assignments or previous courses. Naturally occurring breaks in the score distribution can suggest cut points between letter grades that might minimize the number of students clamoring at your door for the extra point or two needed for the next higher grade. Ultimately, judgments in this area are subjective and should be acknowledged as such when implemented.

6. Do not feel obliged to "grade on the curve" whereby a specified percentage of students will receive each letter grade. To do so can be as arbitrary and capricious as to adopt prescribed percentage ranges for assigning scores, especially in smaller classes.

STANDARDIZED GROWTH

Stenner, Hunter, Bland, & Cooper describe a standardized growth expectation (SGE) as "the amount of growth (expressed in standard deviation form) that a student must demonstrate over a given treatment interval to maintain his/her relative standing in the norm group". To determine an SGE, Stenner et. al. proposed the following three-step method.

— Step 1. The scale score associated with the 50th percentile for a given grade level or the pre-test is identified.

— Step 2. The percentile rank for the following grade level or the post-test associated with this scale score is found.

— Step 3. The difference between the 50th percentile and the post-test percentile is calculated.

When applying Stenner et. al.'s method for calculating SGEs, Haney, Madaus and Lyons point out that the idea of a SGE is analogous to an effect size in that each represents the difference in mean performance of two groups expressed in standard scores. As Glass, McGaw and Smith describe, an effect size represents the difference between two groups in standard deviations. To calculate an effect size, the difference between the mean of the control group and the experimental group is divided by the standard deviation of the control group. Conceptually, the only difference between an effect size and an SGE is that an effect size is used to compare the means of a "control" group and an "experimental" group while a SGE compares the performance of groups of students at various grade levels.

Expected Growth Size

Although an SGE and an effect size are similar, there is one important difference: an SGE focuses on the standing lost when there is no change in test score, while the effect size focuses on the amount of change in a test score necessary to maintain one's standing. When applied in this manner, the effect size method provides an estimate of the expected growth size between two time periods. In the example above, the expected growth size (EGS) between grade three and grade four on the ITBS Composite Language test is.89 standard deviations.

In a well-designed experiment, there is little question as to which group is defined as the control group and which is the experimental group. However, when applying the concept of an effect size to change in test scores between two grade levels, one could reference growth to the pre-test or the post-test distribution. In the case of SGEs, the post-test distribution is used to reference "growth". Note, however, that although SGEs employ the term growth, the methodology actual provides a measure of loss assuming that a student experiences no growth whatsoever. In this way, using the post-test distribution to reference "growth" is fundamentally flawed in that change is placed in the context of where a student is expected to be rather than from where they started.

The situation is analogous to describing someone's progress on trip in relation to how far they still must go in order to reach their destination rather than from how far they have traveled since their departure. In the case of using an effect size to express growth between two grade levels, one might argue that the pooled standard deviation be employed in lieu of the standard deviation of the control group. However, the difficulty of obtaining an estimate of the pooled standard deviation for most standardized tests forces a choice between designating the pre-test or the post-test as the control group. Given the desire to measure change or growth from where a group begins at one point in time to where they end at a second point in time, the EGS methodology references change to the pre-test distribution. For this reason, the pre-test distribution is assigned as the control group.

Advantages

Although an expected growth size is more difficult to calculate, it offers three advantages. First, by expressing change in relation to the standard deviation, growth rates for different tests and different grade levels can be compared directly. Students scoring at the 25th percentile experience less growth than students scoring at the mean. And students scoring at the mean experience less growth than students scoring at the 75th percentile. This pattern explains why the standard deviation for most standardized tests increases as the grade level progresses. Second, once expected growth sizes are calculated for a given test, they can be easily transformed to more common measurement scales. As an example, multiplying the expected growth size by the standard deviation of an Normal Curve Equivalent, NCE, provides the number of NCE points a student's score increases during a given time period relative to the student's initial norm group when s/he maintains his/her current standing.

For the ITBS Language test, the score for a student who maintains a 50th percentile ranking increases 18.74 NCEs between the third and fourth grade. Third, once expected growth sizes are transformed to an NCE scale, changes in an individual's or a group's mean score can be reported in relation to expected growth. Performance on most standardized tests is reported relative to the Norm Group for a student's current grade. If the student grows at the same rate as other students in the Norm Group, his/her percentile rank and NCE will remain the same across two years. However, if the student's rate of growth differs from that of the Norm Group, his/her NCE and percentile rank will change.

The expected growth size can be used to determine the extent to which the student's growth exceeded or fell short of the expected growth size. To do so, the student's current NCE is subtracted from his/her previous NCE and divided by the expected NCE growth rate. As an example, consider a student whose NCE for the ITBS Language test increased from 50 in grade 3 to 55 in grade 4. When divided by the expected NCE growth size for third grade, this five point increase represents 1.27 years of growth. Thus, the student's score increased 27% more than expected.

Limitations of expected growth sizes

Although expected growth sizes provided a sounder approach for summarizing change in test scores than some of the more commonly used approaches, their use is limited to norm referenced standardized tests. Moreover, the EGS methodology assumes that the tests have been vertically equated. When comparing change across multiple years, the methodology also assumes that the tests administered each year provide measures of the same construct based on identical content. Although most norm-referenced tests attempt to meet both assumptions vertical equating and measures of the same construct the extent to which they fail to meet these assumptions impacts the accuracy of estimates yielded by the EGS methodology.

Finally, as with all comparisons of change over time, the EGS method is also limited by the reliability of the scores used to calculate change. Although there is considerable debate over the extent to which low score reliability impacts the meaningfulness of change scores, caution is advised when employing the EGS method for tests with low reliability.

Use of expected growth sizes

To apply expected growth sizes to examine change in the performance of your students, readers are encouraged to use the attached spreadsheet. The spreadsheet provides an easy-to-use template that allows users to calculate expected growth sizes for most standardized tests. In addition, the spreadsheet translates expected growth sizes into expected changes in NCE scores for each grade level. As the attached instructions indicate, two pieces of information are required to use the spreadsheet:

1. Standard Score to Percentile Rank Conversion tables for the standardized test; and
2. The standard deviation for the standard score for each grade level. This information is available in the Technical Report(s) for each standardized test.

Although expected growth sizes are more complicated to calculate, they provide a more accurate and comparable method of examining change in test scores within and across grade levels and on different tests.

COMPUTERS AND TESTING

Computers are really, really good at storing and retrieving information, particularly well-structured information, so it is not surprising that some of the earliest applications of desktop personal computers to testing took the form of "item banking" programs. Today's item banking programs match the expectations that computers will be able to handle text, graphics, equations, and in the case of online administration, time-based (e.g., video or audio) items all with equal ease. Storing our items, of course, only makes sense if we plan to reuse them. If we plan to reuse items, we will want to store information *about* the items as well as the items themselves. For example, we might want to store the instructional objective the item addresses or the cognitive level at which we expect the item to function.

Reflecting their designers' experience in large-scale testing programs, many item-banking programs also store item statistics (e.g., difficulty and discrimination indices), sometimes for each of several administrations of the item on different tests. The tools we use naturally affect the way we work—sometimes for the better and sometimes for the worse. There is a risk to be managed in storing (and presumably using) item statistics in the typical instructional setting.

Test Administration

Item banking is relevant no matter how a test is going to be administered. Online administration of tests, though, offers increased efficiency as well as making feasible options that are not usually feasible with paper-based testing.

Test Scoring

Computers have been scoring tests for about fifty years using response forms that can be scanned by machine. At a minimum, online administration represents a convenience because forms don't have to be transported. In the better online testing systems, even more is possible. Scannable forms are effectively restricted to "selected-response" items (e.g., multiple choice, true/false, matching). Online testing allows students to type in responses. In the case of very simple "constructed-response" items, such as fill-in-the-blank items, the computer can do quite a good job of scoring.

Even for more complex items (short answer or essay), many faculty are finding that grading typed responses online is much more efficient than grading traditional blue books. A lot of the efficiency comes simply from the fact that the responses are typed. In addition, though, some systems allow the grader to enter a comment along with the score for the item. In these cases, it is sometimes reasonable to reuse "boilerplate" comments, which can simply be pasted in.

Recording Test Results

With online testing, scoring and recording are not separate steps. As each item is scored, whether automatically or by hand, the result is entered into a student database. When all the scoring is done, all of the recording is done as well. Not only are the individual students' results available, but summary statistics and graphs are available as well. Computers are still making our lives easier. The ability of a spreadsheet is to store, organize, and summarize test scores. For those who don't find a spreadsheet congenial, easy-to-use grade book programs exist.

Providing Feedback

The final step in the testing process is providing feedback to students. Again, online testing provides remarkable opportunities. Prompt feedback is one of the AAHE Seven Principles of Effective Undergraduate Education. For automatically scored items, instructors can provide item by item feedback or choose to provide feedback at the end of the test. It is possible to provide an explanation for each alternative the student might have chosen so that he or she knows not only whether the answer was correct or not but why. If the items can't be scored automatically, students can still get their results as soon as the scoring is complete instead of waiting for the next time the class meets.

Some of the most exciting opportunities for the use of computers in testing rely on online administration. Feeling comfortable about test security usually comes down to feeling comfortable that (a) the person whose name is associated with the test is indeed the person who took the test and (b) the students were not exposed to the items before taking the test. If that comfort isn't provided through an honor code, we have to establish it through our testing procedures. If all of our students take the test online but at the same time in one or more proctored rooms, we can feel as secure as we do with traditional paper and pencil testing. On the other hand, if students take the test online at a time and place of their own choosing, we really have no control over the identity issue and only very modest control over the seeing-the-test-beforehand issue (through, for example, administering alternate forms).

Computer in Language Testing

The literature on computer-assisted language learning indicates that language learners have generally positive attitudes toward using computers in the classroom, and a fairly large literature has developed examining the effectiveness of computer-assisted language learning. But less is known about the more specific area of computers in language testing.

In reviewing the literature on computers in language testing, there are four recurring sets of issues:

(a) item banking,

(b) computer-assisted language testing,

(c) computer-adaptive language testing, and

(d) the effectiveness of computers in language testing.

Item banking

Item banking covers any procedures that are used to create, pilot, analyze, store, manage, and select test items so that multiple test forms can be created from subsets of the total "bank" of items. With a large item bank available, new forms of tests can be created whenever they are needed. Henning provides a description of how item banking was set up for the ESL Placement Examination at UCLA. While the underlying aims of item banking can be accomplished by using traditional item analysis procedures, a problem often occurs because of differences in abilities among the groups of people who are used in piloting the items, especially when they are compared to the population of students with whom the test is ultimately to be used.

However, a relatively new branch of test analysis theory, called item response theory (IRT), eliminates the need to have exactly equivalent groups of students when piloting items because IRT analysis yields estimates of item difficulty and item discrimination that are "sample-free." IRT can also provide "item-free" estimates of students' abilities. Henning discusses the topic in terms of the steps involved in item banking for language tests and provides recipe-style descriptions of how to calculate the appropriate IRT statistics.

Green outlines some of the problems that might be encountered in using IRT in general, and Henning discusses specific problems that may be encountered with the validity of item banking techniques in language testing settings. Another serious limitation of IRT is the large number of students that must be tested before it can responsibly be applied. Typically, IRT is only applicable for full item analysis (that is, for analysis of two or three parameters) when the numbers of students being tested are very large by the standards of most language programs, that is to say, in excess of one thousand. Smaller samples in the hundreds can be used only if the item difficulty parameter is studied.

Minimal item banking can be done without computers by using file cards, and, of course, the traditional item analysis statistics can be done (using the sizes of groups typically found in language programs) with no more sophisticated equipment than a hand-held calculator. Naturally, a personal computer can make both item banking and item analysis procedures much easier and much faster. For example, standard database software can be used to do the item banking. For IRT analyses, more specialized software will be needed. The following are examples of computer programs that can be used for IRT analysis: TESTAT, BIGSTEPS, and PC-BILOG.

Alternatively, the MicroCAT Testing System program can help with both item banking and IRT analyses. BestTest is another less sophisticated program, which can be used in both item banking and test creation. An example of a software program specifically designed for item banking is the PARTest program. If PARTest is used in conjunction with PARScore and PARGrade, a completely integrated item banking, test analysis, and record-keeping system can be set up and integrated with a machine scoring system. Indications have also surfaced that computers may effectively be used to assemble pre-equated language tests from a bank of items.

Computer-assisted language testing

Tests that are administered at computer terminals, or on personal computers, are called computer-assisted tests. Receptive-response items-including multiple-choice, true-false, and matching items-are fairly easy to adapt to the computer-assisted testing medium. Relatively cheap authoring software like Testmaster can be used to create such tests. Even productive-response item types-including fill-in and cloze-can be created using authoring software like Testmaster. Unfortunately, the more interesting types of language tasks (e.g., role plays, interviews, compositions, oral presentations) prove much more difficult to develop for computer-assisted testing.

However, advancing technologies have many potential ramifications for computer-assisted language testing. Brown outlined some of the technological advances that may have an impact on language teaching and testing: Consider the multi-media combinations that will be available in the very near future: CD-ROM players working with video-image projectors, and computers controlling the whole interactive process between students and machines for situations and language tailored to each student's specific needs....Consider the uses to which computer communications networks could be put. What about scanners and hand-writing recognition devices? Won't voice sensitive computers and talking computers be valuable tools in the language media services of the future?

The new technologies such as the CD-ROM and interactive video discussed in Brown do make it possible for students to interact with a computer. Hence, no technical reason remains why interactive testing like role plays, interviews, compositions, and presentations cannot be done in a computer-assisted mode. Naturally, the expense involved may impose some limits, and the scoring will probably continue to involve rater judgments (thus, further increasing the expense involved). But at least, the logistics of gathering the language samples can now be simplified by the use of computer-assisted testing procedures.

Two consequences may evolve from the current advances in technology: (a) the sophistication of existing computer hardware and software tools will continue to grow, and (b) the cost of the technology will continue to drop (eventually to within reach of all language programs). Hence, the possibilities for developing productive-response computer-assisted language tests will definitely increase. But, why should we bother to create computer-assisted language tests at all? Aren't they really just a sophisticated version of the paper-and-pencil tests that they will probably be modeled on? Two primary benefits can be gained from computer-assisted language testing: Computer-assisted language tests can be individually administered, even on a walk-in basis. Thus group-administered tests and all of the organizational constraints that they impose will no longer be necessary.

Traditional time limits are not necessary. Students can be given as much time as they need to finish a given test because no human proctor needs to wait around for them to finish the test. No doubt, cheating will arise, but such problems can be surmounted if a little thought and planning are used. Given the advantages of individual, time-independent language testing, computer-assisted testing will no doubt prove to be a positive development. Consider the benefits of a writing test administered in a computer laboratory as the final examination for an ESL writing course. Such a computer-assisted test would be especially suitable for students who had been required to do all of their writing assignments in the course on a PC.

In such a course, it would make imminent sense to allow the students to do their final examination writing samples on a computer and turn in the diskette at the end of the testing period (or send the file by modem or network to the teacher). Under such circumstances, the testing period could be quite long to allow time for multiple revisions. Of course, logistical problems will crop up, but they can no doubt be overcome with careful planning. In fact, the literature indicates that computers can be an effective tool for teaching writing. Why not also use it as an effective tool for testing writing?

Computer-adaptive language testing

Computer-adaptive language tests are a subtype of computer-assisted language tests because they are administered at computer terminals or on personal computers. The computer-adaptive subtype of computer-assisted tests has three additional characteristics:

(a) the test items are selected and fitted to the individual students involved,

(b) the test is ended when the student's ability level is located, and, as a consequence,

(c) computer-adaptive tests are usually relatively short in terms of the number of items involved and the time needed.

As Madsen put it, "The computer-adaptive language test (CALT) is uniquely tailored to each individual. In addition, CALT is automatically terminated when the examinee's ability level has been determined....The result is a test that is more precise yet generally much shorter than conventional paper-and-pencil tests". A clear description of how to develop computer-adaptive language tests (CALTs) is provided in Tung. CALT development relies very much on item response theory. While the computer-adaptive language test is taking place, the computer typically uses a combination of item response theory and the concept of flexilevel tests to create a test specifically designed for the individual student taking it.

The flexilevel procedures roughly determine the general ability level of the student within the first few test questions. Then, based on item response statistics, the computer selects items which are suitable for the student's particular level and administers those items in order to get a more finely tuned estimate of the student's ability level. This flexilevel strategy eliminates the need (usually present in traditional fixed-length paper-and-pencil tests) for students to answer numerous questions that are too difficult or too easy for them. In fact, in a CALT, all students take tests that are suitable to their own particular ability levels-tests that may be very different for each student.

One example of the actual development of a CALT is the Montgomery County Public Schools project which is described in Stevenson and Gross. Madsen describes another example of a CALT which was applied to students at Brigham Young University in Utah for testing reading and listening abilities. The Madsen study indicates that many fewer items are necessary in administering computer-adaptive language tests than are necessary in pencil-and-paper tests and that the testing time is correspondingly shorter. For example, the CALT in Madsen used an average of 22.8 items to adequately test the students in an average of 27.2 minutes. The comparable conventional reading test used in the study required 60 items and 40 minutes.

Educational Testing Service (ETS) is providing considerable leadership in the area of what they are calling computer-based tests. That organization is already offering the GRE and PRAXIS as computer-based tests in 180 countries. In 1998, a computer-based version of the TOEFL examination will be released in North America and selected countries abroad, though paper-and-pencil versions will continue to be used until computer delivery is available. Because of recent efforts to develop computer-based versions of the TOEFL, some of the research at ETS has focused on the effects of computer familiarity on TOEFL test performance. For instance, Kirsch, Jamieson, Taylor, and Eignor indicates that, in general, computer familiarity is related to individuals' TOEFL scores. At the same time, Taylor, Jamieson, Eignor, and Kirsch indicates that, after students participate in a computer-based testing tutorial, there is no meaningful relationship between computer familiarity and individuals' TOEFL scores.

Effectiveness of computers in language testing

Educational Testing Service claims the following advantages for their new computer-based TOEFL:

— Further enhancements to test design before 2000

— Greater flexibility in scheduling test administrations

— Greater standardization of test administration conditions

— Portions of test individualized to examinee ability level

— Inclusion of writing with every test administration

— Examinee choice of handwriting or typing essay

— Ability to record multiple aspects of examinee test-taking behavior

— Platform for future innovations in test design and services.

— Judging by what they are claiming, at least portions of this new computer-based test will eventually be computer-adaptive.

Brown looked in more detail at both the advantages and disadvantages of using computers in language testing.

Advantages

— The advantages of using computers in language testing can be further subdivided into two categories: testing considerations and human considerations.

— Among the testing considerations, the following are some of the advantages of using computers in language testing:

— Computers are much more accurate at scoring selected-response tests than human beings are.

— Computers are more accurate at reporting scores.

— Computers can give immediate feedback in the form of a report of test scores, complete with a printout of basic testing statistics.

— IRT and computer-adaptive testing allow testers to target the specific ability levels of individual students and can therefore provide more precise estimates of those abilities.

— The use of different tests for each student should minimize any practice effects, studying for the test, and cheating.

— Diagnostic feedback can be provided very quickly to each student on those items answered incorrectly if that is the purpose of the test. Such feedback can even be fairly descriptive if artificial intelligence is used.

— Among the human considerations, the following are some advantages of using computers in language testing:

— The use of computers allows students to work at their own pace.

— CALTs generally take less time to finish than traditional paper-and-pencil tests and are therefore more efficient.

— In CALTs, students should experience less frustration than on paper-and-pencil tests because they will be working on test items that are appropriate for their own ability levels.

— Students may find that CALTs are less overwhelming (as compared to equivalent paper-and-pencil tests) because the questions are presented one at a time on the screen rather than in an intimidating test booklet with hundreds of test items.

— Many students like computers and even enjoy the testing process.

Disadvantages

— The disadvantages of using computers in language testing can also be further subdivided into two categories: physical considerations and performance considerations.

— Among the physical considerations, the following are some of the disadvantages of using computers in language testing:

— Computer equipment may not always be available, or in working order. Reliable sources of electricity are not universally available.

— Screen capacity is another physical consideration. While most computers today have overcome the 80 characters by 25 lines restrictions of a few years ago, the amount of material that can be presented on a computer screen is still limited. Such screen size limitations could be a problem, for example, for a group of teachers who wanted to develop a reading test based on relatively long passages.

— In addition, the graphics capabilities of many computers (especially older ones) may be limited, and even those machines that do have graphics may be slow (especially the cheaper machines). Thus, tests involving even basic graphs or animation may not be feasible at the moment in many language teaching situations.

— Among the performance considerations, the following are some of the disadvantages of using computers in language testing:

— The presentation of a test on a computer may lead to different results from those that would be obtained if the same test were administered in a paper-and-pencil format. Some limited research indicates that there is little difference for math or verbal items presented on computer as compared with pencil-and-paper version or on a medical technology examination, but much more research needs to be done on various types of language tests and items.

— Differences in the degree to which students are familiar with using computers or typewriter keyboards may lead to discrepancies in their performances on computer-assisted or computer-adaptive tests

— Computer anxiety (i.e., the potential debilitating effects of computer anxiety on test performance) is another potential disadvantage.

Future Directions

Most of the research cited so far has been practical in nature. Drawing on the wider literature of the educational testing field, found that the educational measurement literature on using computers in testing developed very much like the language testing literature has. However at this point in time, researchers in educational measurement have developed well beyond the practical questions of how to item bank, how to definitions and distinguish between computer-assisted and computer-adaptive testing, and how to measure the effectiveness of computers in testing. In short, they are now addressing considerably more technical, complex, and detailed issues.

Examining the types of concerns that have arisen recently for educational testers may therefore point the way for future research on computers in language testing and provide a basis for researchers in our field who would like to begin studying these issues.

CALT Design Issues

A number of CALT design issues need to be addressed by language testers before we can be fairly sure we are using such tests responsibly, including at least the following questions: How should we pilot CALTS? Should a CALT be standard length or vary across students? How should we sample CALT items? What are the effects of changing the difficulty of CALT items? How can we deal with item sets on a CALT?

How should we pilot CALTs? The problem that must be addressed here is caused by the fact that CALTs, because of their adaptive nature, may be different for every student. In classical theory tests, the examinations were the same for every student. Hence, a single examination could be piloted, item analyzed, revised, and then validated during the operational administration. In contrast. a new CALT is created each time a student takes the test. In educational testing circles, the strategy that is used to overcome the piloting problem is called simulation. Using item response theory, testers can simulate the answers of typical students based on the pilot responses of real students. By simulating such responses in various combinations and for different test lengths, researchers can study the probable characteristics of the test under many different conditions and lengths.

Should a CALT be standard length or vary across students? One of the advantages of computer-adaptive testing is that the test can be tailored to each student's ability levels. Such tailoring results in a test that may be more efficient at some levels of ability, requiring fewer items to reliably estimate the students' abilities, but less efficient at other levels, requiring more items to do a reliable job. The issue that arises then is whether the test should be the same length for each student or of different lengths tailored to each student's ability. Stocking indicates that the tailored strategy resulting in different lengths may produce biased scores for students who end up taking short versions. If the test is made to be relatively long for all students, even for those students who will be taking the "short" versions, no such biases may surface.

However, if the test is short for all students, it may be preferable to use the same length test for all students. These important length issues have yet to be investigated for CALTs. Perhaps they should be. How should we sample CALT items? Traditional tests, in order to be theoretically valid, are often designed on the basis of clearly developed test specifications to sample different knowledges or skills that make up a particular domain. Because CALTs will typically be shorter than traditional tests, testing all of the specifications may be impossible. Items could be randomly selected from all the possible specifications.

However, if CALTs are short for only some students, a better strategy might be to develop a sampling algorithm that takes into account the issue of specification sampling by keeping track of which specifications have been sampled for a given student and selecting the remaining items in a way that best fulfills the rest of the test specifications. Such a scheme might even take into account the relative importance of the various specifications. Naturally, any such scheme should be based on research-research that has yet to be conducted in relation to CALTs.

What are the effects of changing the difficulty of CALT items? Bergstrom, Lunz, and Gershon found that altering the difficulty of CAT items slightly raises the number of items that are necessary to test students with adequate precision, but otherwise has little affect on the estimation of their abilities. They did so by studying the responses of 225 students on a medical technology examination. Is there a relationship between item difficulty and test length on a CALT, but little effect on ability estimation in language testing? And if both sets of results are the same in language testing as in the education literature, what difficulty level would be ideal in terms of language test length and precision of measurement in relation to the level of language proficiency of the students?

How can we deal with item sets on a CALT? A problem that occurs whenever item banking is done, even for paper-and-pencil tests, is how to deal with item sets (sets of items determined by reading or listening passages, or sets of items based on item formats, topics, item contents, etc.) Good reasons may exist for keeping certain items together and even for ordering them in a certain way. Wainer and Kiely call these sets of items "testlets."

Unfortunately, using item sets, or testlets, may result in a selection of test items that are not maximally efficient from an IRT perspective. Since such item sets often occur in language tests, especially in academic reading and lecture listening tests, the issue of item sets is an important one in language testing. Hence, investigations should be conducted into the best strategies to use in dealing with CALT item sets, as well as on the relative effectiveness of item sets as compared to independent items. Research might also be profitable on the ordering of items within sets, and indeed, the ordering of items throughout a CALT.

CALT Scoring Issues

A number of CALT scoring issues also need to be addressed by language testers before we can be fairly sure we are using such tests responsibly, including at least the following questions:

— How should we score CALTS?

— How should we deal with CALT item omissions?

— How should we make decisions about cut-points on CALTs?

— How should we score CALTs?

A number of alternative methods have been explored in the educational literature including at least the following:

— Raw scores (a simple sum of the number of correct items)

— Weighted raw scores (in which some items count more than others)

— Scaled scores

Research on which method works best for which purposes when interpreting CALT scores would be very beneficial. Also, when using IRT for the development of CALTs, language testers must grapple with explaining the scoring methods in non-technical terms so that students and teachers can understand the results. Hence, CALT research might profitably focus on how to best convey such IRT scoring information to lay people.

How should we deal with CALT item omissions? On traditional tests, especially those scored with a correction for guessing, students can and do omit items if they are not able to answer them. However, on a CALT, problems arise if the students omit one or more items. How should testers deal with such omissions? Wainer et al. chose to not allow for omissions on their CATs; the students simply could not go on to the next item until they had answered the one in front of them.Another strategy would be to allow omissions but assume that omitted items are wrong. If that strategy was followed, what would be the effect of such a wrong item on the estimation of the items that should follow?

Other problems may arise if students are allowed to omit items. For instance, if omitted items are not scored, students can manipulate the test by skipping items until they find items they can answer correctly. According to Lunz and Bergstrom, such students would receive undeservedly high scores. Another problem is that students can simply omit all items and get a good look at all of the items in the item bank. This would have important implications for item exposure (as discussed below). Another possibility is that students at different language proficiency levels might omit items in different ways. Hence, omission patterns would be linked to language proficiency as measured on such a test and would become a source of measurement error. All of these issues related to item omissions on CALTs need to be researched and resolved in one way or another.

How should we make decisions about cut-points on CALTs? The literature on deciding cut-points is often referred to as standards setting. Reckase has suggested the use of the sequential probability ratio test (SPRT) for making pass-fail decisions in adaptive and other related tests. The SPRT was originally developed by Wald as a quality control device, but both Reckase and Kingsbury and Weiss show how the SPRT can be applied to adaptive tests as well. Lewis and Sheehan suggested using Bayesian decision theory for making mastery/non-mastery decisions on a computerized sequential mastery test. Du, Lewis, and Pashley demonstrated the use of a fuzzy set approach for the same purpose. The SPRT and other methods just described should all be considered in terms of how well they help with test constuction and decision making on CALTs.

CALT Logistical Issues

In addition to the important logistical issues raised by Green, which included system, hardware, human, and software issues, at least three CALT logistical issues need to be addressed by language testers: How can we avoid CALT item exposure? Should we provide item review opportunities on a CALT? How can we comply with legal disclosure laws when administering CALTs? How can we avoid CALT item exposure? Item exposure occurs when students see any given item. Since exposure means that other students who might take the test in the future may know about the exact content of those items which have been exposed, such items should not be used again.

In traditional tests, large numbers of students are tested on one day with a relatively small number of items, all in one exposure. Thus, even though the items could not be used again, they were used rather efficiently to test a large number of students. However, on a CALT, even though each student gets a different test form, unless there is an infinite number of items, whatever items are in the item bank will be exposed rather quickly. If the test is administered on a daily walk-in basis at a computer lab, for instance, all items in the bank could be exposed within a matter of days without having tested very many students. In addition, as discussed above, particularly in a situation were item omissions are permitted on a CALT, students can simply omit all items and get a good look at all of the items in the item bank. Naturally, such wholesale item exposure would have important implications for test security. The steps that can be taken to slow down the process of item exposure are to:

— Have a very large item bank with a wide variety of difficulty levels to meet all item specifications desired in the test

— Have the computer select a number of items which might come next (rather than a single item) and then randomly select from among those possibilities.

— Have the computer select the next item based on complex probabilistic models like those discussed in Stocking, Stocking and Lewis.

— Use simulation studies to estimate the efficiency of different sized item banks in minimizing exposure, then stay within whatever size limits those studies suggest.

— Circulate item banks, or sub-banks, through different testing sites.

— Constantly change the items in an item bank by adding new items and eliminating old ones (especially those most likely to have been exposed).

— Monitor the functioning of items within the item pool by keeping track of students' item performances, and identify items that appear to have been exposed

— Clearly, studies should be conducted into the relative effectiveness of strategies for dealing with CALT item exposure.

Should we provide item review opportunities on a CALT? In traditional paper-and-pencil testing situations, students who have time remaining at the end of the test can go back and review earlier items. Given the fact that CALT algorithms select the next item based on previous item performances, allowing students to go back and review items would undermine the theoretical nature of the test. Lunz, Bergstrom, and Wright indicate that this is not a big problem for CATs, but what about CALTs? Wainer suggests that very testwise students could use reviewing as a way of manipulating the test and gaining an unfair edge. The degree to which these item reviewing issues are important to CALTs is yet to be determined.

How can we comply with legal disclosure laws when administering CALTs? New York state has so-called "truth in testing" disclosure laws dating back to 1979 that require that standardized tests administered in the state be made available to examinees for inspection within 30 days of the administration.

Naturally, with today's communications technology, if a test must be disclosed in one state, it might as well be disclosed in all states and around the world. That requirement does not cause undue problems for paper-and-pencil tests which can be administered to tens or even hundreds of thousands of students in a one month period. However, a problem arises from the fact that a relatively large item bank is necessary for CALTs.

To disclose the entire item bank of a CALT every 30 days, or even to disclose to students only those items they took, would be very costly in terms of development time and manpower to produce, pilot, analyze, and distribute new items. Currently, the New York legislature is considering laws (SO3292-C or A5648-C) that will continue the basic requirements of the 1979 law, but be updated to more reasonably fit with the new CATs and the logistics involved. However, in the interim, research should be conducted into the best strategies for developing new item banks and for phasing out old ones and disclosing them publicly.

8

Remediation and Reinforcement Mechanism

Within the realm of intelligent computer based instruction, student models are frequently collected to aid in pedagogical decision making. The most frequent modelling approach taken is to attempt to measure the degree of the student's ability on a "topic". This measurement commonly takes the form of the probability a student has mastered a topic. This suffices for basic reasoning such as whether to promote the student to a more complex topic, or to control the activity's level of difficulty. However, frequently more complex types of reasoning are needed.

The reality is that most teaching mechanisms are rather ad-hoc. At best it is difficult to attempt to reason about whether a student is confused about topic X or has forgotten topic Y when the only data available are estimates of his ability. Yet the ability to answer such complex questions is a characteristic of a good student model. In order to support such functionality, constructing a machine learning (ML) element on top of a traditional student model. Building the ML element on top of the student model makes it easier to provide inputs that speed learning and generalize more easily, as the student model can be considered to be constructed expert features for input to the learning algorithm. ML algorithms typically exhibit a tradeoff in flexibility and training data requirements. That is, the more flexible (i.e. less assumptions) a particular framework is, the more data it needs to reason effectively. Therefore, having a model that tries to reason about what a student knows at a fine-grained level of detail is likely to be less effective than trying to capture more coarse-gained features. Fortunately, much progress has been made on the former via Bayesian Networks and other formal reasoning techniques while less progress has been made on the latter.

MOTIVATION

This framework is being designed for use in the MFD (Mixed Number, Fractions, Decimals) system. The goal of this system is both to help grade school students learn fractional and decimal arithmetic, and to increase the confidence of students using the system. This system has heuristics that determine if a student needs remediation in a topic, has forgotten a topic, needs to be shown an example, etc. Creating a sound foundation for this reasoning is problematic. Most teachers do not think about individual students at this level of detail, so interviewing instructors is not necessarily the best course of action. It is certainly possible to empirically derive a set of teaching rules by running several studies, and trying to fine tune the parameters.

However, in addition to being expensive, this does not customize interactions to individual students who vary in ways other than the predictor variables gathered. From the student model's standpoint two students could be identical, yet one may learn best from examples while the other prefers to puzzle out problems himself. It is not possible to disambiguate them without the system learning about the student while it is being used. Therefore, we are moving away from hand coding routines that evaluate the student's state and beginning to investigate ML methods. We are considering placing a learning agent on top of the student model, and having it learn the probable long term benefit to the student for each teaching interaction when used in the current situation.

This permits a significant amount of data to be gathered, as the system is not trying to learn about the student's performance in a narrow area, but rather generalize across all of his interactions. To accomplish this, it is necessary to carefully construct a state representation that is neutral across topics. That is, features given to the machine learner should be phrased in terms like "knowledge about this skill", or "recent performance at prerequisite knowledge", not "misconceptions in adding fractions".

THE LEARNING METHODOLOGY

There are several features a learning framework must have to be useful to us. First it must be possible to incrementally update the system in real time (on a classroom personal computer). This excludes many neural network algorithms, as they tend to work best with batch training. There must also be some method for handling stochastic data as students do not exhibit constant behaviour since they forget knowledge, make typos, etc. For these reasons we have chosen to use reinforcement learning as a general framework.

Reinforcement Learning

Reinforcement learning (RL) is a system for providing target values for a functional approximator. It is best thought of as a combination of dynamic programming (DP) and monte carlo (MC) methods. While the RL system is solving a problem it is learning approximate values for each state that it encounters, and in many ways gains the best of both DP and MC. Similar to MC, RL learns based on actual experience. This is unlike DP, which in computing "sweeps" may derive values that are never actually encountered. Like DP, it does not need to know the eventual outcome of an action to start adjusting the estimated values of states. DP requires a strong model to perform such calculations, while RL simply uses its actual experience as a best estimate. That is, it guesses the value of the current state from its guess about the value of adjacent states.

Systems built with RL have outperformed expert humans players in backgammon , and have demonstrated superior performance in elevator scheduling compared to commercial, hand crafted algorithms. These results suggest the potential for impressive performance by these systems. An important point is that RL is not a learning algorithm per se, but rather a method of determining the value of being in a certain state. This value is then used as the target for a machine learner. Briefly, RL provides the machine learner with "rewards" for good performance and no reward for poor performance (alternately, no reward for good performance and a negative reward for poor performance). The learner's goal is to maximize its long-term rewards.

RL is agnostic on which ML algorithm should be used to compute the value of a state. Successful systems have been built using neural networks , linear function approximators (LFA), and lookup tables. Given that the amount of training data is not likely to be large, using a simpler scheme such as an LFA seems prudent. If the problem is small enough, a lookup table that stores learned values may be applicable.

There are two components in an RL system: the environment and the actions. The environment is whatever is beyond the direct control of the learner, while actions are items the agent can select. Note that actions themselves may be stochastic (e.g. actions can be performed incorrectly). The agent examines the current state it is in, and then selects an action to perform. At this point the environment takes over and the effects of the action performed are observed.

Once the reward is received some method of moving the estimate of the previous state towards the reward is needed.

The simplest such method is simply to use the Widrow-Hoff rule : where is the step size (or learning rate) parameter. The main difference between RL and other systems that use this update rule is that RL uses the next state as its target value, while most other algorithms use the result in the final state of the "trial". Waiting until the end to reward the learner has several drawbacks. First many tasks (such as this one) have no clear notion of what constitutes a trial. Additionally, delaying the reward until the last state produces much more variance in the values during learning, and consequently such systems tend to take longer to converge to optimal values.

Some actions such as presenting an example will clearly not have immediate, noticeable effects but are useful in the long run. Fortunately, such problems have been examined in the context of RL. First, since the system is learning to associate the value of a state-action pair with the value of the succeeding state, eventually values will propagate back to the current state. Unfortunately, this process can be slow. Therefore, a set of learning procedures known as TD ([lambda]) have been developed. This adjusts the value of a state-action pair to be equal to a combination on the values of the next several states visited, giving decreasing weight to successive states.

Drawbacks include having to keep track of what states have been visited. This TD framework is a generalized form of other learning algorithms. TD (0) is equivalent to only considering the next state, while TD (1) is equivalent to monte carlo learning, which uses the final outcome in a learning trajectory as a target. Using intermediate values of Lambda controls how far to propagate values, and has been shown to be somewhat better than TD (0) and much better than TD(1). By learning the value of performing teaching actions in a state, the system is learning to customize its behaviour to the student.

Once the systems learns how to compute the expected gain for using each teaching interaction, a teaching policy can be constructed. A first attempt might be to select the action with the highest expected reward. However, this has a large drawback that little exploration is performed. Once an action is found that is slightly better than the others, it will be performed exclusively. A solution is to perform action selection via a Boltzmann machine: initially the temperature is set high, but as the system becomes more accustomed to working with a student the temperature is decreased. This results in more variation in action selection initially, which allows for exploration, but over time the system becomes more greedy in maximizing its reward.

Strengths

As previously mentioned, RL is robust with respect to noisy data. This is due to its learning the value of the current state from the value of the next state (i.e. a "guess from a guess"). In spite of being counterintuitive, this has been shown to give good performance in a variety of learning tasks. An additional advantage is that substantial domain knowledge is not required to construct an RL system, and it easily incorporates the existing knowledge in the student model. Obviously using domain knowledge makes any learner's job easier, but a simple simulation (or observing the actual task occurring) is sufficient for RL. It is possible to use additional domain knowledge to provide hints to the learner. Constructing a good state representation is an example. A program learning to play chess would certainly learn more quickly if it was given features that described "in check", "can capture", etc. Additionally, knowledge can be used to bias the initial evaluation function or to allow the system to construct simulations of what might happen, enabling it to learn without making mistakes on the actual task.

LEARNING PROCEDURE

Thus far, we have outlined a procedure for how a learning system can adapt its actions to fit individual students' needs. However, if the system starts with no knowledge, its initial performance will be random. Thus some method of providing the system with starting knowledge is required. Once this step is accomplished, the system will have a general model of how to teach a domain, but will not take into account idiosyncrasies of the student currently using the system. Given these facts, we propose a two-phase learning procedure with the first phase being done off-line, and the second occurring in real time as the student uses the system.

Off-line learning

There are a variety of approaches for training such a system off-line. The most obvious is to take records of students using a similar system (that does not use ML to select teaching actions), and use these interactions as training data. While straightforward, this has a large cost of running a substantial experiment whenever a new system is being designed.

An alternate course is to use simulated learners. This would entail constructing a weak model of how "typical" students would interact with the system. In order to represent the variance in student learners, several such learners could be constructed. The system would learn from interacting with the simulated learners (simulees). This is tractable problem, as the models do not have to be extremely accurate.

Finally, the system could be biased towards performing certain actions in some states by altering the function approximator's initial coefficients (this is simpler if an LFA is used). The result is that the system will initially perform according to the constructed policy, but will learn when to alter from this path.

In all of these cases, the learner takes a student model as input and decides what teaching action is appropriate; it does not simply learn a model of how to teach that is independent of the learner's level of knowledge. It is likely that some combination of the three techniques listed above will be the most efficient method to obtain good performance. For example, it may be best to build some weak simulee models to get a good first approximation, and then to gather a small amount of training data. In either event, the goal of this is to produce a system that can interact with students and learn from them on-line, and has performance that is good enough to be used by students. By providing these weak initial methods, the cost of determining pedagogical behaviour is decreased (as opposed to constructing a policy by hand).

Given the high cost of hand-coding teaching action selection, Quafafou's NeTutor proposes providing the system with examples, and using machine learning to learn teaching actions applicable to a specific student. A difference between the approach and the one outlined there is that they were concerned with learning symbolic rules while we are interested in numerical techniques. The advantage of using a function approximator is that more data can be considered (only 3 items were used to describe a state in NeTutor) and the system can generalize results more quickly.

On-line learning

Once the system has been trained to have adequate performance, it can be used with actual students. The system (hopefully) has a good general model for how to teach students (with their student model as input), but has yet to learn about idiosyncrasies that the student using the system may have. In order to account for this, the system learns while the student is using it. The system selects an action, the student acts, and a reward is received. If the student learns differently from the standard model, the rewards received will be less than (or greater than) expected, and the system will alter its teaching strategy selection accordingly.

Conceptually, this ML process results a layering of the knowledge about how to teach this student. At the bottom are the raw data recording student actions, above this the standard student model data, then a general notion of how to teach such a student, and finally the knowledge of how to teach this particular student. In order to gather the most from each item of student datum, replay can be used. This technique presents several examples of useful trials. If an action receives a particularly large or a particularly small reward then it is selected to be presented to the system several more times (i.e. the state, action, reward sequence is given to the function approximator several times).

REINFORCEMENT OF APPROPRIATE STUDENT BEHAVIOUR

A critical component of the intervention plan is the pattern of reinforcement for using the appropriate replacement behaviour that the IEP team devises. The team can use information that was collected during the functional behavioural assessment (i.e., baseline data) to determine the frequency with which the problem behaviour occurred and was reinforced. Using this information, the IEP team can develop a plan so that the student is reinforced more often for the replacement behaviour than he or she was for the problem behaviour. As a general rule, school personnel should reinforce appropriate behaviour at least twice as often as the problem behaviour was reinforced.

For example, data collected on Charles indicate that, on average, he disturbs instruction two times during each 55-minute math class. This indicates that Charles is being reinforced for his inappropriate behaviour about every 30 minutes, so his behaviour intervention plan should call for a re-arrangement of his instructional environment so that Charles has an opportunity to engage in and be positively reinforced for appropriate behaviour at least every 15 minutes. It is important that the IEP team carefully regulate the amount of time between "reinforcers." Charles should neither get too much reinforcement, nor need to wait too long for reinforcement.

Finally, the team should make sure the academic expectations are accurate for his skill level so he can be academically successful, as well as behaviorally successful. When trying to determine the best reinforcer to use, knowledge of student preferences and strengths is useful in developing a plan. We might ask a student what types of things he or she likes (e.g., time on the computer, being allowed to run errands), watch for and record any preferred activities, or use an informal survey of reinforcement preferences. It is important to be consistent in the frequency of the delivery of the reinforcer, but it is also good to vary the actual reinforcers routinely, so that the student does not tire or become bored with a particular reinforcer. The amount of reinforcement, in relationship to the amount of effort required of the student to get it, is also an important variable for the IEP team to consider when developing a behavioural intervention plan.

In some cases, it may be necessary to initially offer a student "non-contingent" access to a reinforcer (e.g., with "no strings attached"), especially if the reinforcer is something he or she has never had before. Called "reinforcer sampling," this is one way to let the student know that it is reinforcing. For example, we might allow a student to participate in a highly preferred activity with a classmate (e.g., a computer-based learning activity). If the student enjoys it, access to that activity would later depend on the student engaging in the desired appropriate behaviour. Sometimes, the desired response may call for too dramatic a change in the student's behaviour (i.e., a change the student is unable and/or unwilling to make all at once). If that is the case, the IEP team will need to accept *successive approximations* or gradual changes toward the desired behaviour. For example, John may not be able to handle the pressure that stems from a highly complex academic assignment—especially when he has had too little sleep.

A first step might be to teach John to ask politely to be temporarily excused from a particular activity (i.e., replacement behaviour that achieves the same outcome as the problem behaviour). However, the long-term plan would be for the student to develop increased self-control, to master and complete complex academic assignments, and to solicit peer support (i.e., for desired behaviors). Attempts also should be made to encourage the family to find ways for John to get more sleep.

A final consideration in using reinforcers is the process of *fading* or gradually replacing extrinsic rewards with more natural or intrinsic rewards on a realistic or natural time schedule. Of course, fading will only be a consideration once the student has shown an increased ability and willingness to engage in the appropriate, desired behaviour. The process of fading may be made easier by pairing the extrinsic reward with an intrinsic reward. For example, when rewarding David with points for completing a homework assignment, the paraprofessional also could say, "David, you've finished all your homework this week, and your class participation has increased because you are better prepared. You must be very proud of yourself for the hard work you have done."

POSITIVE CHANGES IN STUDENT BEHAVIOUR

The success of any behavioural intervention plan rests on the willingness and ability of the student to continue to use the appropriate behaviour without excessive outside support (i.e., the intervention). The most basic way to assure maintenance of behaviour change is to be sure that interventions *teach* the student a set of skills. This will require IEP teams to include strategies in the behavioural intervention plan to teach the student in such a way that promotes the "maintenance" (i.e., lasting over time, even when the extrinsic reinforcers are faded) and "generalization" (i.e., using the behaviour in other appropriate settings) of replacement behaviors.

One strategy for doing this is to restructure the social environment to benefit from the power of peer relationships to promote positive behaviour. These behaviors are then maintained though the natural consequences of having and being with friends. Indeed, there are numerous instances in which students have been taught to encourage or reinforce appropriate behaviour and to ignore or walk away from negative provocations of their classmates.

Another way to promote long lasting behaviour change is to use strategies based on cognitive mediation (i.e., thinking through a situation before acting on emotion) and self-management (i.e., using techniques to control one's own behaviour, such as anger or anxiety). For example, students have been taught to apply various problem-solving strategies by engaging in "positive self-talk" (e.g., telling themselves, "I know how to get out of this argument without having to use my fists") or "self-cueing" (e.g., recognizing that her jaw is clenched, she is getting upset, and she needs to ask to be excused). Students also are taught to:

— self-monitor-count the frequency or duration of their own behaviour;

— self-evaluate-compare the change in their behaviour to a certain standard to determine whether they are making progress or not; and

— self-reinforce-give themselves rewards when their behaviour has reached criteria.

For example, Gloria may be taught to count and record the number of times she appropriately raises her hand and waits to be called on during class discussion. She can then determine whether she has met the daily criteria of at least three hand-raises. She then can look at her record of hand-raises for the week and determine if she is making progress toward her goal or not, and collect points to use at the class store later in the week.

Some interventions should be implemented indefinitely while others will eventually need to stop. For example, Bruce is learning to use social problem solving skills instead of getting into fights on the playground (an intervention that we hope Bruce will use forever). He is learning to ask for adult support when he feels like he might get into a fight and his team has decided that he can earn points for the class token economy when he seeks help appropriately rather than fighting (an intervention that must end at some point). Knowing that he cannot get points for the rest of his life, the team has decided to use the technique of *fading* once Bruce has reached criterion.

Bruce's teachers will gradually decrease the use of points or other tangible rewards when he asks for help instead of fighting. This could be done in several ways. First, his teacher could increase the amount of time Bruce has to remain "fight free" in order to receive a reward. For example he may initially receive rewards daily, but as he reaches criterion it could be increased to every other day, then once a week, and so on. Another way to fade the intervention is for his teacher to award him fewer points until he is receiving no points at all.

For instance, Bruce could initially earn 50 points per day for not fighting. This could be reduced to 40, then 30, and so on until he earns no points at all. It is very important to note that the social reinforcement should continue and eventually replace the tangible rewards completely. If this process is gradual and Bruce is helped to realize the advantages of using appropriate social problems solving, remaining fight free will become intrinsically rewarding to him. The success of these strategies may depend on providing the student with periodic "booster" training to review the instruction used in the original intervention plan.

Some students also may need to receive "self-advocacy training" to teach them how to appropriately ask for positive recognition or appropriately call attention to positive changes in their behaviour. This is especially important for students who have such bad reputations that adults and peers do not recognize when their behaviors are changing. Finally, school personnel can support changes in student performance by accepting "just noticeable differences," or incremental changes that reflect the fact the student is taking positive steps toward the desired goal.

EFFECTIVE POLICIES FOR REMEDIAL EDUCATION

Current discussions about postsecondary remedial education reflect differences in the opinions of legislators, educators, and the public as to the purpose and effectiveness of higher education. Concerned parties are asking, how many students need remedial education? Who are they? How much does it cost? Does it achieve its purpose? While these questions require attention, the more pressing issue is that of responsibility. Should the burden of remediation fall on community colleges or four-year institutions? Or should the nation's high schools be held responsible for adequately preparing their graduates?

Informed Policy

In US, a fall 1995 survey conducted by the National Center for Education Statistics (NCES) found that 29 percent of first-time freshmen enrolled in public institutions of higher education took remedial courses in reading, writing, or math. At community colleges, which provide the bulk of postsecondary remediation, the figure was 41 percent. Despite such evident need, the response of some states has been to ban or restrict remedial course offerings.

In 1994, the Trustees of the California State University (CSU) system proposed to shift 90 percent of its remedial education to the community colleges by the year 2007. Strong opposition from community colleges and other groups in California has forced CSU officials to postpone this plan. Meanwhile, Florida legislators have been successful in prohibiting public universities from offering remedial courses. Much of the opposition to remedial education is due to its costs. Often, however, the cost of remedial education seems astronomical because figures are provided outside the context of all instructional costs. For example, in Illinois, the total dollar amount devoted to remedial education provided in community colleges was $23.4 million, yet this was only 6.5 percent of all direct faculty salary costs.

While cost invariably bears on state and institutional policy, effective solutions consider a broader base of information including student demographics, characteristics of successful programs, and program evaluations. Data on students' age, race/ethnicity, extent of necessary remediation, and English as a Second Language (ESL) needs can assist policy makers in allocating their scarce dollars where they are needed most. According to McMillan, Parke, and Lanning, a number of studies document a high level of correlation between student success and the following program characteristics:

— required entry-level testing,

— mandatory placement in basic skills courses,

— continuous evaluation,

— interface between remedial and college-level courses, and

— using technology to offer remediation through alternative instructional media.

A well-designed assessment of programs also can inform the process of allocating public funds and increase accountability. Weissman, Bulakowski, and Jumisko recommend measuring four aspects of program effectiveness:

— course completion success rate, which is the percentage of students earning grades of C or better,

— movement of students from remedial to college-level courses,

— successful completion of college-level coursework, and

— student persistence over a three-year period.

Specific policy areas suggested for review include mandatory student placement into remedial courses, enrollment in remedial courses upon initial entry to the college, and concurrent enrollment in remedial and college-level courses.

Proactive Remediation

Both research and current practice support the use of structured assessment and placement of students in remedial courses. Based on the philosophy of structured open access, the "systematic use of academic standards linked with additional approaches to assist students to reach their educational objectives," this type of proactive institutional strategy has been more successful than an open-door, laissez-faire approach that allows students to enroll in any course regardless of prerequisites. Rather than limiting student achievement, such intervention builds connections among students, counsellors, and faculty.

South Suburban College in Illinois adopted a structured model in the early 1990s that demonstrates that intrusive procedures need not be punitive and can actually foster a caring environment for students with remedial needs. Samples of the 14 policies of the model include:

- Mandatory placement testing for full-time and part-time students who have taken six credit hours.
- Developmental (remedial) courses are mandatory beginning with the student's first semester.
- Students on academic warning or probation status are required to develop an action plan to improve their academic standing.

The San Diego Community College District recently instituted mandatory enforcement of all course prerequisites, including recommended levels of English and math skills. Previously, the district did not insist on the use of prerequisites and students often enrolled in courses inappropriate for their ability levels. Although this system has not been in place long enough to evaluate results, some positive outcomes are evident. Berger notes increases in instructional research conducted by faculty as well as interaction among colleagues across the district. Increases in student success rates, however, remain to be seen.

Collaborative partnerships between community colleges and their feeder high schools are effective means of reducing the need for postsecondary remedial education. By developing a secondary school writing curriculum and an assessment system that relies heavily upon portfolios that follow students throughout high school and to the community college, faculty from the two educational segments can make significant strides in promoting student success. Such a model also addresses growing public concerns that remedial courses in higher education are simply repeating what students should have learned in high school.

The Case of ESL

While the demand for remedial education in general is on the rise, ESL programs have experienced a tremendous influx of students as a result of the recent immigration wave. When challenged by the perennial dilemma of quality versus quantity, the ESL department at Portland Community College in Oregon decided it could provide both. Its successful action plan focused on meeting faculty development needs and overcoming three major impediments facing many ESL programs in community colleges: 1) lack of understanding of who ESL students are and what they need, 2) outdated assumptions about ESL instruction and student services, and 3) scarce public funding.

Clarifying the needs of ESL students as well as the purpose and structure of the program has far reaching implications for students' financial aid status as well. Aid policies constructed to protect the integrity of public funds do place limits on the uses of these dollars for remediation. College officials can craft effective programs that allow ESL students and those in remedial/developmental programs to legally benefit from financial aid, but they must be aware of the restrictions that apply.

INDEX